AUGSBURG SERMONS

SERMONS ON
GOSPEL TEXTS FROM
THE NEW LECTIONARY
AND CALENDAR

AUGSBURG SERMONS

GOSPELS

SERIES B

AUGSBURG PUBLISHING HOUSE
MINNEAPOLIS, MINNESOTA

AUGSBURG SERMONS—GOSPELS—SERIES B

Copyright © 1975 Augsburg Publishing House

Library of Congress Catalog Card No. 75-2844

International Standard Book No. 0-8066-1489-7

Scripture quotations unless otherwise noted are from the Revised Standard Version of the Bible, copyright 1946, 1952, and 1971 by the Division of Christian Education of the National Council of Churches.

Manufactured in the United States of America

Contents

6

8

10

Introduction

The Calendar and Lectionary introduced by the Inter-Lutheran Commission on Worship (ILCW) in Advent 1973, has become one of the most popular liturgical tools for contemporary worship and preaching. It is the answer to many requests in Lutheran churches for a revision of the church year and a new lectionary.

The church year calendar has been modified and modernized. The lectionary has been extensively overhauled by drawing on parallel efforts by the Protestant Episcopal, Presbyterian, and Roman Catholic churches.

This new lectionary has proved to be just what preachers have been asking for

The New Church Year Calendar

This new calendar is similar to all previous calendars in that Easter is still the heart of it, and the Gospel still tells the story of Jesus Christ throughout the year.

The revisions in the new calendar are these:

- The *gesima* Sundays, sometimes known as pre-Lent, are now listed as Sundays after Epiphany. The season of Epiphany is therefore lengthened, which makes possible a fuller development of Epiphany themes.

- The Sundays between Easter and Pentecost will be known as the Sundays *of* Easter, rather than *after* Easter.

- The Latin titles for the Sundays of Lent and Easter have been deleted.

- Passion Sunday has been moved from the Fifth Sunday in Lent to the Sixth Sunday (Palm Sunday).

- The Sundays in the Pentecost-Trinity season have been numbered *after Pentecost* instead of *after Trinity*.

- In color terminology, *purple* replaces *violet*, and *red* is suggested for use during Holy Week.

The New Lectionary

The new lectionary presents a three-year cycle of lessons for the church year. The texts designated for a specific year will be chosen alternatively from Series A, Series B, or Series C of this lectionary.

This lectionary follows the traditional pattern of appointing an Old Testament lesson, an Epistle, and a Gospel for each Sunday. During the Easter season, however, a reading from the Acts of the Apostles replaces the Old Testament lesson.

Perhaps the outstanding feature of the lectionary is its use of a *Gospel of the Year*. In each series, one of the Synoptic Gospels is featured, providing continuity to the reading and telling of the Gospel story throughout the entire church year. The reading of the *Gospel of the Year* is interrupted annually by the insertion of the Gospel of John from Easter Sunday through Pentecost. Certain festivals for which only one Gospel is appropriate (the Epiphany for example), also are outside the domain of the *Gospel of the Year*.

Series B in 1975

The Lutheran churches in America will receive their first exposure to Series B of the new *Calendar and Lectionary* beginning in Advent 1975. Mark is the *Gospel of the Year* in this series and thus will be the primary source for most of the sermons preached in 1975-76.

The *Gospel of the Year* approach enables the pastor to study the Gospel of Mark in depth and to share his insights with his congregation through his sermons. This will help make visible the uniqueness of each of the New Testament Gospels. The same kind of organized in-depth study and proclamation of the Gospels is continued in Series A which features Matthew and Series C which is based on Luke.

The first volume of *Augsburg Sermons,* based on the Gospel texts of Series C, was published in the summer of 1973. The second volume, Series A, Gospels, was published in 1974. The enthusiastic response to those sermons, plus the wide acceptance of the new *Calendar and Lectionary,* provided the encouragement to issue the present volume based on the Gospel texts of Series B. This book, like its predecessors, is offered in the hope that the sermons, the calendar, and the lectionary will contribute to the renewal of preaching.

HE MADE ME A WATCHMAN

First Sunday in Advent
Mark 13:33-37

On this first day of our new church year the most important word Jesus has for us is "Watch!" In this brief text of only five verses the word "watch" appears four times. Count them! The text begins and ends with the admonition "watch!" That is the way this new year for our congregation could profitably begin and end . . . with the admonition "watch!"

As Jesus spoke these words he was sitting on the Mount of Olives looking across the Kidron valley to the temple. The inner circle of his disciples, Peter, Andrew, James and John, had asked him about the future of the church, for he had just told them that the temple, that magnificent focal point of Israel's faith, was to be torn down. His answer to their inquiry was clear. The focal point of the faith of the church could not be a temple made with stones. Rather the focal point of faith was himself. That meant faith and trust must always look to God alone. So his words for the inner circle of his disciples applied not only to them but to all in the future who would exercise care for the church. "Watch" that the church trusts in God and not in some temporal thing.

In speaking as he did to his disciples, Jesus made them watchmen for his church. If we are to gain anything from this text on the first day of our new year, it can only be insofar as we see ourselves as watchmen for the church. In the last line of this text Jesus said, "What I say to you I say to all: Watch."

The spiritual "Go tell it on the mountain" is absolutely right when one of its verses reminds each of us to consider that Jesus "made me a watchman."

Watch Out!

What does a watchman do? A watchman in biblical times was a person with a better vantage point than the rest. A watchman tried to analyze the situation and then warn the community of any impending danger to its life. A watchman on a city wall kept a position on the periphery of the city. From such a vantage point he could watch out for any dangerous development either without or within the city. A vineyard often had such a watchman placed in a tower from which he could watch out for any impending danger.

The job of the watchman was most important at night when most of the community was sleeping. It was also important during non-threatening times when the people dropped their guard and became apathetic.

As one reads the New Testament he quickly concludes that the disciples did take seriously their role as watchmen for the church. Just as the prophets of the Old Testament analyzed the dangers facing the people of God and repeatedly warned, "Watch out, your faith is misplaced," so the disciples of Jesus, from their vantage point, kept "watching out" for the church.

In days of persecution their function as watchmen was not as crucial as in the days when such persecution abated. Apathy was always seen as a greater danger to the faith. It was in those days that the church seemed to fall asleep. It could forget the real focus of faith. It was often confused as to what its real mission was. Sometimes it lost its sense of time and could not see beyond the concerns of the day. It was at such times that the disciples needed to say to the church, "watch out."

The first disciples knew the importance of "watching out" from first hand experience. They themselves had fallen asleep in the Garden of Gethsemane. The Lord himself served as their watchman. "Watch and pray, that you may not enter into temptation," he said, "for the spirit indeed is willing but the flesh is weak."

How easy it is for a congregation to begin another year with a perfectly willing spirit but with very weak flesh! We live in comparatively "good times" for the church. The enemy for which we need to "watch out" is not so much without as within. When we back off the congregation's business-as-usual, stand at the periphery, find a vantage point and look honestly at the situation, we find the danger is not one of being attacked, but one of being asleep. One contemporary watchman calls the danger, "church somnambulism" . . . sleep-walking.

Where is the flesh weak in our congregation? In what area of our life are we asleep? What aspect of our congregational life will just "sleep-walk" into the next year unless some among us assume the role of watchman and say "watch out," "wake up."

Watchword

Oftentimes the cry "watch out" is dismissed as the work of an alarmist or a disgruntled critic unless it is connected with a watchword. A watchword has two meanings. It can be a secret word used as a countersign or password among members of a society. Such a watchword may have been necessary in days when the Christian community was in danger from outside its membership. At present I think our need is for a watchword of the second meaning. That is, as the dictionary puts it, we need "a motto . . . used as a rallying cry."

It is not enough for the contemporary watchman to analyze the situation and yell "watch out." Nothing will change. He needs to add a reason why the congregation must awaken itself to its work. That reason for the church is put very simply by Jesus. There will be an accounting. So the watchword of the church is: "The Lord is coming" . . . and there will be an accounting for our congregation.

I was very fortunate as a youth. I grew up on a farm. That meant there were many chores for us after school. It also meant we could play basketball. Our barn was so arranged that we had room not only for a hay mow but also for a full basketball court. My father was not opposed to our playing. In fact, he helped us erect the backboards. But he also expected that we would have our chores well underway by the time he came in from the field. Our great problem was not in realizing that we had work to do. It was in keeping track of our time and in keeping a balance in our activity. My brothers and I would begin playing, forgetting that when our father came home there would have to be an accounting. Sometimes we would ask my youngest brother to serve as a watchman. He would listen for the sound of the tractor or the happy tune of Dad's whistle. It wouldn't be enough for our little watchman to say to us, "You had better watch out!" In our preoccupation with other things that cry could go unheeded. But there was a watchword, a rallying cry, that sent everybody to his job. And that watchword was: "Dad's coming!"

It wasn't out of fear that we scrambled to our positions for we loved our father and knew that he loved us. We scrambled to our work because we wanted to give him a good accounting of our time. We didn't want to betray the trust he had in us. We understood that our spirits were willing to live and work "under him in his kingdom" so to speak. But our flesh was weak. We bowed to the temptation to play too long. What really caused us to wake up and heed the time was the watchword: "Dad's coming!"

Jesus gave our congregation a similar parable. He likened our situation to a man (that is, God) who leaves for a while and places his servants in charge (that is, we who are the church). Each servant has responsibility for a portion of the work. Knowing the temptation that can overcome his servants while he is away, the master commands the doorkeeper to be on the watch. "Watch therefore—for you do not know when the master of the house will come—lest he come suddenly and find you asleep."

He is coming. There will be an accounting for us. He has made us watchmen. It is not enough for us to identify the areas of ministry in which our congregation is asleep. We must continually sound the watchword "Jesus is coming." Not that we should be frightened by his appearing but rather that we do not want to disappoint the Master who has entrusted the work of ministry to us.

Watch Over

The role of the watchman in the congregation is best filled by those who are willing to act on their own advice. To yell "wake up, watch out, Jesus is coming, get to work" may be sound advice to the congregation but credence is given only to such watchmen who themselves "get to work."

There were those times when our little brother would try to trick us. "Dad's coming!" And we would scramble to our work only to find that we had been tricked. You could tell when the watchword was genuine by watching the watchman. If he went to his work, we knew his words were to be believed.

It is true that Jesus made us watchmen over the church. Though we do not know the hour when he will return to his household, we do know that he is indeed coming again. The watchword is true. And it makes a difference in the way the church works when it believes the watchword to be true . . . and no false alarm.

When the watchmen themselves stay on the periphery of the church and do nothing but critique the church for its inactivity, they lose their credibility. You can believe the watchman when he himself takes his place in the center of the church's life and mission.

I have observed the way parents deal with their children in potentially dangerous situations. I've seen parents at the seashore yelling from a distance the constant reminders, "Watch out, a wave may come and sweep you away." But those often-repeated warnings from a distance soon lose their effect and sometimes even produce an opposite effect. More effective is the parent who not only watches out for the child from a distance, but who watches over the child while becoming involved in the child's work and play.

It is important that we see our job as watchmen in Christ's church in this same way. To watch over the church, not just to watch out for it, implies a willingness to move from the periphery into involvement at the heart of the church's life. To watch over the church is to love the church.

In the familiar verse of Psalm 127 it is contended that "unless the Lord watches over the city, the watchman stays awake in vain." In addition to the obvious meaning of this familiar passage I am taken with the way God's activity with his people is described . . . as "watching over." One of the proverbs describes God as "watching over your soul." The writer of the letter to the Hebrews describes the work of church leaders as "watching over your souls."

I am sure that Jesus' inner circle of disciples who first heard this text and who later in the Garden of Gethsemane so needed the services of the watchman, had good reason to take up the role themselves. And I know from their performance that they knew their watchword would go unbelieved if they themselves did not act on it. So we find them in the center of a vital church life. It was not their idea of the role of watchman to remain on the church's periphery. They were in the midst of the people "watching over their souls."

What better way to begin the new year than for each of us to understand that Jesus has made me such a watchman.

LARRY A. HOFFSIS
Old Trinity Lutheran Church
Columbus, Ohio

OUR ROLE IN GOD'S DRAMA

Second Sunday in Advent
Mark 1:1-8

As people of faith, we have the conviction that the Bible is of central importance. Yet, simply saying that sets us in a dilemma; because, the truth be told, although we are people who know the Bible to be significant, and people who read it some, most of us have the nagging wisdom that we should read it more. Perhaps one reason we don't is that we simply don't know how to read it so that it makes sense. For many Christians sporadic attempts to read Scripture have been cut short when they gave up in confusion or despair. Still we have the poignant suspicion that if we could make sense out of the Bible, then it might make sense out of the whole span of human history, and it might even make sense out of my strange, chaotic life.

The Biblical Drama

But how do we get at it? The best advice I can think of is to emphasize that the Bible has a story line. It is fundamentally a drama of God's dealing with his people, a recital of "the mighty acts of God." If you can get the plot line fixed in your mind, the odds are that the scenery and the cast will fall into place. Lose the story line, and the biblical narrative is reduced to a jumble of peoples and places and things that come at you with little recognizable order. It is as if the whole biblical drama were placed on a roll of movie film, and some mischief maker with sharp scissors took it out of the cabinet one night, cut up the film so that every frame was cut apart from all the other frames, and, having done that, threw all the frames into a basket and swished them around, so that when you reached into it for a daily devotion or a text for a Sunday or a Bible lesson, you get only a single unrelated frame. Isn't that often the way we study the Bible? We take a frame, and study it carefully, unaware of what went before it or comes after it, not knowing where it fits in the story line.

No wonder we get confused! It is simply not true that Moses and Paul can swap places and have the story still make sense. You can't take a Psalm of David and put it where the Gospel according to Luke is, and put Luke where the Psalms are, without throwing everything out of whack. You can't put Joshua in the New Testament, and you can't put Revelation in the Old Testament. It just won't go.

The Entry Point

But, let's go further. Even if we get the pieces of the story line all in place, we still need to find an entry point into the drama; an entry point through which we can get at its rhythm and reason, where it has been and where it is going. For Christians that entry point is the gospel, the good news about the person and work of Jesus Christ. He is at the *crux* of the drama, and please remember that in Latin that word means *cross*. If you want to get at the crux of the biblical narrative, and consequently of the human experience, you can get to it only through the cross of Jesus Christ.

Mark and the Gospel

The best way to do that is to go straight to the witness of the New Testament. Take Mark, for example, the gospel which we will in effect read through during the coming church year. Without fuss or feathers, beginning with chapter 1, verse 1, Mark marches right into the drama, and says "here it is!" (read Mark 1:1-8). As you can see, Mark is the no-nonsense evangelist. He's got a story to tell, and he gets right to it. "Here begins the gospel of Jesus Christ, the Son of God." Only eight verses, and already we are deep into the biblical drama. For Mark with his customary bluntness declares that you can't understand what preceded Jesus unless you look back at it through him, and you can't understand what unravelled after Jesus unless you look forward to it through him. He is the entry point.

Thus, Mark, as you know, doesn't begin with the birth of Jesus. Indeed, that event obviously did not seem significant to him. Further, he won't even allow us to begin with John the Baptist. He understands that John's dress, diet, person and message were meant to provide echoes of the ancient prophetic promise that God would send another Elijah to signal that the coming of the Messiah was imminent.

Thus, Mark directs us to look back through Christ to John, and back through John to the prophets, and—in very truth—back through the prophets to the mind and heart and will of God himself.

That's why Mark's opening words are, "Here begins the gospel of Jesus Christ, the Son of God." Gospel. You know, of course, that in its old English origins, that word means "God's story." That's what the gospel is. It is nothing less than God's own story. Is it not an unfortunate habit, therefore, that we use a shorthand identification and call it Mark's gospel? For that is not what it is. It claims itself to be the Gospel according to Mark. Scripture is clear. It declares that what we are reading is nothing less than the Gospel of God concerning his Son; to which Mark, Matthew, Luke, John, Paul, Luther, you and I, all bear witness. This is God's story of what he is up to in the human scene, and it is God's affirmation that he now intends to sweep us up, despite our undeserving, into what he is doing. There may be a variety of witnesses, but he is the author.

Declaring that a drama is underway, Mark immediately confronts us with the testimony of John the Baptist that we must repent. We are to turn away from our practice of knocking over the scenery and colliding with other members of the cast, from hindering the drama. We are rather to get back into the story line and conform to what the author has in mind. It means, quite simply, that God has something going on, and we are meant to be a part of it.

Even a moment's reflection makes clear that none of us ever begins at the beginning. When I was born, I brought with me a genetic inheritance, and I entered into a family tradition, and the human story. All of that was behind me. It is something out of which I cannot escape, and which I cannot truly deny. I didn't just drop in; I was placed in the flow of things, and I have the insistent hope that my life will be woven into what follows me also. As every parent, I pray that the influence of my commitment and values may inform and affect the children and grandchildren who will come after me. That whatever God allows me to invest in the life of this congregation, both in your individual lives as its members and in its corporate life as an institution, will have some continuing good effect. Like you, I care that my life not simply be dropped into an abyss.

The Bible declares that, although we come into the drama at a certain point, we are not unconnected from what came before us and what follows after us. We have been born into the human stream, and we have been baptized into the community of faith. We are part of God's continuing drama.

The Prompters: Repent

That conviction makes us ask what he means us to do at the point at which we have been placed into the drama. Let me put it this way. We are meant to be prompters. Like John, we are, among other things, to serve as prompters for the rest of the actors on the stage. We have been informed of the author's intention so that we can pass it on to the other members of the cast. To say it in more traditional terms: we have been baptized to be the means by which God confronts his world with his Word. We are to prompt, as John did. Every place we are, we are to ask, "It this the way God wants his drama to go?" We are to be the people who press that question on God's behalf in the shop, at home, in school, in the lab, in the operating room, the service station, in the union or Board of Directors meeting, our town's housing authority, our nation's foreign policy, and—no less—the life of our congregation and church. Are things going the way the author intends them to go?

In every place and all the time, the prompter is to insist, on God's behalf, that the fact that life is unfair, although an accurate description of the way things are, is a condition unacceptable both to the Christian and to his Lord. We are to share God's own distress when his scenery is despoiled, and his cast is ill-treated, and his drama has departed from his intention.

Isn't that what the call to repentance is? It is to be aware of the effect of disobedience. Scripture's insight is that God allows us to choose whether to help his drama along or to get in its way. Remember how Peter, after he had made his confession of faith that Jesus was the Christ, urged Jesus not to go up to Jerusalem? Jesus' immediate response was: Peter, you are an obstacle to me; you have missed the point of the drama; you are getting in the way when you tell me to avoid Jerusalem and the obedience that is required of me.

So we, too, are often obstacles for God in the daily routine of our lives. God has sketched the outline of the plot, but he has not written all the lines and has not hemmed us in with full and detailed instructions. Rather, he has honored and trusted the cast to improvise in ways that are appropriate. Thus, our first calling is to be prompters; by our words and our lives to say to the rest of the cast, "Wait a minute, this is the way God intends the human drama to go."

The Prompters: Good News

But we have a further word for the cast. As God's spokesmen, we have also been commissioned to tell them, "Don't get discouraged!" John's testimony was that this Jesus would be able to go beyond the call for repentance; he would give new and solid reason for hope.

Think of it again in terms of a drama. Now and again you read about a play that "bombed" in its try-out in New Haven. It did so poorly that the producers closed it down without bringing it to the city, so that they wouldn't lose more money. The backers' prudent decision was to abandon the project and, thereby, avoid further loss.

The gospel of Jesus Christ, the word of forgiveness, is that God is not about to close down his drama, to scrap it, to say, "Well, that's it; I'm not taking any more losses." The good news is that God is willing to pay the price to keep the show open, and human history going, even if the price is the gift, the obedience and the crucifixion of his Son, Jesus Christ. The cross of Jesus Christ is the evidence of how much loss God is willing to suffer. That's the good word the prompter can say to the cast. There is reason for courage; there is reason for commitment; there is reason for hope; it is possible for our lives to be laced with joy. The author has given clear evidence that he is prepared to see his drama and his people through to the end.

The result of all this is what so many Christians have found. That when the Bible begins to make sense, I find that it is really making sense out of me, and why I draw breath, and why we are together on this globe. I begin to see human history whole, as the setting in which God works out his mighty acts, and I begin to see my own life within the context of God's purposes.

For, if God is not random in purpose or capricious in deed, then there is a rescue from the one-frame mentality we spoke of earlier. I can be set free from the preoccupations which hold me captive; this one bill and how I am going to pay it; this one ballgame and who is going to win it; this one date I'd like to have during the Christmas vacation; this one stock I bought or this one business transaction I'd like to complete; this one meal I must prepare for the family; this one stencil I have to cut; this one friendship, this one antagonism; even, this one last Christmas present I still must buy.

We were not born or baptized to be confined in such one-frame anxieties or lost in such one-frame confusion. We are the people who know that life is not simply and sadly a cosmic hoax. We are the people who can rejoice in the morrow because we see it in the glorious sweep of God's activity and drama. We are the prompters, the stewards of the mysteries of God, privileged to speak God's Word to God's world. Amen.

FRANKLIN D. FRY
St. John's Evangelical Lutheran Church
Summit, New Jersey

DO YOU RECOGNIZE JESUS?

Third Sunday in Advent
John 1:6-8, 19-28

"I baptize in water," John replied, "but among
you, though you do not know him, stands the one
who is to come after me" (John 1:26f., NEB).

We are getting a lot of confusing signals these days. It is like the biblical phrase that refers to the cry "Peace, peace," but there is no peace.

Like the time of revolution whose description opens Charles Dickens's novel *A Tale of Two Cities*, it is "the best of times" and it is "the worst of times."

We have trouble in such a time, a time like ours, with identity. That crisis of identity is evident in role confusion, so that husbands and wives don't know what is expected of them. But also workers, once valued and proud of their skill, may now feel so separated from the end-product that they don't know where they belong. Children, particularly teenagers and college-age people, give evidence of similar confusion.

We have trouble these days recognizing both who other people really are and who we ourselves are. With this goes considerable confusion about how to measure why a particular action or attitude is important or unimportant.

One early Sunday morning during the days of President Franklin Roosevelt's popularity, the phone rang in the office of the church which the president often attended.

The minister answered and heard a voice on the line inquire: "Tell me, sir, do you expect the president to be in church today?"

"That I cannot promise," said the minister, "but we do expect God to be there and that should be reasonably good reason for attending."

We all need reminders like that to set our feet on reality. Our motives easily become very mixed and unstable, so that we give God less than the place he deserves.

Some years ago a man named Bruce Barton wrote a book which became rather popular. It was titled *The Man Nobody Knows* and its author later served in the U.S. Congress. The book was about Jesus Christ and sought to point out many things about him that we fail to note.

Unfortunately, from a Christian standpoint the book was not all good, but the title *The Man Nobody Knows* is an intriguing one. Ask yourself: "Do I really know Jesus?"

Perhaps it is true that many people, also church people, do not know Jesus as they should. In part this is because they will not take time to find out. They are too busy, they say.

But we read in history that Susanna Wesley, though she was the mother of 17 children, spent one hour each day shut up alone in her room, praying to God for them.

Two of her sons, John and Charles Wesley, became great leaders in a spiritual movement in England known at Methodism.

Advent, a time of spiritual preparation for Christmas, offers all of us the chance to reexamine our spiritual life and especially our relationship to God through Jesus Christ.

Recognizing Jesus Then

In what sense, we ask, was the statement of our text in John 1:26 true in John's day? Was it simply that Jesus had not yet stepped forth into the rightful role as Messiah which he would soon claim? Or was it that John hinted at some darker, more difficult, kind of non-recognition of Jesus.

Surely when we hear the Old Testament lesson for today in Isaiah 61 which describes so beautifully what the Messiah would do, we are reminded of the time in Nazareth when Jesus applied Isaiah's prophecy to himself. His townsmen did not welcome the identification. They resented it. Far from knowing Jesus at that point for what he was—and claimed to be—they rushed at him in violence.

John the Baptizer's followers, sincere as they may have been religiously, were in temperament not much different from the people of Nazareth. But John now gave them a chance to be brought forward to faith in Jesus, gently and slowly. John let them know that they were imminently close to a grand discovery, if they could make it.

Many of John's hearers were eager to see the Messiah God would send, but they did not know Jesus was that Messiah. Their problem was *ignorance*. It was a common problem then, and it is a common problem now. Then people who expected God to send a Messiah were usually looking for the wrong kind of person. They wanted someone to make life easier for them by changing the government, by making it easier to find a livelihood, or by at least cheering them with hopeful thoughts.

Ignorance needs to be reckoned with. There are still many people living in our neighborhoods who have never had a substantial conversation about Jesus Christ with someone who knew what he was talking about. There are many others who have heard a lot about Jesus but not from people they trust. Such, too, are ignorant.

We may also be sure that many who heard John's words, as well as those who heard Jesus himself, still did not believe Jesus was the Savior. Their problem was *unbelief*.

Often we do not recognize how strong unbelief is. We treat it too politely, that is, we act as though a little courtesy, a mild suggestion on our part of a less than radical change, could accomplish what we cannot do at all, namely, turn a heart from the power of sin to trust in God. Only the Holy Spirit himself can enlighten, call, and convert. But we can speak of the danger of unbelief and proclaim, in word and deed, both the judgment and the mercy of God.

Others who heard John speak and looked around for Jesus expected something else. To them Jesus did not look like or act like a Messiah. He came humbly without great ostentation. As time went on, though Jesus spoke beautifully and healed many of diseases, he also spent a lot of time with what seemed the wrong crowd, those who had stained reputations and belonged to low-level groups. For some, the problem was *self-righteousness*.

Those who learn to trust in a kind of decency that stems from rules, customs, and rituals instead of a heart dependent on God because of human weakness or failure, easily fall prey to self-righteousness which makes Jesus seem superfluous or nothing more than someone's personal preference.

Still others stumbled at the problem that because Jesus was one of their own number, he couldn't be great!

In speaking to those who heard him John said: Jesus "stands among you." Never! The Messiah they expected had to look it and act it according to their expectations. *Pride* was their problem—as it is for so many today.

Not only the church, always seen for the weaknesses which it certainly includes, but even Jesus himself, as he is portrayed in the Bible, does not suit many people. Their pride makes them want a Savior more tolerant of their weaknesses and more grateful for their attention. They do not want to be called to account; they call God himself to account. They do not want to follow Jesus; they want to plan his program.

Church Recognition of Christ

Can it be that for us, who want to be faithful and humble believers, Jesus stands unrecognized also?

The church, certainly our church, claims to recognize Christ. Our creeds and confessions testify to our understanding of him and faith in him in terms we find unmistakably clear. Our hymns and prayers offer Jesus recognition and express nothing but the highest confidence in his power and mercy.

Well and good, that is as it should be. What of our lives? Do we bear as clear and as consistent testimony there? Or are we often faltering, forgetful, and forsaking? Unless we realize that Jesus in fact often stands among us unrecognized, we are indeed in danger.

Prophecy in the Scripture says that many will confuse Jesus with themselves and miss his holiness. It is necessary to hear the accusing words of Psalm 50 directed also toward ourselves. The psalmist speaking for God, says: "If you meet a thief, you choose him as your friend; you make common cause with adulterers; you charge your mouth with wickedness and harness your tongue to slander. You are forever talking against your brother, stabbing your own mother's son in the back. All this you have done, and shall I keep silence? *You thought that I was another like yourself,* but point by point I will rebuke you to your face."

Too easily we make our faults our virtues, easy tolerance of weakness and of evil, and then complete the foolish self-justification by ascribing these "virtues" also to God. Again and again we must be advanced to the concept of Jesus as the "altogether-other one." Paul's exhortation and prayer in the Epistle today are exactly appropriate: "May God himself . . . make you holy in every part, and keep you sound in spirit, soul, and body."

Another Old Testament prophecy indicates that we must recognize Jesus as one who suffers. When we look away from the consequences of our sin in such a way that Jesus is only seen as triumphant, we miss that message and do not recognize his cross. In Isaiah 53:3-5 we read: "He was despised, he shrank from the sight of men, tormented and humbled by suffering; *we despised him, we held him of no account,* a thing from which men turn away their eyes. Yet on himself he bore our sufferings, our torments he endured."

On the other hand, sometimes we do not recognize Jesus for what he is because we cannot reconcile his humanity with his divinity. We make him less Lord of all in our lives than he ought to be. In verses 10 and 11 of this same chapter (John 1) he is so described: "He was in the world; but the world, though it owed its being to him, did not recognize him. He entered his own realm, and *his own would not receive him.*"

Perhaps our greatest failure to recognize Jesus occurs when we fail to see him in the helpless and hopeless—or hopeful—expressions of those in need. In Matthew 25:35 ff. Jesus' words are presented: "I was hungry . . . I was thirsty . . . I was a stranger . . . naked . . . sick . . . in prison. *Anything you did for one of my brothers here, however humble, you did for me.*"

What to Do?

By God's grace and the Holy Spirit's working our eyes have been opened, and we recognize Jesus. We do not always see him in our midst, and we do not always recognize him as we ought, but we do know him and love him.

What are the consequences in our life? Often not what they might be. We hold too closely to our pride, our self-righteousness, and we yield too easily to our weaknesses.

"We will not accept into membership anyone with any reservations whatsoever. We will not accept into our membership anyone unless he is an active, disciplined, working member in one of our organizations." That was Lenin's requirement for communist party members. How does our dedication and commitment to Jesus Christ compare with this?

We must see Jesus as Savior in the way that he is Savior. We must not make him suit us but must rather change our lives to conform to him. He is our faithful, sacrificing Savior, whose death reconciled us to the Father in heaven. He is our glorious, risen Lord, whose resurrection and present rule over all things makes the future secure for those who trust him.

Our lives must pattern after his, a goal we shall never attain but by the Spirit's power may advance toward. Whenever we recognize him, wherever we see him, we want to respond to him in faith and follow him in hope and love.

As we follow him, with benefit and joy to ourselves, let us also openly gladly, and faithfully point others to him as we testify, "Behold, the Lamb of God who takes away the sin of the world" (John 1:29).

Advent can help us recognize Jesus. Let it not be as John said, that one stands among us whom we do not know. And knowing him, let us follow him.

OMAR STUENKEL
The Lutheran Church of the Covenant
Maple Heights, Ohio

THAT'S THE POINT OF CHRISTMAS!

Fourth Sunday in Advent
Luke 1:26-38

I saw an ardent young Buddhist come to the open temple in Tokyo at high noon. First he clapped his hands together sharply, apparently in an attempt to awaken his deity. Then he carefully tossed a coin into the treasury box that stood before him in a further attempt to win his god's approval. A brief moment of prayer and he was gone, his countenance visibly unchanged.

I noticed the worshiper of Kali outside a temple in Calcutta. The temple priest with unblinkingly cold eyes guillotined the two goats that had been brought as a sacrifice. Again, that moment of worship over, the one with the sacrificial offering slipped away. I noticed once more a face impassive and unchanged.

In both instances I felt like shouting, "You needn't run off somewhere to find God; you needn't follow the cry, 'Go here,' or 'go there.' You need not seek out holy places, or cover the world to find God. He's here!"

The Miracle of Christmas

God is here. Wherever you are, wherever I am.

That's what Mary discovered right in her own home, and that can be for us the contact point of Christmas. Isaiah, seven centuries before the Christ came, points to this by calling the Christmas child by the name, "God with us."

God with you! Isn't that a mind-blowing thought? God here, in the very earthly form of Jesus. You can find him in that simple stable box, a visible witness to the fact that all people in their very earthly identities are completely worthy and capable of receiving God's Christmas gift of himself.

For God came to Mary when she was alone, without any go-between: no priest, no husband, no temple, no ritual, no bureaucrat, no legal form. A face-to-face encounter came seeking, searching, wanting, demanding. God's invading Spirit ignored all of the barriers created by men and accepted by them as reality. The way into the heart of this one responsive person, Mary, was wide open to God.

God's Open Road

Notice how God pays no attention at all to the value judgments we place on human worth. We love to measure people by their economic status. "How much are they worth?" we ask, and we mean, "How much money have they got? What kind of home do they live in? What kind of car do they drive?" The answer to these questions usually determines how much power we think these individuals have in the community and the amount of respect we think they can command.

But Mary was abysmally poor. She could only provide the minimal offering of two doves for her own post-natal purification rite. Perhaps Jesus had witnessed his mother's frantic search for one lost penny when he was a boy and that vivid recollection became the basis for one of his parables of the kingdom. In her poverty, that one lost coin was terribly important to her. Her surprised delight at finding it, her celebration with her neighbors, stayed in his memory.

Poverty, you see, is no spiritual barrier to God. Mary's son later said, out of his own experience, "How blessed are the poor in spirit, for theirs is the kingdom of heaven."

Just as her poverty was no barrier to God, neither was Mary's extreme youth. She may have been fifteen or sixteen years of age when God's surprise announcement came. Perhaps you have felt that only ripening years can experience the real fullness of his coming. The Old Testament record puts its heaviest accent on age. Older men were to rule. The hierarchy of age controlled religious experience.

But in Mary, God reveals that he is no respecter of persons, young or old.

How many young people have we known who have found it much easier to identify with the living God than those much older? Before my own mind walk teen-agers who live in a constant awareness of his presence. Mary constantly identifies with her Lord's promises. God is so important to her that her urgency matches his when he speaks. Her potential mission begins to consume her. Delightedly, she reaches out for this great gift, tasting its promise, appreciating its depth, loving its expectancy. After only a moment's hesitation, she makes it all her own.

Poverty and youth yield to God's will. Being a woman does, too. Religious and civil subordination to men had been the historical role of the Hebrew woman. Mary understood this. Study of the Torah was denied to females in her world; participation in the mysteries of the synagogue and temple were for men only. She knew that there could not even be a prayer meeting for women unless ten Jewish males called it and were present. Even if 10,000 women were gathered together, the presence of the tenth male was more important than all those thousands of devout women, and without him no prayer meeting could officially take place!

But God plays no favorites and the most significant meeting between God and a human takes place with one young woman. Mary finds herself selected for a key role in God's great plan and agrees to become the fulcrum of the ages. She nurtures and instructs the divine Word made flesh, her flesh and blood. Mary becomes the forerunner of all those mothers who brought their children to Jesus even in the face of rebuke from the disciples because they read the real heart of Christ better than they did.

The Singing Faith

Mary still makes our hearts sing as she throws open her life to let her faith swing against faith, to let it hope against hope, to let it soar until she radiates anticipation even of a future that will demand all the resources that she can muster from God.

To be sure, the angel says, "Hail, O favored, O graced one," but can you find it easy to accept the fact that she is "favored" of God when you see what happened to her? A smelly, drafty stable as her delivery room? Abject poverty and a daily struggle for survival? A refugee in her teens from Herod's murderous horrors? An early widowhood? A sword to pierce her heart as the son of her body hangs crucified?

If that were the promise held out to you, wouldn't you scream back, "God, please, don't favor me like that!" We know such cries. Your spirit as well as mine has called them out. One person, so crushed by the pressures of life, put this personal sob of despair into a large sign on a wall where 400,000 cars sweep by each day, "Can't you hear me calling?"

A famed black writer summarizes it well when he asks, "Do you know what the saxophonist is saying when he socks his instrument down at the local nightclub? He's crying, 'does anyone love me? Does anyone care if I'm around?' "

Jesus prophesied that before the end comes the love of most people would grow cold. The world has a reputation for coldness and unfeeling brutality. But when even God seems to say goodbye and to leave you to capricious fate, what do you do?

The characteristic of Mary's personality that elevates her to supreme importance in the sight of God is that quality of remaining open to new possibilities from God's hands. After that first hesitating request for further information, "How can I be a mother when I'm not married and haven't had sexual intercourse?" she moves right on to receive everything from God, even the suffering which was to share equal time with her joy. God's promise becomes a new reality in her life, a reality which supersedes all other realities.

Why should any of us expect more from life than our Lord received at its hands? His only inheritance was a borrowed cross. The world may fashion a cross for you and many of you have experienced suffering for Jesus' sake. In the mystery of grace you learn that this, too, is part of the favor of God. Nevertheless, I've seen many of you writhe in pain because of the responses people have given you. One of you fought for honesty in your business, and because of it your partners destroyed you and your firm went into bankruptcy. But you accepted your lot with courage and started again, going on in the spirit of Jesus "who for the joy set before him endured a cross."

The Hope of Christmas

Love alone sees the potential and the lover cuts away at anything that destroys the relationship between self and God. The sculptor chips away all irrelevant material until the real image is brought forth. The process can be hurtful but also amazingly redemptive. Jesus said, "Blessed are the meek for they shall inherit the earth." The meek are disciplined, those who have brought all other drives under Christ's control. The biblical picture is of a wild horse who is bridled without any destruction of power. Those wild drives are simply redirected under the command of the one who holds the reins. Everything works together in disciplined beauty.

Do you marvel at the sheer audacity of God, daring to invest so much in so seemingly small a person? Are you aware that the whole plan of world redemption pivots on one seemingly insignificant girl? Do you realize that all the future years are to be shaped by her lonely response? Doesn't this give you hope?

She found favor, the grace of God, and she bore God's Son in her human body. God hasn't really changed that approach. The record says that to as many as received him he gave power to become children of God. And Paul exults, "Christ in me, my hope of glory!"

Isn't this the very point of Christmas?

A letter came from a college woman fighting her way through cynicism and doubt. The worship experience with us loosed a chain of events which led to a searching of her own spirit and a longing for personal peace. She concluded her letter, "Pray for my new relationship with him. He's not dead; he's not just another picture on the wall. Jesus is alive for us and, thank God, *with* us!"

God says to you today, "Hail, O favored one, the Lord is with you!" He comes, striding roughshod across all barriers, to share his life with you. Believe it! That's the point of Christmas!

ERLING H. WOLD
St. Olaf Lutheran Church
Garden Grove, California

GOD IN OUR MIDST

The Nativity of Our Lord—Christmas Day
Luke 2:1-20

"And this will be a sign for you; you will find a babe wrapped in swaddling cloths and lying in a manger" (Luke 2:12).

It is surprising that the shepherds didn't ask further directions from the angel. Among the many babes in the crowded city, there should have been further directions to mark the Christ out. But obviously, there was one place where no one in his wildest imagination would look for a baby . . . precisely in an animal manger. Animals and human beings might live in the same house in rural Palestine, but within the house, one drew the line of space even if he couldn't divide the odors. The manger was the private possession of the animals. And it was here that the shepherds came.

Of all the Christmas cards I have received, one I cannot get out of my mind at Christmas time. It came from an elderly lady of eighty, a former parishioner of mine, who lived on in a farmhouse on the edge of town that had seen better days. She was always surrounded by chickens, and pigs running between the house and the fence with an occasional stray cow complicating her life. She and her sister were all that was left of the family, and they tried to make it alone without the help of younger strength. But they were always falling over chickens and breaking a limb or a hip. And here was their card to me, wishing me a Merry Christmas, and scribbling:

"Our Lord comes to us, even in the midst of our mess." I knew immediately what she meant . . . for the memory of that impossible mess was still fresh in my mind. Faith like that is rare to behold.

But I would guess the reason why this card keeps popping up in my imagination is that, as the years pass with all of us, the accumulations of a life-time seem to crowd in on our sense of order. Each clean-up becomes overwhelmed at the size of the mess; retirement itself is just one massive clean-up—or else a slow death in the midst of the mess. And we have somewhere in our minds the conscience that says that we can only expect the visit of the Holy One if the mess gets cleaned up. Yet the message of Christmas and this precious card is that Christ comes in the middle of the mess. The spontaneity of the story leaves no room for preparation. Haste is necessary to really take in the marvel of the birth. The shepherds must run to find the child in a manger and catch the glory of the moment when God's Son appears in an animal's feeder.

Growing up in America with its clean division between barn and house, I didn't realize the exact nature of the manger till I visited European villages where human beings and animals mingle in sleep and where the odors are a lingering part of the rural home. Then I understood, for the first time, Luther's earthy descriptions of our Lord's first home.

If this were merely the story of a hero's birth, we could pass it by. Legend is full of stories like this. Then the hero grows away from it. But the story of the manger is really the setting of our Lord's ministry. When he emerged as an adult, teaching, you will remember he came to the synagogue in his home town Nazareth and announced his text from Isaiah:

> The Spirit of the Lord is upon me because he has anointed
>   me;
> he has sent me to announce good news to the poor,
> to proclaim release for prisoners and recovery of sight for
>   blind;
> to let the broken victims go free,
> to proclaim the year of the Lord's favor.

And then he simply announced that the prophecy was now fulfilled; he was in a movement which brought the power of the kingdom right to those who were caught in the social mess. People couldn't understand this. For after all, wasn't religion made up of acts of scrubbing up, and getting well dressed? Wasn't the kingdom supposed to be the crowning touch for those who were on tip-toe, rather than some moving power to those who were already hopelessly tied up in their own failures?

You remember how Jesus spent all of his time with the messy people in the back alleys, while the religious waited impatiently for him on the front sidewalks. And he replied, "The Son of Man came to minister to the poor and the sick and the lepers."

The church does not allow us to forget this in Christmas time. We sing the Song of Mary:

> He hath put down the mighty from their seats,
> And exalted them of low degree.
> He hath filled the hungry with good things;
> And the rich he hath sent empty away.

The great Epiphany Psalm 72 echoes the same theme:

> He will be the deliverer of the poor,
> a friend to those who have no one.
> For humble people he is within reach,
> He gives hope to those without rights.
> Their blood is precious in his eyes,
> he ransoms them from the house of slavery.

I love that one verse, and believe my Christmas well-wisher knew it too:

> "For humble people he is within reach."

Scholars today are really groping behind the written gospels for the figure of Jesus, lost in the oral traditions about him. What was he really like? What actions and words that we have are absolutely genuinely his? And their lines of exploration all seem to cross over at the messy places in his society. There he could be found in the midst of the mess, announcing the wonderful good news about the availability of the Father's power, bringing the forgiveness of sins and the removal of men from the oppressing powers of the mess. The messiness itself is the exact place where the good news of God's forgiving power does its first work. My former parishioner had hit the nail on its head when she suspected Christ would come in the midst of the mess.

Christians throughout the world are finding the same message.

I remember the dark pessimism that hung over the mission of the church in the late fifties and early sixties. The rise of nationalism throughout the world had brought forth the old religions in a huge burst of power, overcoming the lands where Christian missions were established. Meetings were held to discuss what would become of the weak younger churches . . . it seemed that the whole Christian mission was dying.

The churches themselves reexamined their Bibles in the light of their world situations and they discovered a Jesus they had not suspected. They found him in the middle of their oppressed situation, in their mess, and discovered him as the Liberator of the oppressed, the friend of the poor. Today, these churches in South America and Africa speak to us about their Lord in world terms. They have taught us to find Jesus Christ in the face of the poor, the hungry, the bound. He comes in the middle of our mess.

We cannot close what we have to say without setting this in a world context. No one can think of the manger scene today without remembering the original Bethlehem, now threatened with war. A Jewish writer in the *New York Times* (December 22, 1974) described typical Jewish approaches to the critical situation of its survival. He found in their history two approaches to such crises: first, the mass suicide of the nation in self-defense, second, the imagined conflict in the ultimate clash between good and evil:

> Jewish tradition tells us that problems can have a natural or miraculous solution. To the never-ending Arab-Israeli wars, Masada and Armageddon are natural solutions. The miraculous solution is peace. Israeli's acceptance by its neighbors remains the cardinal natural objective, but its realization would appear to require time of Messianic dimensions. Still, it is sometimes an imperative of realism to seek the impossible.

Unsuspectingly, this writer put his finger on exactly the Christian claim and message. It is the transformation of life in the power of the Spirit at the heart of the messiness. It is the Messiah taking upon himself the pain and suffering of the situation and announcing the forgiveness of sins. It is truly a miraculous solution for God's Son himself works in the midst of the mess . . . his name shall be Emmanuel, that is *God with us.*

HENRY E. HORN
University Lutheran Church
Cambridge, Massachusetts

DON'T EXCHANGE THE GIFT!

First Sunday after Christmas
Luke 2:25-38

History has a strange way of repeating itself. Assuming that that is true of the current post-Christmas activity, the gift exchange enterprise has consumed much time, energy, frustration, aggravation, and produced perhaps very little real satisfaction. We are here today to urge you with all of the persuasion we can apply under the blessings of God's Holy Spirit that you do not exchange the gift—the real gift of Christmas.

You Really Shouldn't Have

One of the more common cliches spoken by the recipient of a gift to the donor is: "You really shouldn't have." Now, while that is normally considered a compliment, suggesting that the gift has been most extravagant or that the recipient is really not worthy of such great kindness, what is often meant is: "You really shouldn't have because this isn't what I want. It's the wrong color, the wrong size, the wrong style. You really shouldn't have"! That that is the meaning of "You really shouldn't have" is obvious now by the post-Christmas dash to the store at which the unwanted item was purchased. Without pursuing this too far, it is quite possible that some people remember their Christmases past by the things they got via the gift exchange route. Again, I want to issue this warning—don't exchange the gift!

There is a gift—the gift of Christmas—that is not to be exchanged. Of this gift from God we might say: "You really shouldn't have," but it was the only way God could win us back to his everlasting love. This gift, the gift of his Son our Savior, is the only gift that brings peace—real and lasting and living peace for now and forever. Don't exchange that gift.

Just Another Baby Boy

For many, Christmas is nothing but a baby. If that was all there had been to the first Christmas, just a baby, there wouldn't have been a second Christmas, nor this one just celebrated. If the average Publican or Pharisee or Sadducee had happened by the Bethlehem manger scene recorded in the Gospel of Luke he wouldn't have been terribly troubled—"it's just another Jewish baby boy. Mazel tov. Good luck to him." There was really only one person beyond the select and special few of whom we read in the Christmas gospel, who saw in Christ more than "just another baby" who might have been exchanged for a thousand other babies. That one was Herod.

Advised that the baby whose birth drew unusual visitors from distant lands was not just a baby who might be exchanged by a number of other babies, Herod set about to have the newborn king of the Jews slain. His pogrom was clumsy and heartless. One doesn't chop down an apple tree to pick an apple, and yet it was that sort of illogical program of wholesale slaughter Herod devised in seeking to assure himself the security of the throne over against a baby boy who posed as a threat to him. All baby boys two years old and younger were to be killed.

The senseless slaughter that evoked "wailing in Ramah" is observed on this date by ancient appointment. Tradition has given this 28th day of December the name: The Holy Innocents. For more than 15 centuries Christians have been recalling that little band of unwitting martyrs. But, as we said before, for most of the residents and visitors in the city of David, Christ was but another little baby boy.

Unfortunately for some, the Christ of Christmas is just one of many elements that go into the making of Christmas. Making him that it is quite possible that he actually runs the risk of being exchanged for something else.

But that isn't the way Simeon saw it. Simeon, we are told in our text, saw in Christ the One desired. Simeon realized that by having Christ and the peace that the Christ brings, he had all that he wanted . . . all that he needed for time and for eternity. Simeon wasn't interested in exchanging the gift. Nor should we be.

Peace Assured

We know so very little about this holy poet, but what we do know about him is important. The words that describe him are so acceptable: "righteous—devout—looking for the consolation of Israel (that is, the coming of the Savior)—the Holy Spirit was upon him." Because all of those things were true about him, he understood why the gift of Christmas was not to be exchanged. Because of his intimate knowledge of God it didn't strike Simeon at all strange that he should be directed to the temple of Jerusalem. Nor did he consider it spectacularly unique that he should be able to select the proper trio from all the other husband-wife-infant combinations that peopled the crowded temple courtyard.

We can rest assured that Christ wasn't the only infant brought to the temple by his parents that day. After all, every mother came to the temple 40 days after the birth of a male child for proper ceremonial purification. It wasn't that Mary and Joseph and the infant were identified by some chubby little cherub choir hovering above as they moved into the area or that Mary and Joseph were equipped with identifying halos. That wasn't necessary. People very close to God—those who are constantly concerned about living more closely to him and his Word—will find it very easy to be led by him. That was the experience of Simeon. And then also, although there are no words of dialog recorded of that exchange between Mary, Joseph, and Simeon, it would seem that the Bethlehem parents sensed a deep spirituality in this man who stood before them with his arms outstretched. Having cradled the holy child in his arms, he addressed the Father of this child, Almighty God, our heavenly Father. Those words we have as part of the rich treasure-trove of our liturgy.

In some of the more contemporary orders of the Holy Communion the Nunc Dimittis, as this poem of praise and thanksgiving uttered by Simeon is known, is omitted. While it is true that the Western Rite never did include it as part of the eucharistic worship, there is meaning in its employment. As Simeons of today, we respond to the promptings of the Holy Spirit when we join with the fellowship of redeemed in our public worship. As the Simeon of old, we come to the inner sanctuary of God's holy temple, our house of worship, and in faith we stretch forth our arms to receive the gift. And having thus received him in the Holy Communion, we can return to the world with the assurance of peace. "Let us depart in peace, according to your Word." Don't exchange the gift, that gift.

After Simeon spoke those wonderful words of peace and salvation for all the world through faith in Christ Jesus, he directed a word of blessing to the parents of the gift and then, specifically to Mary, he spoke words that concerned the manner in which her Son would reveal the hearts of many people. It is true that energy restrictions have imposed something of a brown-out of Christmas lights, especially in the residential areas. But the electrical displays of yesterday were not necessarily indications of the hearts of the residents in the gaily gleaming homes. Not so with the gift. The gift of Christmas reveals who we really are. What you think of Christ is the question that we answer in the manner in which we live the gift in our relationships to our neighbors in all the world.

The Revealer of Hearts

After those words of Simeon, the report goes on to state that a frequent visitor to the temple named Anna, a pious woman known for her spiritual disciplines approached and spoke words of thanksgiving to God for providing the redeemer of the world. Earlier, it is stated that Mary and Joseph marveled at that which was spoken to them by Simeon. No doubt they reacted in the same way to the words of Anna. What is our reaction? That is best illustrated in the way in which we value the gift. Would we exchange the gift?

The world in which we live at this moment is very much like the shops that have been filled with exchangers of gifts these past days. The decorations of the season have lost some of the attraction. For many with the jaded taste of the abundant life, there is little that holds appeal. The p.a. system's droning of carols sounds dated. Where has the melody of life gone? The whirly tempo of the rat race crowds out the melody of life. The packages being brought into the stores are not as attractive as they were when purchased. Brown paper bags transport unwanted merchandise. In many instances the price tags on unsold stock have already been adjusted to bargain price levels. So, many of the things for which we have worked and toiled in this world as securities over against another day are becoming less and less valuable as each turn of the inflation cycle is completed. They are possessions that lose their value in a world where values are slipping more and more. But don't exchange the gift.

Don't exchange it? you ask. If we aren't to exchange it, what are we to do with it? This is a gift that is to be shared, for only in the sharing of it will we be able to keep it. Only in the sharing of it will we be presenting to others that and that alone which provides gladness for sorrow.

Share the Gift

This gift has been prepared before the face of all people. You've heard that before, haven't you? But have you accepted it? You know, only as we appropriate the promise of God—his peace, his lasting and living and loving peace, will we be convinced that the gift that is not to be exchanged is indeed the gift that is to be shared. Have you shared the gift?

God wants you to have this gift and to keep it. That is good of him, isn't it? But you will hold it and keep it only as you share it. And share it you will as you realize that this gift is the only gift that can effect the healing and the help that the weary world needs, as it has always needed it, and as it has never needed it before. In this world so dark with sorrow and tragedy and suffering, the gift of light is needed. There is something marvelous about a fireplace, isn't there? We can sit before the blazing logs by the hour and feel as though the time spent wasn't at all wasted. The beauty of the flame doing its entrancing choreography is intensified the more when it is shared with loved ones, friends and neighbors. So also the blazing love that flames from the heart of God is something that is more meaningful when shared. Are you interested in sharing the gift? Is your church congregation, your denomination?

No doubt many of us have chuckled at the revisions innocently made by children who repeat what they hear when they speak the Lord's Prayer through their little lisping lips. There was that version done by a little lad who prayed: "Lead us not into Penn Station." That's an old one. We heard a more recent innocent innovation the other day. A curly-haired girl of four prayed: "Forgive us our Christmases."

Is this a Christmas to be forgiven? Or is this a Christmas in which we have by the grace of God seen in the celebration of the Savior's birth a gift, the most priceless gift that can be kept only by sharing? Let us then clasp him to our heart, as did Simeon. Let us more deeply live the peace of which the Christ came to live and to die and to rise again. Above all, let's not exchange it. Let's share the gift!

CYRIL M. WISMAR
Clifton Lutheran Church
Marblehead, Massachusetts

YOUR NAME, RELATIONSHIPS, DESTINY, AND BEHAVIOR

The Name of Jesus
Luke 2:21

And at the end of eight days, when he was circumcised, he was called Jesus, the name given by the angel before he was conceived in the womb.

The Name of Jesus

The name of Jesus described his identity. His identity was described in terms of relationships. The angel Gabriel said to Mary, "Behold, you will conceive in your womb and bear a son, and you shall call his name Jesus." An angel gave the same message to Joseph when he said, "Joseph, son of David, do not fear to take Mary your wife, for that which is conceived in her is of the Holy Spirit; she will bear a son, and you shall call his name Jesus, for he will save his people from their sins."

Jesus' Names and Our Names

The name of Jesus identified him as our Savior. Identity has to do with relationships. Jesus' given name described his relationship to us and to all men as our Savior.

Our last name describes our relationship to our families. Names are meant to tell a story. Otterness describes a piece of land on a fjord in Norway. Otter stands for a sea otter. Ness means a nose or point. Thus, Otterness was a point of land on the fjord where the sea otters lived. The families that lived there took the name of the land.

My grandfather could also have taken the name of Olson, because he was Ole, the son of Ole. This was the tradition for the last name in Scandinavia, and also the tradition for the Jewish people at the time of Jesus. Peter was known as Simon, bar Jonah, or Simon, son of John. James and John were known as sons of Zebedee.

Jesus had a double identity. First, he was the Son of man by birth of the Virgin Mary, and second, he was Son of God by conception of the Holy Spirit.

In other traditions, people got their names and their identity from their work. Many have names like Baker, Smith, Banker, Fisher, and other names that describe work or a profession. I have noticed that most people, today, get their identity from their jobs. First, people ask your name, and then they want to know where you work, and then where you have come from. This is an effort to establish your identity. Jesus came from Nazareth in Galilee, and he also came from his Father in heaven, and his job was to be our Savior.

Personal Names and Impersonal Numbers

Jesus' given name described his purpose in life, to be our Savior. Our parents have also given us a personal name. It may or may not have something to do with a purpose our parents had in mind for us. Our parents' hopes for us and what we actually do with our lives may be far apart. But they did give us a personal name.

Governments, institutions, and businesses keep on giving us numbers instead of names. We are known by social security numbers, employee numbers, credit card numbers, military service numbers, and tax numbers which tend to make us nameless and faceless people. Being a number destroys us, because it establishes no personal relationships. We can be identified only by the computer.

The Relationship God Wants for Us All

A wonderful description of the relationship God wants between us and himself is found in the first chapter of Ephesians. In verse three, Paul says that God the Father has blessed us in Christ with *every spiritual blessing.*

The first blessing is that he chose us in Christ before the foundation of the world that we should be holy and blameless before him. Jesus was given a name before he was conceived in the womb. We were chosen by God before the world was ever created.

This means that God has taken the initiative. As Jesus said to his disciples, "You have not chosen me, but I have chosen you," even so God chose us before the world was created, because that is when he decided to send his Son as our Savior.

This is really good news. When children choose up teams, everyone wants to impress the captain to choose him. He says that he can run, catch the ball, or do something better. He tries to impress the captain with a reason to choose him. Not so with God. God decided that he wanted us to stand in special relationship with him before the foundation of the world. It was then that he chose to send his Son to be our Savior.

We do not need to impress God. He has already decided. He wants you and me to belong to him. He has chosen us in Christ to be holy and blameless before him.

The second blessing is that God destines us to be his children. This is God's will for us, to stand in special relationship to him as his children. God, the Father, wants to have the same relationship with us as he has with his Son, Jesus Christ. This is a mind stretching thought. Most of us do not think highly enough of the destiny God has in mind for us. John speaks of this in his first epistle when he says, "As he is, so are we in this world." It is hard to believe this, especially when we are keenly aware of our own sinfulness.

This special relationship with God can only be accomplished by his glorious grace which he has freely bestowed upon us. God has looked squarely and realistically at our sins, and he has taken action to help us through Jesus Christ.

The free gift of God's grace is difficult for us to accept. In my junior high confirmation class, I offered anyone in the class a one dollar bill. No one came up to receive it, even after a lot of repeated offers. Then, I asked why no one came. They answered that they did not want to accept the dollar because it was too expensive for me, and made them feel guilty. I said that I also knew it was expensive and wanted them to receive it with gratitude and not with guilt. If we can not receive a gift with gratitude, we can not be children of God. We are to trust God's promise, and receive his grace with gratitude. With this explanation, in a short time, I had given away fourteen one dollar bills.

God's gift of grace is tremendously expensive, but it is still free. Receive it graciously with gratitude and be happy about it like the confirmation class.

The third blessing is that in Christ, we have redemption. Redemption means to be brought back. A favorite story of mine is one I heard about a boy who made a small sailboat and then took it to the lake. He set it in the water and the wind caught the sail, taking it some distance across the lake. By the time the boy got to the other side, someone else had already picked up the sailboat and taken it home. Some time later, this boy saw his sailboat in the window of a pawn shop, and it was for sale. He went in and bought it. Then he said, "Now, I own you twice. First, I made you. Then, I bought you back."

This is what God has done for us. First, he made us. Then we became lost in our sins, and he bought us back in Jesus Christ. This is the relationship that God intended in the first place. He brings us back to himself in the forgiveness of sins. This is what Hosea did for his unfaithful wife. First, he married her, and then he took her back many times in forgiveness. Finally, he found her for sale as a cast out whore, and bought her back for about fifty cents because he still loved her.

The description of God's grace is extravagant. Paul speaks of God's grace which he has lavished upon us. The word lavish brings to my mind the picture of strawberry shortcake, with a great abundance of strawberries and whipped cream running from the top and over the sides of the dish, far more than necessary. This illustrates God's forgiveness and grace. They are not just barely enough. They are far more abundant than our sins. They are lavished upon us in the generosity of God. We continue to live in the lavished grace of God.

The fourth blessing is that God has let us in on the mystery of his plan to unite all things in Christ. This unity means the restoration of harmony in all of God's creation. We experience a part of this now; and the complete fulfillment of God's plan will take place when Christ comes again. When we are falling apart now because worry and anxiety have gotten the best of us, Christ is able to hold our shot nerves together in his grace and forgiveness. Faith in his promises to help, strengthen and guide us, will hold us together through thick and thin.

When people are falling apart, meaning broken marriages, torn up families, and ruined friendships, Christ is able to bring back and hold these people together. The secret is the forgiveness of sins. Only forgiveness in Christ can unite people who have fallen apart. After they are reunited, they can only stay together by continued forgiveness and living in grace. Grace is God's power and help for imperfect people to keep on loving one another. God's love is not idealistic love, but realistic and gracious love.

Idealistic love always leads to alienation, because you are disappointed in the behavior of another person and fail to remember, as God remembers our frame, "that we are dust." Gracious and realistic love takes into account that all of us need forgiveness and strength for our weakness. Our only hope for unity is the gracious love of God in Jesus Christ.

Our Identity and Our Behavior

The name of Jesus Christ, the Son of God, establishes his identity. The Son of God became a human being, Jesus of Nazareth, to become our brother and Savior. As someone has said, "He came to be a partaker of our humanity, so that we might become partakers of his divinity."

The destiny that God has in mind for every single one of us is to stand in the same relationship to him as his Son, Jesus Christ.

When our oldest daughter went away to college, we did not give her a lot of instructions. We simply asked her to always remember who she was. We were not asking her to remember that she was our daughter, but we were asking her to remember that, by grace, she was a child of God.

Knowing and remembering who you are determines how you behave. Jesus always knew and remembered who he was, and that determined his behavior. He said, "I and the Father are one. My will is to do the will of him who sent me."

Whatever your name is, I want you to know that by grace God has chosen you to be his child. Whatever your name is, I want you to know that by grace you can behave like a child of God, and people will see and know that Jesus Christ is your brother.

JAMES R. OTTERNESS
Lutheran Church of the Risen Lord
Odessa, Texas

TO SOLVE THE RIDDLE OF GOD

Second Sunday after Christmas
John 1:1-18

Few words in scripture have gripped the human mind with the power of the opening lines of the Fourth Gospel:

> In the beginning was the Word
> And the Word was with God
> And the Word was God . . .

The language is so simple that theological students who are learning Greek usually begin their study of the New Testament here. Yet the thoughts are so vast that the lines seem to have a magical power. The Western church used it for centuries as a blessing for the sick and for the newly baptized children. It was even placed in amulets and hung around the neck to protect one from sickness. In the present series of lessons for the church year, it is the only one that remains fixed throughout the three-year cycle.

It's seductive, though, to be so entranced by the mysterious repetition and simplicity of these words, that we forget their importance. Like all human words, they are meant to bear a message, and that message becomes clear only at the end of this passage:

> No one has ever seen God;
> It is God the only Son, ever at the Father's side,
> who has revealed him.

Jesus Christ has solved the riddle of God.

Riddles are not simply childish jokes. They have a long history in humanity's quest to understand the world. Have you heard of the "Riddle of the Sphinx?" The ancient Greeks told of a monster which came to the city each year with a riddle. "What speaks with one voice, but walks on four legs, on two legs, and on three legs?" If no one could answer, the sphinx would capture a victim and carry him away for dinner. Finally the hero Oedipus answered the riddle by saying that *man* crawls on all fours when he is small, walks on two legs when he is grown, and hobbles with a cane when he is old. By answering the riddle, he saved the city.

We still use the idea of "riddle" in this serious sense when we talk about the "riddle of life" or the "riddle of suffering."

For many people *God* is a riddle. They would pose the question like this: "If there is a God, why do the innocent suffer? Why is there so much pain and sorrow in the world?"; or they ask "Why does God demand so much of us, when he didn't create us perfect in the first place?"

We ought to take these questions quite seriously, because they remind us that the existence of evil and imperfection becomes an acute problem when we dare to talk about a *loving* God. Even the church calendar poses this riddle when it places observance of St. Stephen's Day and Holy Innocents Day right after Christmas Day. It's as though we barely have time to hear the angels sing about "peace on earth" before we are reminded that people like Stephen were stoned for their Christian faith, and that a king so feared the coming of Christ that he tried to kill all the children under two years of age. For a Christian, then, the riddle would be: "What kind of a God would let himself and his followers be pushed around by a hard and cruel world?"

We are not the first ones to puzzle over this question. The Gospel lesson for today reminds us that confusion and misunderstanding have clouded the good news of God from the beginning. "He was in the world ... yet the world knew him not," says our text. "He came to his own home and his own people received him not." The rest of the book of John repeatedly calls attention to the fact that people misunderstood Jesus—from Nicodemus asking "How can a man be born again when he is old?" to Pilate impatiently snapping, "What is truth?"

And yet the answer to the riddle was there. That's the way it is with good riddles. When you *really* understand the question, you already have the answer. Do you remember that old favorite about "What is black and white and read all over?" The secret to that riddle was the sound of the word "read." Once you understood that it did *not* refer to a color, the answer to the riddle made sense. Or take the one that went:

"Railroad crossing, look out for the cars.
Can you spell it without any R's?"

When you realize that the task is to spell "it" rather than "railroad crossing," the answer becomes self-evident.

The riddle of God is a lot like that. Once we grasp the keyword, questions about his power and his will can be answered. The text for today says that Jesus is that key "word"; "And the Word became flesh and dwelt among us." When we try to solve the riddle of God from any other starting point, we run into a dead end. That's what Jesus meant when he said, "No man comes to the Father but by me."

How does Jesus solve the riddle? He shows us how God's power differs from our usual concept of power. For us, power means the strength to have our way, no matter who opposes us. We use it in words like "power-play," or "power-hungry." In a community, the people who make decisions and can enforce them are called the "power structure." We consider our nation a "world power"—or even a "super-power"—because our nuclear arsenal is so big. Nobody would dare to challenge us. Power is the ability to eliminate the opposition.

If that's what "power" means, then God should have the power to blot out evil, protect his followers, and eliminate suffering. But Jesus Christ shows us that God expresses his power in a different way. Instead of destroying suffering, he shows that suffering cannot destroy us. Prisoners of war have testified that the best resource they had against torture and abuse was the absence of fear. When they fretted about their reactions, the enemy had them in his grip. When they rose above the fear of the moment, they became free—though they had no power of their own. Christ met human anger, betrayal and even death, not by becoming angry himself, but by accepting the worst we could dish out— and proving that it could not destroy him. His resurrection illustrates how God's power works. It does not eliminate death. It simply takes away death's finality.

Jesus spent much of his ministry urging people to see that suffering does not go unnoticed. God marks the fall of the sparrow and the plight of the leper. God's way of dealing with our suffering is to accept it, to share it, and then to use it. And that's the way he dealt with our sin, too. He took it upon himself and used it, in the cross, as a means of breaking sin's hold on the world.

So Jesus becomes the key to understanding what a loving God can do for a suffering and sinful world. Perhaps in the year ahead we can remember that:

> Not with swords' loud clashing
> nor roll of stirring drums
> But deeds of love and mercy
> the heavenly kingdom comes.

HUGH GEORGE ANDERSON
President, Lutheran Theological Southern Seminary
Columbia, South Carolina

THE DARK SIDE OF EPIPHANY

The Epiphany of Our Lord
Matthew 2:1-12

How many of you are afraid of the dark? Only the children will raise their hands and admit that it's good to have mother or an older brother go up the dark stairs first and put on a light at the top. At eighteen months, my little girl slept alone on the second floor of an enormous, creaking farm-house-parsonage. She was most comfortable in the darkness. It is not natural to be afraid of the dark. In my daughter's case such fear is something she will probably learn from her world and will probably teach to her children.

What a blessing it would be if the only form of darkness that assailed us was the dark at the top of the stairs or the shadowy, spooky garage we were conditioned to fear as children. What a different world it would be if mankind were not enshrouded in the darkness of ignorance, hatred and unbelief. And what a life —were there no mysterious, dark closet called death.

Epiphany is a season of light, but also one of darkness and flickering shadows, a time Christians set aside to remind themselves and the world that Christ has overcome every evil power associated with our public and very private versions of darkness.

The Darkness Prefigured

There is something about the story of the Wise Men that has always made me feel uneasy, but I have never known why. On the surface it has an almost story-book quality that has captured the imagination of generations. Consider the lore and tradition surrounding the subjects of "We Three Kings of Orient Are." It doesn't really matter that the title to that song is inaccurate on three counts, namely, that there were not necessarily three, Scripture specifying no number; that they were not kings but "magi" or wise men; and that they came more probably from Persia than the Orient. Likewise tradition has assigned names to the magi: Caspar, Melchior and Balthasar; and ages: twenty, forty and sixty; and races: white, yellow and black. All the pretty *fiction* that has grown up around the *fact* of the Wise Men almost obscures the all-important dark side of the story. For in the background, behind the wondrous babe and the eastern sages lie evil, terror, and malignity without motive.

That evil centers in the figure of Herod. He is so bad that his sinfulness seems at first a caricature. He initially strikes us as the buffoonish villain in a melodrama complete with ill-fitting brush mustache—until we get a glimpse into the depths of his fear and the horrors it produces. After his conversation with the magi, Herod "was troubled." The Greek word can mean, "he was terrified." What was it about a baby that could terrify a king? Everyone knows an older brother or sister can be threatened by a new baby, but how a king? What was it about a baby that could incite this king to Hitler-like genocide? The same king who with sugary hypocrisy had said, "When you find him, let me know so I can worship him," later slaughtered all male children in Bethlehem under two years of age. It was Herod's Epiphany massacre. And it's the first indication of the evil Jesus would arouse in man.

Jeremiah had a vision of the evil when he wrote:
> A voice is heard in Ramah,
> lamentation and bitter weeping.
> Rachel is weeping for her children,
> she refuses to be comforted for her children,
> because they are not (Jer. 31:15).

Even the jolly Christmas carol "We Three Kings of Orient Are" surprises us by injecting a note of doom in the unfamiliar last stanza:

> Myrrh is mine, its bitter perfume
> Breathes a life of gathering gloom;
> Sorr'wing, sighing, bleeding, dying,
> Sealed in the stone-cold tomb.

Myrrh, the spicy gum of an Arabian tree, appears in only one other significant role in the New Testament. Jesus' secret disciple Nicodemus brings myrrh mixed with aloes to prepare the body of his Lord for burial. Myrrh for birth, myrrh for death. What a miracle! God protects his Son from one terrified king until the time would come when another king, this time a Roman procurator equally terrified of Jesus' authority, would have him crucified.

This is the dark side of Epiphany with its own message for us: Jesus has come to confront the great evil in this world head-on. Throughout his ministry Jesus encountered opposition; throughout the history of the church, Christians have met persecution. In the book of Revelation we discover that this hatred for Christ will not diminish with time but will intensify and grow like a cancer in history until at the end of history the antichrist will be loosed upon the earth, combining in himself all the hatred, paranoia and evil of a thousand thousand Herods. The darkness hates the light. You can bet Herod hated that star.

The Darkness Defeated

Epiphany is the season of the star. The Old Testament lesson for today sounds the theme, "Arise, shine; for your light has come" (Isa. 60:1). A recent magazine article tells of a city of 40,000 people named Tromsø, located in the northernmost reaches of Norway. It is an ordinary city except from November 25 to January 21 when the sun does not rise above the horizon. During this two-month period of perpetual night the article says, "the mentally unstable may slip over the edge into a temporary state of profound mental disturbance. Even those who are emotionally healthy the rest of the year may become tense, fearful and pre-occupied with thoughts of suicide." During the period of darkness the least desirable elements in humanity come to the surface: envy, suspicion, egotism. The citizens long for the light and hate to be alone; they install neon lighting systems around the windows of their homes and brood until finally on January 21, celebrations begin, schools are closed, and they welcome the sun over the horizon with shouts of "There she is; she's back! She's back!"

There's a town that would value the words of today's Old Testament lessons and would appreciate the dark and the *bright* side of Epiphany. And there *is* a bright side. Matthew is announcing through the story of the Magi that the Jewish baby born in a manger is the Lord of the Gentiles too. We are not preoccupied with the Jew-Gentile dilemma as Matthew's first readers were, but we can rejoice that Christ came for people of all races and all socio-economic levels. He calls people who are not *just like me*. Jesus is King of kings and Lord of lords. The wisdom of the world falls on its face and worships the wisdom of God. All nature, represented by the star (we will let the astronomers argue whether or not it was Jupiter and Saturn in conjunction), rejoices in his birth, just as nature would quake and grow sullen at his death.

Throughout the coming weeks each Gospel lesson will provide a mini-Epiphany, a little glimpse into the divinity of Jesus. Next week, for example, at his baptism, we will hear the voice of God say, "This is my beloved Son." As Christians we pray that our lives would follow the pattern of Epiphany, that the light of Christ would grow brighter and brighter in our hearts until faith in the risen Christ is translated into a face-to-face vision of the Son of Righteousness.

As beautiful as the light imagery is in Scripture, there are also, as the Norwegians name them, murky times, periods of darkness when the light of Christ is dim, and all the Herods in our world and the Herod in us seem to be gaining the advantage. I can only grieve when I see the Epiphany process working backwards. It disturbs me when I see people who once had the light of Christ in them now living in the shadows of doubt on the periphery of the church. It saddens me to see young people reared in Christ who now feel they have outgrown Christ the way one outgrows braces or a high school prom. Why has the light failed? Or has it?

It is a truism to say that there are many factors in a twentieth-century person's environment which militate against a strong Christian faith: sure there are drugs; and when hasn't there been sex? And of course violence is everywhere. But in addition to this unholy trinity there is also something in ourselves that tells us we really do not need the light of Christ, nor the glory of the open tomb. There is a gross enemy of Christ in each and every one of us that will let us worship only what the tyrannical crowd approves as cool. The enemy suggests reverence only for that which fulfills our own ambitions or gratifies our own desires.

When we affirm Christ's resurrection victory over all forms of darkness, we begin with the private and work outward to the public. We begin with the insecurities, anxieties, and deep-seated hatreds which feed upon themselves in us and cause us to wound other people. These are the very powers of darkness which dissipate in the light of Christ. Living in a society that revels in seeking out the sordid side of life, we celebrate the little visions of Christ that keep us going and keep us struggling in the battle against the larger and more public forms of darkness in the world.

The Wise Men came to worship Christ. Their kind of worship, the kind that gives to God the very best man has to offer, does indeed afford the epiphanies we need to carry on the work of the church. In fact, as his children of the light, we become a part of those epiphanies for others as we reflect his light. "Let your light so shine before men that they may see your good works and glorify your father in heaven." All are needed in this Epiphany task: wise men, housewives, businessmen, shepherds, students, so all of us can join in celebrating the season of the star. "Arise, shine; for your light has come."

RICHARD LISCHER
Prince of Peace Lutheran Church
Virginia Beach, Virginia

JOHN'S, JESUS', AND MY BAPTISM

The Baptism of Our Lord—First Sunday after the Epiphany
Mark 1:4-11

Identity Crises. We seem to have a lot of them around these days. Parents are scolded for permitting their children to develop an attitude of low self-esteem. We must not let them grow up feeling worthless. Teachers are told they must be continually encouraging their students. A system of rewards and punishments will, we are told, "modify" behavior.

It is most tragic to encounter a person constantly betraying feelings of worthlessness. It may be caused by parental rejection in early childhood, or a traumatic experience as a child.

Yet pouring soothing oil of commendation over deeply troubled psyches does not often reach the area of the wound.

We do need a good self-image, but that seldom results from superficial and mechanical application of verbal praise. Our egos cultivate a taste for encouragement. Like cracker jacks—the more we eat, the more we must have.

Social Identity Crises

Parallel to propping people up constantly with praise, is the penchant we have for turning adolescents in upon themselves. We continually tell them they must find their real personhood. It almost seems there are two kinds of people in the world—those searching for self-identity, and those busy attending the needs of others. The latter are too busy to have time to continually gaze at their own navels. And the really wondrous thing is that they find in the needs of others a crystalline mirror that gives them a revealing image of their own identity.

Our modern identity crises are, no doubt, deepened by a pervasive absence of identity among middle class, white people. Many are bored, fascinated temporarily by technological toys, or off on an occult experience if it doesn't demand too much. And then there are the more familiar forms of escape. It may be that that is why we are so frightened by black, brown or red power movements. Perhaps it is not the portents of violence so much as that we see others "getting it together" ethnically or personally.

Identity is a problem. For the Christian, there is nothing in God's promises that deals so searchingly with this question as an understanding of Baptism.

Today we consider three Baptisms—John's, our Lord's, and our own.

John's Baptism: Repentance for the Forgiveness of Sins

Some people would probably accuse John of having an identity problem. After all, didn't he say: "I am unworthy"? He said he was unworthy of being a *latros*, the lowest of the low servants of the household. He was not worthy to wash feet or bear cups. Today, we tip those who wait on tables or shine shoes, and one never tips an equal. John truly must have had a bad case of low self-esteem.

Yet John had an identity. He refused to be regimented to the rigors of studying under a rabbi, and perhaps some day becoming a Scribe. He refused becoming attached to the orders of being a Pharisee or Sadducee. John looked around and saw a people fallen into a deep pit of spiritual paralysis, who had not the nerve to overthrow the occupation forces. He knew they didn't need more rules to follow, or ideas with which to play. He saw death and decay. There is reason to believe that the Jewish people were in their lowest ebb of religious life.

And so John reached back into the history of his people and assumed the "role" he knew was most needed for this hour. He would be a prophet, but more than a prophet. He could see that what was needed was repentance. No matter how painful for him or damaging that might be to fragile egos. He did not choose the soothing oil of commendation. He chose as his tool the cleansing water of renewal.

John's Baptism: A New Act

Some interpreters associate his water baptism with the proselyte baptism being practiced by some Jews who wanted a rite of passage for Gentile converts. But that was a ritualistic, ceremonial washing. John practiced a baptism that was entirely new. He called people to be baptized who were sorry for their sins, most all of them Jews. He dressed and ate like a prophet who would call for repentance. It was not because he was disagreeable that he wore a hair shirt. He wore one—like Elijah—so no one would mistake his message. He loved his people, but he knew they were dead in their sins. He did not give up his Jewishness, but ate foods—locusts and honey—that were kosher. He was not an ascetic so much as he was a prophet calling people back to their human identity as the forgiven people of God.

But he was more than a prophet in the Jewish tradition. He sensed that there was a new aeon dawning. They were trembling on the brink of the promised messianic age. This called for a new kind of baptism—a baptism unto the forgiveness of sins.

John had an identity. He was called to bring people to repentance and announce the good news of forgiveness! His feelings of unworthiness, especially in the company of the Christ, were insignificant as he came to know that God is a God of forgiving love, and was ushering in an even greater age of power and promise.

Jesus' Baptism: Identification with the Human Race

Even the Gospel writers seem a trifle embarrassed that Jesus chose to submit to the baptism of John. John certainly was. They knew his claim to innocence. Commentators on this text speculate in long involved paragraphs why Jesus should need the baptism of repentance for the forgiveness of sins. The only interpretation that makes any sense is the emendation in Matthew's story in which Jesus says this is done to "fulfill all righteousness." Jesus wanted to identify with us. It was his insatiable love for human beings like you and me that he submitted to John's baptism. Again and again, he goes out of his way to show us he was truly human. He identified with the dregs of humanity—prostitutes, quislings, and persons with whom we would not be even seen. He was tempted in all points, and he lived his life in all points, like us.

This was an act of identification with the human race. This was the anointing of the beloved Son who would usher in the new aeon. This is proclaimed in our second lesson for today in which Peter explains to the Gentile Cornelius that the new humanity begins with the baptism of Jesus (Acts 10:37). He is anointed with the Holy Spirit and turned loose to reveal to us what God is really like, and what true humanity is like. He identifies with us that we may have an identity.

The Church's Baptism: The Gifts of Forgiveness and the Holy Spirit

John's baptism was for those who longed to repent and be forgiven. This was still a preparatory act. John said a curious thing. He would baptize with the gift of forgiveness, but the Christ was to baptize with an even greater gift. Now we know that Jesus himself did not baptize. He was to commission his church to baptize not only with the gift of forgiveness and cleansing but also to bestow the gift of the *Holy Spirit*.

Many questions about baptism still divide the church. Oscar Cullman, the exceptional N.T. scholar, effectively dealt with such issues as infant or adult baptism, whether faith precedes or follows baptism, and the difference between "water" and "spirit" baptism: "Those who dispute the biblical character of infant Baptism have therefore to reckon with the fact that adult Baptism for sons and daughters born of Christian parents, which they recommend, is even worse attested by the New Testament than infant Baptism . . . and indeed lacks any kind of proof." (*Baptism in the New Testament*, p. 26). Yet infant baptism is not easily accepted on the basis of exposition of Scripture or argument. It comes to us only by faith. Indeed it is the most beautiful and explicit image of the operation of sheer grace we possess in the church. It is God working while we are yet helpless (Rom. 5:6).

Baptism Bestows Two Great Gifts

When the din of arguments about baptism recedes, we are left with the striking fact that there are two basic gifts bestowed on us in our baptism. One is the forgiveness of sins, in which we actually participate in the death of Jesus Christ, even as we walk with him in newness of life through the power of his resurrection (Rom. 6:4). The other great gift is that of the Holy Spirit. In Galatians, Paul reminds us that we are adopted as children by means of forgiveness, and this means that the Spirit is sent into our hearts (Gal. 4:4-6). God saves us "by washing of regeneration and renewal of the Holy Spirit" (Titus 3:5). We were baptized by one Spirit into the oneness of the body of Christ and "all were made to drink of one Spirit" (1 Cor. 12:13).

Thank God, the church is becoming much more aware of the work of the Holy Spirit and his gifts. The Scriptures are very clear about the importance of his gifts. But we must be equally clear that those gifts do not come by a special or additional baptism. We who are baptized possess the gift of the Spirit. We have it now. We live with that bold assurance.

And so we also have an identity. We are the forgiven followers of Jesus Christ empowered by his Spirit. We are baptized, therefore we are forgiven. We are baptized, therefore we are empowered by the Spirit.

Our fellow Christians in the Third World of Asia, Africa and Latin America often are puzzled by our continually asking the identity question: "Who am I?" They tell us in the first place the question should always be: "Who are we?" The latter question is much closer to biblical truth. Third World Christians tell us: "You Western Christians are too hung up on your individuality." Our baptism tells us we are adopted into a people of God. And when we are tempted to fix our attention on our own worthlessness we must, with Luther, write in large letters across our hearts "I am baptized!" Then a new understanding of self-worth can emerge. Identity is not based on being bathed in the soothing oil of commendation, but on having been cleansed by the water of our baptism by which we become participants in the death and resurrection of our Lord. We are baptized. We are the forgiven followers of Jesus Christ, empowered by his Holy Spirit. Baptism bestows a deeper self-worth, by which we can say: "I'm not OK .... you're not OK .... with God .... *That's* OK!" Amen.

L. DAVID BROWN
St. Paul's Lutheran Church
Waverly, Iowa

DOORS TO DESTINY

Second Sunday after the Epiphany
John 1:43-51

God offers each of us a glorious destiny! "He destined us in love to be his sons" (Eph. 1:5).

God intends great things for us, but he won't force them upon us. He wants everyone to be made whole and free—to be saved. He offers the truth that makes us free. But our destiny is not predetermined. We can refuse it or simply miss out on it.

God Acts

God works in many ways to call us and to invite us into our future. In Christ he came that we might have life and have it abundantly. In Christ he lived to reconcile the world to himself. At any moment, in any place, God may open for us doors to destiny. God acts through Christ, through Christians and through circumstances to "gentle us" toward the kingdom prepared from the foundation of the world. But the question is: Do we recognize God when he is trying to assist us?

T. S. Eliot said that "destiny waits in the hand of God." But God doesn't wait. God beckons through doors that he opens.

Let's look at the events by which God drew Nathanael to Jesus and offered him his place in the beginnings of the Christian church. By going through these doors Nathanael entered a life-transforming future. He found his "place." His life was fulfilled in the purposes of God.

Through Friends

First, we see that God opens doors through our friends. Sometimes we say, "It isn't what you know but who you know." Of course, what we know is not to be discounted. It does make an important difference. At the same time, friends and acquaintances make possible many things that wouldn't come about otherwise.

Think about it. Sometimes the door a friend opens is an opportunity for a good time, like going fishing or snowmobiling or to a play or concert. Sometimes it may be to a new experience. When I was in high school an announcement was made at the morning general assembly. We were told that try-outs for the debate squad were to be held that evening after classes. I was somewhat interested, but I didn't make up my mind about it, not until one of my friends said to me during lunch period, "Rey, are you going to the debate meeting today?" That friend was interested too, so we decided to go together. Just that little bit of encouragement opened a whole new experience for me that lasted through both high school and college. It led to friendships. It resulted in travel to new places. It added excitement. It produced skills. Through it God shaped my destiny. Ever since I've been grateful for the door that opened wide because of Tom. As Emerson wrote, "A true friend is somebody who can make us do what we can."

Note then what happened to Nathanael through his friend, Philip. Philip had answered Jesus' invitation, "Follow me." Jesus had really impressed him and in a special way. So Philip found Nathanael and said, "We have found the very person Moses wrote about in the book of the law, and of whom the prophets also wrote! He is Jesus of Nazareth, the son of Joseph."

So Philip shared a great spiritual find. He came to a friend and expressed his enthusiasm. He described in very specific terms the great discovery that he had made. He wanted his friend to be in on it.

Whenever a friend tells us about his Christian experience we ought to pay special attention. When, with excitement, he describes an experience with Jesus Christ, we ought to come on the alert. God opens doors through friends who tell enthusiastically what Jesus Christ means to them. Mrs. Browning, the poet, asked the novelist, Charles Kingsley, the secret of his life. Kingsley replied, "I had a friend!"

John Henry Jowett, a great and sensitive pastor, originally had no intention of becoming a minister. When he told a respected church school teacher his decision to enter law, this friend said, "I had always hoped you would go into the ministry." By that simple word, Jowett found his destiny.

Through Questions

God also opens doors through questions openly expressed. Nathanael wasn't ready right on the spur of the moment to respond to his friend's excitement. Most people wouldn't be. After all, Israelites had waited a long time for the deliverer expected by the prophets. A lot of leads had turned out to be dead ends. Furthermore, Philip's announcement had come without introduction. When friends surprise us with their enthusiasm we sometimes don't know what to do with it. We're embarrassed because it rather overwhelms us, especially if it's something as personal as religion.

So Nathanael picked up what may have seemed a minor point and asked a question. Philip had said Jesus was from Nazareth, which was just another small town fairly close to Bethsaida. Possibly there was friendly rivalry between the two villagers and the people joshed one another about it. So Nathanael asked, "Can anything good come out of Nazareth?" The question seems to be partly serious and partly a way of stalling for time. It expressed the best Nathanael could think of at the moment. He didn't pretend to have accepted his friend's testimony. Neither did he reject it. If he had doubts, his question was a way of letting them come out; it was a way of getting more information; it set the stage for Philip to say something more.

Questions openly expressed and directed to the right people can be God's door-openers. You remember how the Samaritan woman asked Jesus, "Where do you get that living water?" As a result, she and we have Jesus' promise: "Whoever drinks of the water that I shall give him shall never thirst; the water that I shall give him will become in him a spring of water welling up to eternal life."

Even if questions represent doubts, they should be openly expressed. Francis Bacon said, "In contemplation, if a man begins with certainties, he shall end in doubts; but if he be content to begin with doubts, he shall end in certainties."

Through Invitations

This brings us to a third way God opens doors, namely, through invitations offered and accepted. Philip understood his friend. He didn't reject the question. He didn't deny his friend's right to ask. In Christian circles there must always be room to ask questions and to let them lead to affirmations. "Doubt comes in at the window when inquiry is denied at the door."

So Philip offered Nathanael another open door: "Come and see!" Invitations can be so much better than arguments. Some things can't be demonstrated simply by argument. They have to be experienced. In matters of faith each of us must make his own discoveries. We must see for ourselves. Only then will we appropriate and appreciate.

Some of life's best unfoldings happen when we go along with someone who already has made a life-changing discovery in the kingdom of God. Then the adventure becomes a mutual discovery program. What's real about God for others should always receive our respect. When an invitation is offered, then it's up to us to make the next move. Many miss the great future God intends for them because they simply are too preoccupied to come and see. The artist, Sigismund Goetz, painted a picture showing Christ on the steps of St. Paul's Cathedral with the crowd blind to his presence. One man, buried in the sports page of the newspaper, almost brushes Christ as he passes. A scientist is too busy with his test-tube to notice the Lord. A couple, bent on pleasure, hurry into a taxi and don't see Jesus. An orator shouts at the crowd about the rights of men, with never a look at the great brother of all. Only a nurse catches a glimpse of Christ, but she too passes on.

Nathanael was interested enough, open enough and practical enough to accept Philip's invitation. God illumines those who are willing to look for themselves. "Behold, I stand at the door and knock," says the Lord, "if any man open the door I will come in to him and sup with him and he with me."

Jesus Christ: the Door

Most important of all of the doors God opens is his Son. No one comes to the Father without him; no one reaches his full destiny apart from Christ. But if we enter by Christ we shall be saved. We shall go in and go out and find both the food and the pleasure by which to live.

The very moment Jesus saw Nathanael he said, "Here is a real Israelite; there is nothing false in him!" How surprised

Nathanael must have been at this amazing statement. Jesus knew him! More than that, Jesus knew what kind of person he was!

Jesus also appreciated Nathanael's good qualities and understood his spiritual struggles. "Here comes a man who really deserves the name Israelite. He is incapable of any of the deceit that Jacob showed. He is transparent in every way. He neither hides his questions nor underestimates the enthusiasm of a friend."

When we come to Jesus Christ and he confronts us, we meet one who understands us through and through. He senses our problems. He appreciates our strength and our achievements. He knows our potential. The New Testament and the history of the church are full of persons who have had this kind of experience of Christ. Like Nathanael they have asked, "How do you know me?" They have received answers like to that given to Nathanael: "I saw you when you were under the fig tree, before Philip called you."

His Personal Touch

Even when we are unaware of Christ, or ignoring him, or rejecting him, the Lord sees us and our situation. To him we are individuals with unique characteristics, circumstances and possibilities. Doors open all over the place when we realize this. Lights come on; the future beckons; life begins to flower and bear fruit.

Jesus is the man of amazing insight and charisma. He is the person of wonder and mystery. So great his grace that before we even consider him he is concerned about us and treats us as persons. We need to pay attention to him until this realization dawns deeply and intensely within us. Augustine said, "God loves each one of us as if there were only one of us to love."

We need to focus steadily on Jesus until we feel his personal touch. Then doors swing wide open and we are moved to go through them out of free choice. Then we arrive at our own discovery of Christ; we make our own response to him; we have our own enthusiastic convictions to share.

Our Personal Response

Nathanael responded: "Teacher! You are the Son of God. You are the King of Israel!" He had found the Divine Instructor, chosen and anointed by God. He had come to see Jesus and discovered that he was seen by him.

Sir James Barrie tells the story of Jess, whose brilliant son, Joey, was killed when a cart ran over him. Joey was going to be a minister and his first sermon was to have been on the verse: "Thou God seest me." Twenty years after, Jess was telling about it. "Aye, but that day he was coffined, for all the minister prayed, I found it hard to say, 'Thou God seest me.' It's the text I like best too. . . . I turn't it up often in the Bible. . . . But juist when I come to 'Thou God seest me,' I let the Book lie in my lap, for once a body's sure o'that, they're sure o'all."

Quickened Expectations

When we go through the door of personal commitment to enter the realm of faith, Jesus sets our sights on the future. He quickens our expectations.

Jesus said to Nathanael: "Do you believe? You will see much greater things than this! You will see heaven open and God's angels going up and coming down the Son of Man." What this statement meant to Nathanael I'm not sure. It probably reminded him of Jacob's ladder. It must have given him a sense of wonder.

With Jesus Christ there's always something more. There's always something to which to look forward. No matter what our age or our circumstances, there's always room for spiritual growth. We may stop growing physically, but with Christ our destiny can unfold daily. "The path of the righteous dawns more and more to the perfect day."

For Nathanael this meant a daily walk with Christ. After the crucifixion, he became a missionary, first in Jerusalem, then in Asia Minor and then in southern Russia. Tradition says that he died as a martyr. His sights were set upon the kingdom of God.

God has great plans. He invites us to be a part of them. Before us he opens doors and *a* door and *the* door is Jesus Christ!

REYNOLD N. JOHNSON
St. Mark's Lutheran Church
Minneapolis, Minnesota

THE TIME HAS COME

Third Sunday after the Epiphany
Mark 1:14-20

The clock and calendar dictate much of our behavior. It's time for the news; time for school; time to go to work; time to gather all the forms for Internal Revenue. The time has come to face mounting unemployment and massive inventories that threaten our national economy and personal security. We can no longer ignore the prophets of doom who point to bleak and unpromising prospects. The new year has already lost its magic glow; and the moment of reality has come as the Epiphany star comes down.

Christ stepped into just such a setting. The once popular preacher of the wilderness had fallen into disfavor. The Baptist's call for repentance had been silenced by the bars of Herod's prison. Mark reports in terse phrases: "Now after John was arrested, Jesus came into Galilee, preaching the gospel of God, and saying, 'The time is fulfilled, and the kingdom of God is at hand, repent, and believe in the Gospel'" (Mark 1:14-15). *The time has come*—and Jesus comes to you and me.

For a Good Word

The time has come *for a good word*. Evidence surrounds us arguing loudly for despair and discouragement. Energy shortages, dwindling resources, inflation or recession, violence in our community and around the world—all these threaten our time. Realism requires that we acknowledge the fact that we face risks to our survival. Yet there is no need to draw the curtain on mankind in the midst of the tragic drama. There is a gospel sound; there is a good word that comes from Jesus in our time, too.

It's a word of hope that Christ offers. God comes among us with the sure word of the gospel that assures us of his love and presence. The restoration of confidence is possible for those who live in the power of the living Lord. The case for optimism rests on the promise of the gospel that "he will not leave us or forsake us." It knows that the Spirit gives the gifts that are necessary to bring meaning and purpose to life that comes under the love of Christ.

Isaiah knew the good word: "The people who walked in darkness have seen a great light; those who dwelled in a land of deep darkness, on them has light shined." The prophet describes our hope as the light of Christ shines on our darkness and death. Here in the light there is brightness and the potential for joy. Here in life that is given meaning by the grace of Christ is the key that will unlock the gloom of our time. That is the gift that you and I bring to our family; it is the offering that we give to our daily setting. Ours is the good word of hope. It is the clear word of confidence in Christ.

Norman Cousins says, "Hope cannot be ordered into being. Men in a condition of despair cannot be commanded to generate glorious dreams. But they can be encouraged to rediscover themselves" (SR/World 12/14/74, p. 5). Christ "came proclaiming the gospel of God" that encourages us to rediscover the potential that our Father gives us. He brings hope as he offers to give us daily the new start in forgiveness and grace.

That word of hope springs from the word of love that Jesus brings. The time has come for that good word to be sounded loudly and clearly. "God loves you! He loves you just as you are—with all your imperfections, failures, and rebellion." The Lord who loved the impetuous fisherman, Simon, Peter, loves us in our spasmodic bursts of discipleship too. The Christ who touched the diseased and healed the wounded still offers to reach out for those who will let that gift of love come to them.

The time has come for us to repeat the good word that God loves you and to make it personal and specific. *You* matter and *you* are worthwhile in the sight of God. No matter what others may think or say—how they may treat you or respond to you —how you manage on the ladder of life—God comes to touch your life with his love in Christ and you are worthwhile. That is a difficult gift for many to accept because we have been conditioned to devaluate ourselves. It's "just not Christian to say good things about yourself."

One of the stalling points for our council members at the recent retreat was completion of the sentence, "The thing that I like best about myself is. . . ." Some were not sure that they should be able to discuss their strengths and contributions. Weaknesses are more easily focused. Is it because our weaknesses may offer convenient excuses for evading involvement in the difficult situations of life? Surely you and I can accept ourselves and live with the blessings that God has given to us when we hear the good word of his love. "I believe that God has created me. . . . He has given and still preserves . . . all that I need for daily life." It's time for a good word of hope to come from all those who know that love through Christ.

For a Strong Faith

The time has come *for a strong faith*. "The kingdom of God is at hand, repent and believe in the gospel" was the core of Christ's call as he came into Galilee preaching. Jesus pointed to God's reign and invited his followers to enter the kingdom. Here is the Father and the relationship that all of us share as sons and daughters linked in his family. That main theme needs to be echoed among those who are without personal attachments and solid relationships. It needs to be offered as the strong and sure base that binds us to the living God who establishes his covenant with us. At our baptism, that contract was clearly stated: "The

Lord God who has begotten you again of water and his Spirit strengthens you with his grace unto life everlasting."

Strong faith focuses on participation in that kingdom with the love that Christ gives to us as his baptized children. It is not merely learning stories about Jesus and his ministry that constitutes faith. Instead those who know that biblical story are freed to live with the gift of life and grace. We are given a place on which to stand, a foundation on which to build. That faith understands possibilities; it does not merely count probabilities. It can risk openness and encounter because the life that comes in Christ has direction and it has a clear goal.

In his book *The Spirit of St. Louis,* Charles Lindbergh described the feeling of disorientation and its relationship to keeping alive. Lindbergh was lost in the fog in his flight across the Atlantic in 1927. He could not get his orientation and he panicked. He describes the moment this way:

> Subconsciously, without understanding the full significance of my action, I adopt a basic rule for the flight. Somewhere in the hidden recess of my mind I have discovered that my ability rises and falls with the essential problems that confront me. What I can do depends largely on what I have to do to keep alive, to stay on course. If there was no alternative, I could fly blind through fog during the night and day. The love of life is sufficient guarantee for that. But there is an alternative, the alternative of climbing faster, and that I choose. My head is thrown back to look upward. My neck is stiff. What of it? Hold on to those stars. Guide on them. Don't let them get away.

You and I can fly blind night and day. The love of life and the instinct for survival are sufficient reasons for that. But we have the option of holding on to the stars to orient ourselves to life's deep need of faith to guide it. Here is the One to whom that Epiphany star leads us. Before we permit that light to fade away for another season, let's give it a chance to guide us to Christ and his blessing and power in life.

The time has come for a strong faith that knows life is filled with possibilities for those who "repent and believe in the gospel." Jesus adds the gospel promise to the resounding call for repentance that had come from John the Baptist. He called for recognition of sinfulness as emphatically as John had done. Yet he makes this significant change in the theme: "Believe in the gospel." It is incumbent upon those who know the name of the Lord to come in confession and to receive the word of assurance and absolution. The liturgy begins with that note of reality and gospel each week.

But those who "believe in the gospel" can rise from that kneeling posture and stand up tall in the sure Word of forgiveness and new life. As he spoke the invitation "come and follow me" at the shore of the Lake of Galilee, Christ calls each of us to share in that company of disciples today. Here we are partners in the gospel community as we share life with one another. Here we know the strengthening and supporting arm of others in our times of weakness and sorrow. Surely we are linked here in that kind of gospel community that makes life worthwhile and significant. Our membership in this parish is more than adherence to doctrine and support of a program. It is living in the gospel truth of Christ's forgiveness and sharing that blessing with all who need to know that he also cares for them.

For a Clear Witness

These are the disciples who know that the time has come *for a clear witness*. As Jesus called Simon and Andrew from their fishing nets, he said: "Follow me and I will make you become fishers of men." He still calls his followers to "fish," to share the kingdom with others. He expects that we will actively reach out with the gospel and share the invitation to come and share in Christ's love. He wants his disciples to win others to that body of believers, to share the gift that we have from him.

That clear call has been muffled in many settings as we hesitate to speak to others about Christ. It has been distorted in those who choose to tell their own stories and focus on personal "conversions" rather than on the experience of God's grace in Jesus. The fishermen have frequently chosen to sail smoothly and safely across the waves of daily encounters rather than facing the uncertainty of letting down the nets. It is easier to share a few dollars with Jesus than it is to walk out to the streets of our city and suburbs with the substantial gifts that will raise men out of the watery wastes in which they are wallowing. The gospel of forgiveness and life can only be meaningful if we also witness to his love in what we are and do by his power.

Witnessing is a spontaneous and natural reaction to life's experiences. Those who know that Christ is alive in their lives and who have experienced his love will be quick to share that blessing. Having heard the good news and knowing the love, grace, and power of God in their own lives, these followers of Christ are "fishers of men." But that kind of witness will come only when Christ is really alive in the lives of people in the parish. It will be the characteristic of this congregation to share with others what they experience here. That genuine and enthusiastic word is contagious and it is beginning to come from you. You can be the single most important factor in our sharing the gospel with this community.

That kind of fisherman is not trained or programmed. To witness is not some task that is separated or a skill that is learned. The good news flows freely from the words and actions of faith in the life of persons. The call of the gospel is a call to be a partner in this community where we experience the grace of God among us. It is a genuine invitation to join in this community of believers, where we have found God's strength that lifts us and makes each day worthwhile and full.

Witness is genuine only when it flows from what is alive in the person who gives it. It is real only when it reflects the Spirit that motivates us. To join the fellowship of those who are truly "fishers of men" is to respond to the love that Jesus shows to us. It is to reach out with that love to those whom we know best. Of course, there is risk in witnessing to those who know us well. It is always possible for them to test the truth of what we say about Christ's presence and the way in which his life touches ours.

A clear witness comes from those who follow Jesus. That needs to be re-emphasized in many places today because "evangelism" is no longer a favorite focus. How often do you share the gospel with others? To whom have you witnessed of the power and love of Christ? Surely this is the call that comes to all who risk discipleship. It is the primary privilege that we have as we follow our Lord. He calls us to be "fishers of men."

The time has come for a good word: a word of hope and love in Christ. In a time of strong faith, those who are followers of Jesus are spontaneous witnesses who share his love as disciples. Thus the Epiphany star need not fade—but it hangs there on the horizon to guide us to the eternal Christ. It shines on as the light that leads us to the Light of the World in the face of all darkness. Amen.

REGINALD H. HOLLE
Parma Lutheran Church
Cleveland, Ohio

THE SECRET OF LIFE

Fourth Sunday after the Epiphany
Mark 1:21-28

It doesn't take much thought or very much living to learn that life is dangerous. We must live out our days without a guarantee of protection from such external dangers as environmental pollution, unwarranted attack from others, communicable disease, and genuine accidents.

The dangers and difficulties of living would be much easier to handle if they only existed outside of us. When we feel hostile toward others, depressed or discouraged, tempted to go against what we know is right and decent, we are facing the dangers from within. I cannot imagine the feelings and thoughts a person must have who concludes that each individual is left to his or her own resources in attempting to avoid as many of these dangers as possible. It seems to me that such a person walks a very frightening, lonely and dark pathway through life.

A profoundly different outlook on life is reflected in the "Prayer of the Day" for this Fourth Sunday after the Epiphany. How I wish many people whom I have come to know and love could pray with the author, "Almighty God, you know that we are set among great dangers and that we think our knowledge and our power are greater than they are. Protect us and in ways beyond our strength guide us through all dangers and temptations; through Jesus Christ, your Son, our Lord. Amen."

Jesus and the Demons

While the prayer we have just considered recognizes the external and internal dangers of living, it focuses not on them, but on Jesus. It is precisely what Mark does in the beginning of his Gospel when he writes about a demon-possessed man who met Jesus in the synagogue at Capernaum.

Not long after his baptism and temptation, Jesus, accompanied by a small band of his newly recruited disciples, approached the substantial town of Capernaum which was located on the northern shore of Lake Galilee. As soon as the sabbath day arrived, he went to the synagogue and took the opportunity to teach those who were gathered there.

His teaching and his presence "astonished" his hearers. They were used to hearing traditional texts of scripture and traditional interpretations of them. The words they heard coming from Jesus so amazed them that they asked one another, "What is this?" A new teaching!" But the text makes clear that their amazement was not limited to the uniqueness of the teaching but also to the tone of authority used by Jesus.

The tension and excitement which Jesus had created was greatly increased by the sudden appearance of "a man with an unclean spirit."

Mark makes it clear that the poor man facing Jesus had somehow been invaded by a force from outside of him over which he apparently had no control. He had in fact been possessed and was not himself.

What or who is an "unclean spirit"? People who suffer from what we know as mental illness were no doubt considered to be possessed by some malevolent spirit or spirits. Certain kinds of mental aberrations result in uncleanness of varying degrees and kinds. Many people of former times did not hesitate to regard all illnesses as being the result of some form of possession. The Bible does not provide the answer to the phenomenon it describes.

The question which has been asked through all the ages is, "Whatever possessed him or her to do that?" The experience of possession from outside the self is not related to people who hold certain religious beliefs or who have lived in certain centuries. It is the universal experience which testifies to the fact that human personality is open to invasion from the outside. We are not only invaded by the words and ideas coming from other persons, but by the power of their personalities. We can assert that God and whatever you name his adversary does not exist, just as we can deny the existence of angelic beings related to God or evil spirits related to God's adversary.

To judge the meeting of the poor possessed man with Jesus as a quaint Bible story which need not be given serious consideration is to fly in the face of the agonizing concerns of modern men and women. There is a renewed interest in the occult, possession and related subjects to which our media bear ample testimony. People continue to search for a secure haven from the dangers and the unpredictability of everyday life. They also search for the secret which makes life in this world worth the living. It is that very secret which Mark is trying to share with all the children of God who walk the face of this earth.

The Secret of Life

Mark records that the possessed man shouted, "What have you to do with us, Jesus of Nazareth? Have you come to destroy us? I know who you are, the Holy One of God." Incredibly, Jesus immediately silenced the demon or demons and commanded them to leave the poor man. After "convulsing him and crying with a loud voice," they left. They also left those who were present in the synagogue of Capernaum that day more astonished than before and with further motivation to ask about the uniqueness of Jesus' teaching and to reflect upon the authority which he clearly commanded.

Interpreters continue to pay attention to the fact that Jesus so quickly silenced spirits who were identifying him as the One who was sent to men from God.

When this gospel is seen in light of the entire Gospel of Mark, the answer is not long in coming. Jesus did not want to be known as a "Mr. Fixit." He did not want people to find room in their hearts for him because he was a miracle worker, because he could be called upon at any time to place bandages on the wounds of life, or because he could remove all the dangers of being a person in the world.

The message Jesus came to bring was proclaimed to free men and women who could choose to enter into a new relationship with God and with each other or could choose not to. Jesus did not come proclaiming that he would remove people from all the cares, troubles, tragedies and mysteries of this world. Near the end of his ministry he prayed that those who followed him would not fall into the hands of the "evil one" but would remain faithful and continue to have his "joy fulfilled in themselves" (John 17:13).

To persons whose lives were cluttered by everyday cares and who wondered whether life was worth the living, he proclaimed that all mankind was fashioned in the image of the living God. He proclaimed and proclaims through all of his followers that God is love and love is the building block upon which lives must be anchored if they are to stand against the dangers from within and from without. Jesus came to tell you and me that the love of God and the love which we give to each other contains an eternal dimension. It is a love which knifes through the darkness, pushes back our fears, emboldens our steps and makes every day of our pilgrimage through life worth the effort.

Whenever I consider this passage from Mark, a man's smiling face appears before me. His name is Feimau. He lives on the Island of Yap which is part of the Western Caroline Islands of the Pacific.

In 1961 I joined a Protestant Missionary, Edmund Kalau, on the Island of Yap in order to assist in the dedication of a church which had been built with the financial assistance of Air Force personnel who had been stationed on the Island of Guam. The Yapese were amazed that "warriors" who did not know them cared enough to contribute to the church they were trying to build. They asked Pastor Kalau if it would be possible for a representative of those people from far away to join them for the dedication of their chapel. I always shall thank God that I was chosen to be that representative.

Since weather conditions prevented me from leaving the island, I joined Pastor Kalau as he traveled from village to village preaching the gospel. On one trip we traveled with another visiting missionary, Feimau, and a native interpreter. The journey we made was an extremely difficult one. The jungles of Yap are dank, dark and foreboding. Though it was mid-day, it was so dark we had to use flashlights.

We were halfway to our destination when we decided to stop for a rest. Feimau, a handsome bearded man of approximately 65 years of age, looked at me and broke into one of the most beautiful smiles I have ever experienced. Through the interpreter, he said, "These jungles are very dark. For almost all my life I walked them in fear of the demons. From my childhood on I was taught that demons lived in the rocks and trees of these dark jungles and lay in wait for those who pass by." I reflected that life was difficult enough without having to live with such teachings and with such fear. My reflections sent a cold shudder through me in spite of the tropical humidity and temperature.

Feimau broke the serious look which had covered his face and began to smile again. As he began to talk, tears filled his eyes. He said, "If I wanted to express to you what it means to be a Christian, I could do it in one word. That word is *Light!* Even though I do not understand Yapese, I heard him repeat the word several times with a joy that would defy written or spoken description. "I no longer walk in fear on these jungle paths. There may be demons or there may not be demons, but I am Christ's and that is enough."

I never shall forget Feimau nor the witness he made to me. At this writing he is still witnessing to other Yapese about the Light which has come into his life. I believe that he personifies the wisdom of Jesus' silencing of the demons. Pastor Kalau did not proclaim Christ by promising to Feimau that the dangers of the world would be removed or that a spell could be cast which forever would prevent the invasion of evil spirits. Pastor Kalau told him of the Word which the men and women of this world need to hear. He told Feimau that the Word was Jesus Christ in whom there was life and light. He told him that "the light shines in the darkness and the darkness has not overcome it" (John 1:5). I thank God that Feimau was able to receive this testimony and has the opportunity of sharing it with others whose paths are not illuminated by the light which has come into his life. Feimau was found by the secret of life.

Power for Living

The interpreters will continue to deal with the meaning of "unclean spirits" and recorded cases of demon possession. I believe that all the generations of men and women never will be able to set aside once and for all their fascination with the occult and with the strange forces or powers which pervade both the universe and the hearts of people. The debate will continue as to whether evil forces which can influence persons are real or simply the fear of them. Christians believe that both possibilities are realities, but the result of either possibility is distress, darkness and despair.

Christians of this generation join Mark in proclaiming that the divine power which Jesus manifested in Capernaum exorcised the unclean spirits which tortured the man whom he encountered. Whatever powers exist in the creation and in the hearts of people, they do not compare with the power of the living God. In this conviction and as a result of his experience with Jesus, Feimau stood smiling in the middle of a dark and forboding jungle. We can do the very same thing.

We all have our jungles and they all have their dark, foreboding places, but we also walk through them with one whose teaching carries authority and whose power is infinite. We walk into the future with all its improbability bearing a radiant smile on our faces for the sake of all those with whom we come in contact. We cannot keep for ourselves the gift that was given to be shared with others.

So many persons cry out with the demonic of Capernaum, "What have you to do with us, Jesus of Nazareth?" He has everything to do with them as he does with us. Our lives and the churches to which we belong are called to share the powerful, darkness-shattering Word with others. The very darkest places of society and the hearts of persons need our witness most of all. Despite all the dangers of life it is a life worth the living when Christ comes to dwell with us.

JAN C. WALKER, Assistant to the President
Northeastern Pennsylvania Synod—LCA
Wescosville, Pennsylvania

A DAY IN THE LIFE OF JESUS

Fifth Sunday after the Epiphany
Mark 1:29-39

One of my grandmothers had a habit of putting most of the nice gifts she received for Christmas or her birthday into a large old trunk. She would always say that they were too nice to wear or use. She died at about ninety-four with a trunk full of unused gifts.

The book of Revelation says of Jesus, "He is the One who is, and who was, and who is to come." We enjoy celebrating Jesus' birth and discussing many of the stories of when he was the man of Galilee. We bury our dead friends and loved ones in the hope of the resurrection promised by the One who is to come, but what about the One who is? We may talk about our faith and claim to have a faith, but I ask you, do we live with a faith full of unused gifts? These gifts are Christ's promises and power for living now.

As Christians we stand in worship and confess our faith. We sing songs like "My Faith Looks Up to Thee." These may be more words in a worship service than reality in our lives. On Monday morning we may face our life as if he were not present.

When the weather is difficult or there are bicycle problems I drive my son on his morning paper route. I get out of the car and throw some of the papers on customers' porches as we move down the streets between six and seven in the morning. As I drop the paper on people's porches, I guess in a symbolic way, I am putting at their doorstep the world's published problems and crises for that day.

All of us wake up in the morning to a world in crisis and pain. We wake up to our personal "today" with its plans, responsibilities, opportunities, decisions and emotional and physical pains. We may ask ourselves whether faith is meant to be an everyday source of strength. Does God care how life in our everyday world can be?

Let us turn to our Gospel text in Mark 1:29-39 and consider what it is saying and whether it speaks to our question. One may ask why the Gospel writer included these experiences out of the many other unrecorded experiences in the three year ministry of Jesus.

Mark tells the experiences of a day in the life and ministry of Jesus. Mark had, previous to our text, told what had happened while Jesus and his friends were worshiping in the synagogue in Capernaum on a sabbath day and our text tells us what happened after the service. Is there an important connection between what goes on in the service and what happens after the worship service?

Our text begins as Jesus left the synagogue and went directly to the home of Peter and his brother Andrew. Peter's mother-in-law lived there also. Because Peter's mother-in-law later assumed the responsibility of being the hostess, one can speculate that it was really her home and that Peter's family together with his brother lived with her. It was not uncommon to be invited after the service for some refreshments at the home of a friend who lived near the synagogue. It was illegal to walk too far on a sabbath. James and John were also invited to come along with Jesus. When Jesus arrived at Peter's home he was told of Peter's mother-in-law's fever. Jesus willingly went to where she lay and took her hand and helped her up and the fever left her. She then got busy and served Jesus and all of her guests.

Our text describes what happened at sunset which ended the sabbath. Healing was considered work and therefore forbidden on the sabbath. Actually, Jesus did something illegal by healing Peter's mother-in-law before sundown. As the sabbath ended, many people from the town came to the front door of Peter's house hoping that Jesus would come out and heal them. Jesus was willing to do this. He proclaimed not only in words but by his healing acts and the casting out of demons, that the kingdom of God was invading this world to win it back to God. Jesus confronted Satan's power in the arena of people's everyday lives.

Jesus slept overnight at Peter's home and while the household was still sleeping he got up and took a walk out in the countryside to a lonely place and here spent time in prayer. It becomes evident as one reads the gospel stories that Jesus did this often and that prayer was important in his daily life as the man from Galilee. When the rest of the household got up for breakfast Jesus was not around so Peter went out looking for him. Others followed Peter in his search for Jesus. When they found Jesus they told him that everyone was hoping to see him and that he should continue to stay with them, but Jesus told the group that he wanted to go on to other villages and carry out his mission in the midst of many towns and villages.

As we reflect on a text I think it is important that we let it give us a lesson for our life in our "today." I am sure our text has many lessons for all of us, but I want to underscore several.

God's "Yes" for Today

First, Jesus is God's "yes" in our "today." Many years ago I went back to the college from which I was graduated, for its homecoming events. I remember watching the traditional tug of war between the freshmen boys and the sophomore boys. At the center of the tug rope was a mud filled pit about twenty feet long and ten feet wide. Once you took hold of the rope you could not let go, and therefore, the losers would be dragged through the muddy pit. The struggle began with thirty or forty on each side. It wasn't too long before the freshmen pulled the slipping, sliding sophomores through the muddy pit. After it was all over and we were walking away I observed a sophomore dripping with mud from head to toe, meeting a fellow sophomore dressed in a nice suit with a girl friend on his arm. All the muddy sophomore said to his classmate was, "Where were you when we needed you?"

In the midst of life's crisis and pain I'm sure many of us want to say to God, "Where are you, God, when I need you?" Our text is proclaiming that Jesus is God's "yes" for our "today" . . . the One who is!

Peter said, "Come home with me," and Jesus must have responded with "yes." The household wanted Jesus to do something for Peter's mother-in-law and Jesus said, "yes." Many people gathered outside the door of Peter's home, waiting to see Jesus with their sick or possessed people and Jesus was there with his "yes." I find our text saying that Jesus is God's presence for life today. He is present to touch us in our "today"—in today's pain, depression, anxiety, decisions or whatever our day may bring.

A Guide to Renewal

Second, Jesus is a guide to daily renewal. One day after attending a meeting in Minneapolis I boarded a DC-10 for Chicago. The ground crew had pushed the plane away from its loading gate into the taxi area and here evidently is where the pilot starts all engines and then proceeds to the assigned runway for take-off. Our plane on that particular day seemed to delay a longer than usual time before starting for the assigned runway. Finally after about ten or fifteen minutes the captain announced over the public address system that he was unable to get one of the engines started and therefore the delay. Even if it were possible to advise the captain, I am sure no one on that plane would suggest that we ignore the third engine and proceed on our journey with only two engines that were working. I feel that many days we launch into the decisions, stresses and business of our day with only a part of the resources available to all of us for living each day; resources needed for body, mind and spirit. All of us have needs in order to remain as healthy and alert people every day. Our needs include such items as food, funds, and friends and quietness to meet our physical and emotional diet.

The medical profession tells us that one of modern man's quiet killers is hypertension and we all know that crowded schedules and social calendars are the order of the day. In our area if you want to invite several couples over on a Saturday night you had better get your invitations out six or eight weeks in advance. We are an active generation. We allow our schedules to become very crowded and the pace catches up to us sooner or later. There are many factors that can give a person hypertension, such as diet, worry or stress. However, if we were to add to our schedule for the day a few minutes of being quiet and alone like the example of Jesus we might experience some interesting results in greater resources for daily living. I believe that we could gain something personally in body and spirit by developing some of the methods of the ancient arts of meditation and relaxing of the whole person. Whether we always recognize it or not, we are only whole persons when we experience an every day relationship with God. I think Jesus in his Galilean life style demonstrated that need. His life and ministry as a man was dependent upon the power and presence of the Holy Spirit. Just as a good breakfast at the start of our day is important to our physical health so Jesus started many days with a time apart for prayer and quietness so that he might experience that all important relationship with God. As there are times for busy activity with people, in the expression of a meaningful life, so are there essential times of quietness and being alone with one's thoughts and prayers. Think of it in terms of your own personal renewal each day.

A Concern for All

Third, Jesus had a concern for all. Peter and his friends came looking for Jesus with the concern that many wanted him to be around. Jesus responded by directing his new day to other towns, synagogues and people. Yes, Jesus is a man for all people; people like those in the Capernaum community, the Galilean fishermen, and Peter's mother-in-law. Jesus traveled to meet these people where they were. He is for you.

Jesus in using the term, "we," enlisted everyone who would follow him as a part of the task force in his generation and in our generation to carry his claims and promises to every village and town. The people of God have a message that Christ cares about people no matter who they are or where they are in life. The message is, "Jesus the One who is, meets us where we are; where we are in our ups and downs, our joys or sorrows, our pain or pleasure." I think all of us are interested in telling our friends about a good restaurant that we have visited or some interesting places we have traveled. I have known people with serious illness who have been greatly helped by certain doctors and methods of treatment. From then on they seem to take every opportunity to encourage others with similar problems to try the same doctor or treatment.

Jesus had a strong desire to tell his story and to touch people where they are with the proclamation of the coming of the kingdom of God. He wanted his followers to catch the same enthusiasm and to get the good news out to all. This good news is that Jesus Christ is the One who was, who will come, but also the One who is. Our personal Redeemer in our "today." Jesus Christ wants to be understood and desires his presence to be felt and known. Faith is not just an experience in the worship service, but Jesus, the One who is, may be experienced now in our "today!"

KENNETH L. STANGELAND
Grace Lutheran Church
Elmwood Park, Illinois

PROOF POSITIVE; PROOF NEGATIVE

Sixth Sunday after the Epiphany
Mark 1:40-45

The word is quick to judge the genuineness of man's convictions. Easily it is assumed that because a person has done something good that that is his nature, or because one has been involved in something unpleasant that that is his trait. The judgment is too hastily made, and the assumption, fortunately, not divine.

You would not want your errors to dominate your virtues in the eyes of others, nor your good to so veil your weaknesses that the reality of your own humanity is denied. Still, we are often trapped by this quick and easy method of ascribing haloes to some and horns to others. It was President Kennedy who said "Sincerity is subject to proof," and so it is, but the proof is the product of the negative as well as the positive.

Scripture may be seen as similar to a roll of exposed film. As it is developed the negative is clearly seen, but it is also only as that negative is printed that we realize the proof that is hidden within. Good and evil, gospel and law, love and hate are not disconnected realities, but often appear as Siamese twins, or at least reactions of one to the other, much as peace trails war, and bust follows boom.

Paul Tillich explained in this way, "The character of human life, like the character of the human condition, like the character of all life, is 'ambiguity': the inseparable mixture of good and evil, the true and false, the creative and destructive forces—both individual and social."

As the leper confronted Jesus with his anguished request, the negative of disease was met by the positive of cure. The negative of the law was met with the goodness of the gospel. The evangelical tour of the Savior had to be scrapped, but no one was prevented from seeking him out themselves, and they did so. Here again Kennedy's comment that "sincerity is subject to proof" is proven.

The true story depicted in *Sugarland Express* indicates the merging of good and bad much like the blurred dyes mingled in a madras print. They are actually inseparable. Recall how strong the mother instinct was in LuJean, who talked her convict husband into escaping a pre-release facility to claim their baby Langston before he could be adopted by his foster parents, a reputable couple, in Sugarland, Texas? Good pursued a wrong course, and the action wound up tragically in the death of LuJean's husband, but inevitably she got her baby back. Negatives produce positives, and positives are proof that negatives exist.

Did not Good Friday kill, while Easter gave new life?

As we focus on the leper, we are made aware that genuine Christianity is not a matter of total obedience, but faith and trust, and the goodness of a God who says to the needful soul's plaintive request, "If you will, you can make me clean," "I will; be clean." Summed up in the words of Carlyle Marney is the truth of this encounter and our own, for "we remember that we cannot talk of a Christ who matters without talking of the one obsession of His life—to know and do the Father's Will." It is more than a miracle manifested here, but proof positive from the proof negative that grace is a gift, and joy its hallmark.

The First Negative: Man's Condition

Developed from the film that is our text is a negative that illustrates in black and white and shades of grey the condition of man.

Separated from society, alienated and exiled to a life without family and friends, the leper could not live within the city walls, eat with his fellow Jews, or be touched by them, for he was thought to be unclean, his illness the result of some grievous sin.

Jesus was not blind to that man's plight, but neither was he blind to the plight of man in general. As the Second Adam, he came to remove the sting of the First's disobedience, to conquer sin, and offer mankind life without eternal blight. Jesus transgressed the laws of the Jews by touching the leprous man, but his heart filled with compassion so that he could not stick to the ceremonial code. It happened many times, and not least of which was the compassion that he had for the crowd that nailed him to the cross. He did not differentiate between the recognized need of the one, the leper, and the unrealized need of the other, man in general. Jesus touched the man and the positive was proven immediately in the miracle of health.

Michelangelo's Sistine Chapel ceiling depicts God touching Adam with life, and the result was the same for the leper. He came alive from the death of isolation. Naaman, the Syrian general, gained new life when he relented and dipped in the waters of the Jordan the seven prescribed times. Paul knew the fullest power of life when in that brief blindness after his encounter with Jesus on the Damascus road he was made to see clearly the Messiah. Up to then, he was enmeshed in the death struggle of the law, in a yielding to hatred, and willingness to murder to erase that which he didn't understand. Ananias laid his hands on Paul and instantly he saw again. Out of the negative was produced the positive by a holy touch.

I visited with a woman whose father, an Episcopal clergyman, had died some years before. Her comment was that "a little piece lives on in every person that he touched, and he touched a lot of people." A young lady that I had had to suspend from school on several occasions, and was finally expelled after I left, wrote some months afterwards of her great joy in discovering Jesus. Through the illness of her father, the touch of Christ came to her. "I feel great," she wrote, "No more problems at all. I find myself praying when there's nothing to pray, and then I think how lucky it is to be *alive*." Out of the negative was produced the positive by a holy touch.

Is that not the meaning of daily confession? We come as did the leper to ask for cleansing, knowing fully it is God's will that all men be washed of their iniquity. His absolution was one four-word proclamation: "I will; be clean." The leper in all of us is made whole again. Helmut Thielicke reminds us that "Only he who dies and rises again with Christ can credibly bear witness to the death and resurrection of the Lord." Too often, "we merely act 'as if' he had risen again," and that's the movie-set facade we need to tear down.

We could lament sin totally were it not for the fact that it drives us to ask Jesus for his touch of healing, his hand of life and forgiveness. Yet before the day passes, there is need anew to repeat the healing for the positive picture is proof the negative exists. Man's condition will always require the touch of Jesus. On that genuine Christianity must focus totally.

The Second Negative: The Force of Law

The picture may seem cloudy, but study it. Jesus responded to the leper's condition with "compassion" (KJ), "pity" (RSV), "warm indignation" (NEB), "sorrow" (Beck), but no sooner had he pronounced his benediction of health than the Lord's gentle tones became strident. We are told that the Greek word translated variously as "stern" (NEB, RSV, Beck), "stringent" (Williams), and "strict" (Phillips) actually implies he was "very angry with him." The cordiality changed, and Jesus instructed the man to fulfill the law. He was to show himself to the priest, make the appropriate offering, and thus be adjudged cured by the proper authority.

Scholars debate this confusing and contradictory change in the Lord's attitude. They attempt to formulate arguments that will either soften the tone or explain away the personal anger Jesus vented, as well as the physical shove he gave him. His robust and vigorous lifestyle is thus thinly veiled by such well-meaning apologists, but Jesus requires none of these. The words he spoke, his change of attitude, and the fire of his action toward the healed man were not contradictory.

Paul Tournier helps me understand this change in Jesus as he writes, "Even when the Word of God strikes a man without warning, when there is a sudden conversion, an inner call, which changes all at once the direction of his life, he perceives that God has been speaking to him for a long time, that the dialogue was already going on in the darkness of the unconscious before it broke out into the full light of day." God spoke in the Old Testament via the law. The cured leper could not possibly comprehend the magnificence of Christ's gospel without facing up to the real burden of the law. It was the negative of the law that produced the vivid picture of the gospel of love with contrasts too distinct to deny. Where legalistic practices had reduced faith to a mere technicality, and had introduced a rigid understanding of religion as a mechanical experience, Jesus' compassionate healing could only be understood as pure grace, and the application of the law as futile without the heart of faith.

Here is where we can sympathize with the healed man. He knew the freedom from bondage that came with the healing. Now

freed, he celebrated the event with obvious joy. He relished sharing his changed condition with the priest, I'm sure, but to keep
silent about what had happened was a request he could not
possibly fulfill. Jesus, I believe, attempts to show us that we can
make a curse out of our God-given cures of acknowledging only
the place of the law, without simultaneously celebrating the joy
of grace. It was not *his* obedience or disobedience that saved him,
but Christ's.

However it is to be explained, one must see that the leper's
failure to keep quiet, as Jesus commanded, benefitted others. It is
a dangerous thing to suggest, perhaps, for people grab all-too-
quickly at such ideas, thinking to sin more is to actually sin less.
The negative of the law produced the positive of grace, and that
grace freed the leper to tell the world the exotic wonder of his
cure. Though it was grace that triumphed, we recognize the tension between obedience to the law and the genuine response of a
truly happy soul.

It was the other way around for Jesse Craig, the hero of Irwin
Shaw's novel, *Evening in Byzantium*. Hospitalized with a violent,
life-sapping ulcer attack, and eventually cured enough to leave the
hospital with the doctors' advice to change his lifestyle, he refused
both to abide by their law, and to celebrate God's grace. He returned immediately to his old, death-assured pattern. The leper
was not so foolish. He told the world his story, and the world was
that much richer.

If he was the uncontrolled emotionalist that some charge, it
seems to me he was perfectly normal. As we have been told,
"Mature people are made not out of good times, but out of bad
times." The leper seems to prove that to me, and the button he
was wearing must have read, "Please be patient. God isn't finished with me yet."

Out of the negative implications of the old law, grace was fully
experienced in the positive proof that Jesus, and Jesus only, cured
the man of his leprosy and was ready to forgive future disobedience.

The Third Negative: Tour Cancelled/Ministry Widened

We may lift up one more negative from the developed roll that
shows that success often is the result of change, and change that
often is not desired. It's true that success, despite its downplay by
younger generations, is still courted wildly by huge armies of
men. They seek to advance more quickly than advisable, but is it
their drive that eventually puts them into the seats of responsibility, or attests to their genuineness as persons?

Jesus had intended to evangelize the whole of Galilee, yet the witness of the leper became so widely known that he was unable to move inside the towns because of the great crowds that followed him. Instead of going to *them,* they came to *him.* The planned tour schedule had to be cancelled. From this negative we get the picture that the villagers and farmers, the fishermen and the distressed organized groups to seek him out. Isn't that the continuing dream of the church? We know the greater success in evangelism is where people are already aware of their need. An alcoholic can't conquer his problem if he denies he has one. Others can't be persuaded for Christ if they are convinced they have no need. Those who have finally reached that state where they know that in themselves there is no answer, and in the isms, and avant garde pursuits of their contemporaries satisfaction is unknown, they are the ones who treasure the gospel as it is entrusted to them. Jesus had them coming to him in droves, largely due to the disobedience of the leper.

It was Jesus' custom to tell people not to spread the word of the miracles. He wanted people to treat such events as external signs, whereas his reliance was on internal ones. It was altogether possible that they might misinterpret physical and material blessings. It would feed their concept of a "worldly Christ," rather than a spiritual one. The notoriety gained from the miracles changed the quiet, personal ministry Jesus embarked upon, causing throngs to seek him out, yet he reached the masses in a way that could not have happened had it not been for the willingness of the cured to point the way to Jesus.

When plans change, and yearnings are no longer plausible, it's marvelous to see how often the results are far beyond what we dreamed possible. Moses was content to shepherd his father-in-law's sheep, but God had a different destiny for him. Ruth was happy to glean in Boaz's field, but God opened the door to greater happiness and marriage. Jonah fought against doing God's bidding, but God pushed him into the greater role nevertheless. Peter, Andrew, James and John were perfectly happy catching fish, but Jesus gave them greater joy in fishing for men. So it was that God changed the paths of Augustine, Luther, Wesley and countless others, paths that led to successes far greater than they had imagined.

And so it is for us. Change challenges. Change widens our ministry, and puts us all the more in the hands of God, trusting him, for he alone knows the future he wants us to conquer for him. It is not "drive" that succeeds, but Christ.

We are not the same anymore when we feel the influence of one another. That's part of the dynamics of life. Jesus accepted it, perhaps, with some reluctance, as is often our reaction, but change for him was a widened ministry, and a greater triumph. Was not the leper's life changed also? And for what reason? That he might continue to show us even today that the proof positive of God's continual, healing love is that he changes negatives into pictures of joy.

I recall climbing late one night to the top floor of Dana's Old Main with the school photographer to quickly develop pictures he had taken that evening that we intended including in a publication I was editing. In the darkroom, he went about his tasks efficiently and I waited to see the negatives in the dimness of the red light only to discover he had developed the wrong film. Instead of Lauritz Melchior singing at a concert, we had the Dana Vikings making baskets on the home court. There are negatives that will never produce the positives we're seeking, but if we want proof positive that real Christianity is based purely upon the goodness of God, the grace of the Lord Jesus Christ, we need print only the negative of the leper's healing.

In a stirring novel about pastors who served a single parish in a Swedish hamlet over a period of several hundred years, Bishop Bo Giertz writes sympathetically about a pastor who was late in preparing his sermon for Sunday, and as he was pondering that morning what he would say, he was called to the bedside of a dying parishioner. He returned to the church just in time to conduct the service, hastily grabbing a book of sermons that lay on his desk. Although not given to reading his sermon, he did so that day in desperation, sensing the power and might of the Word he was proclaiming.

"Like hammer blows aimed with unerring precision against the head of the nail," wrote Giertz of the pastor's preaching, "the words 'Jesus only,' recurred again and again and sank ever deeper into the consciousness." It was the story of the Transfiguration, when the three disciples and Jesus were on a high mountain. They saw in their vision Elijah and Moses with Jesus, but then suddenly they saw Jesus only. When we print the negative of life as God-in-Christ sees it, that's the sole picture we see, Jesus only. He is the proof positive that grace triumphs and in the leper, as in us, grace is our only claim. Neither works nor words achieve anything. Jesus only. And in that is health and wholeness and happiness.

RICHARD ANDERSEN
The Community Church of Joy
Glendale, Arizona

BODY LANGUAGE—LISTEN!

Seventh Sunday after the Epiphany
Mark 2:1-12

One of the most difficult achievements to accomplish is to equate actions, life styles and behavior patterns with words. So much of life seems to be as Shakespeare contended long ago: "A tale told by an idiot, full of sound and fury, signifying nothing."

Words! Words! And more words!

Everywhere words! Flashing on the TV screens. Imprinted in magazines and newspapers. Flickering through neon signs. Blinking in advertisements. An abundance of words available and in usage. Of course, our difficulty is not with words; it is with meanings and communication.

Meanings and Communications

The story is told of a psychiatry professor who made it his ambition in life to let all his students know how important it was for them, as budding psychiatrists, to always practise love in their profession. The one element in life which must always be displayed to your clients is love. One evening, one of the professor's students, having had difficulty with one of his assignments, strolled over to the professor's home. This particular evening, the professor, rather than preparing his lectures and seminars for the next day, as he was prone to do, thought he would relax and repair the broken sidewalk in front of his house. He was just putting the finishing touches on the floating process when the student arrived. The general few words of greeting were exchanged and during this time three boys who were playing football in an adjacent schoolyard came bounding around the corner of the house with their big feet right into the freshly-poured concrete. In a split second, the professor picked up his shovel and ran after the rascals, but their legs rapidly outdistanced his, and he didn't catch them. Upon returning to his home, he could be heard mumbling and grumbling in his beard. To all this the student replied with a query: "Professor, I thought you told us to love our people. I hardly saw you display love!" To this the professor answered rather dryly: "In the abstract—yes! In the concrete—no!"

Getting our words in line with our actions is difficult. Recently I read the book *Body Language* by Julius Fast in which he forthrightly and accurately postulates that our bodies don't know how to lie. Movements of the body give off messages of their own which may amplify and confirm or contradict and deny what we say.

Saying what we mean—that's the challenging responsibility of any communicator. Putting into action the message of our words—that's the demanding role of being obedient to the Word. For example: in Frances Ridley Havergal's famous hymn "Take my life and let it be," we identify more readily with the "let it be" than we do with "take my life."

The Word Became Flesh

"And the Word became flesh and dwelt among us." That's what Christmas and Epiphany—and Easter—are all about! The message of God is incarnational—dwelling in the flesh. God does not communicate in a vacuum; he proclaims his message through a vehicle. The birth of Jesus—sentimental as it might be—is God's chosen way of revealing to the world his fabulous love for all his dear children. The Epiphany revelation started with the three Wise Men from the East who came with their most precious gifts: gold, frankincense and myrrh, to adore the Christ child and to worship God whose Word, through the shining star, became a lamp unto their feet and a light unto their path. The Epiphany continued with Jesus' incarnational ministry, as his life style and behavior patterns sought to remain true to his Father's will. The Word became flesh and dwelt among us.

Throughout that public ministry, the occasions are many when people crowded around Jesus very closely to hear what he had to say and to bear witness to his ministry. There was usually a lot of commotion as people found a place to stand or sit. But once the hustle and bustle of the crowd was over, a sudden hush set in, for Jesus—whose life style matched his words—taught and preached as one having authority. It was as though Jesus said: "Listen!" and when he did, all eyes were glued to him. Listen! A sower went out to sow. . . . The kingdom of heaven is like. . . . There was a father who had two sons. . . . Jesus taught in the manner of the teachers of his time. He liked to use stories and he was a skillful storyteller, commanding the respect, attention and response of his listeners. The Word became flesh and dwelt among us: body language—listen!

And people came to him from every quarter. It is obvious that they recognized Jesus for who he was.

The Spirit of the Lord Is Upon Me

When Jesus came back to Capernaum—either to return to his own home or to that of Peter—word spread quickly that he was back in town. It is quite likely that Jesus had not seen his friends for some time. So almost immediately great crowds gathered at the house—crowds so large that the house was overflowing. As usual, Jesus seized the opportunity to preach the Word.

Suddenly he was interrupted by four lads who, failing to be able to break through the crowd, cut a hole in the roof of the house and lowered into Jesus' midst a paralytic. Ingenious persistence! We do not stretch the meaning of this story when we stop to admire both the ingenuity and the persistence of the bearers. To Jesus the problem of the crowds became an opportunity, to bear witness to the Gospel. To those who brought the paralytic, the problem of the crowds became an opportunity to exercise their ingenuity and persistence to see the Lord and King of life. Like the Wise Men of old, they persisted. They brought their friend to the Lord. And they were not disappointed.

Jesus not only lived in the midst of crowds; he also met the pressing needs of the crowds. His return to Capernaum was no exception. I suppose there's only one thing worse than being rushed off your feet by cares of the needy and crying crowds. That is not being rushed at all. Being rushed off your feet, being rushed to death often means being rushed to life, being brought into healing, restoring, helping relationships with other alive and dynamic persons, and with God himself. Such was the case with the four lads in Capernaum. They came to Jesus recognizing him as the one who could help their friend. They came believing. They came knowing that if anyone is in Christ, he is a new creation. They came because they beheld in Jesus the alive power of the Holy Spirit, even as Jesus himself said:

> The Spirit of the Lord is upon me,
>   because he has anointed me to preach good news to the poor.
> He has sent me to proclaim release to the captives
>   and recovering of sight to the blind,
>   to set at liberty those who are oppressed,
>   To proclaim the acceptable year of the Lord
>   (Luke 4:18-19).

They came believing that the Word became flesh and dwelt among us; they came ready to submit their lives to the power of the Holy Spirit in order to be healed.

My Son, Your Sins are Forgiven

Seeing the faith of those who came with the paralytic, as well as the faith of the paralytic himself, Jesus pronounces six words: "My son, your sins are forgiven." Jesus was a man of few words. But every word was meaningful. Indeed he spoke as one having authority—as one being about his Father's business—but foremost as one who had the love of God in his heart. "My son, your sins are forgiven." For someone plagued with guilt and sadness and suffering, what a tremendous message to receive as the grace, love and mercy of God are revealed in an open and personal ministry by him whom we call "Emmanuel—God with us!"

Whether in fact the Saviour knew something about the paralytic that is left out of the records, we do not know. But we do known that "psychosomatic" was a word meaningful to his day. It was believed that illness was a result of an evil spirit or was a punishment or consequence of sin. It may well be that the paralytic himself believed that his paralysis was due to sin. Whatever the details, the paralytic knew to whom to go for healing. Jesus saw that he needed more than physical mending; he also needed spiritual restoration. Hence Jesus says: "My son, your sins are forgiven."

Almost immediately Jesus was tested as to the soundness of his theology and the verity of his claim. With a contemptuous curl on their lips—probably with upturned moustaches—and with a scowl on their faces, some scribes "were sitting there, questioning in their hearts." Questioning? More like accusing! They were not able to see Jesus' ministry with open minds and receiving hearts. They could see nothing but a departure from their tradition. While claiming to be evangelists for God, they turned out to be men of empty words. Their behaviour patterns spoke a body language which was different from love. They and their tradition were everything; the need of man and the mercy of God were nothing. That is a devastating type of blindness. But it can happen to any of us when anything: our prestige, our possessions, our beloved customs and traditions, our institutions, etc.—become more important than does a loving concern for God's merciful work through persons. From such shortsightedness our prayer must be: "Good Lord, deliver us!"

Fortunately Jesus perceived their scheming spirits and their questioning and tricky minds; he confronted them directly with the question: "Why do you question thus in your hearts? Which is easier, to say to the paralytic, 'Your sins are forgiven,' or to say 'Rise, take up your bed and walk'? But that you may know that the Son of man has authority on earth to forgive sins—he said to the paralytic—'I say to you, rise, take up your bed and go home.' And he rose, and immediately took up his bed and went out before them all." God is not mocked. He knows when we are sincere or when we are playing games. Jesus recognized the genuineness of faith in the paralytic as well as the lack of genuineness in the scribes.

What at first appeared as a sign which would give rise to opposition—especially from those who were questioning—now stood as a sign of God's power. And they all stood with amazement. "We never saw anything like this!" A miracle occurred. The Word became flesh and dwelt among us, full of grace and truth. A life was committed in spirit into the hands of God and healing took place; the paralytic arose and walked. Alleluia! Praise to the Lord! Thanks be unto his holy name! No matter whether we speak of the human body in its totality or the spiritual body of believers—the body of Christ—Jesus, the Saviour, brings healing, renewing, restoring power and love to our midst. Indeed, if anyone is in Christ, the old has passed away; the new has come. The body language of which Jesus speaks is the incarnational language of love: "Lo, I am with you always. . . . My Son, your sins are forgiven. . . . Rise, take up your bed and walk. . . . [My] Word is a lamp unto [your] feet and a light unto [your] path."

Incarnate in Us

To us also has been given the power to enable God to be alive in us. Through the power of the Holy Spirit, God has chosen us to be his witnesses wherever we are, to be his channels of communication in life, and to be his vehicles of merciful service to others. As we respond in faith, great things can happen; with God all things are possible. Our body language—both as individuals and as fellow-members of the household of God—surely ought to be the incarnational language of the gospel. It can be, if we let the Holy Spirit guide us. If we are excited about our faith in Christ Jesus, we will discover fresh and new experiences with the Lord daily as we discover further his presence, meaning and purpose in our lives through his loving grace and through the lives of others. God's Word becomes flesh in us!

Then life will not be as a tale told by an idiot, full of sound and fury, signifying nothing; rather it will be as a life lived for Christ, full of creativity and newness and aliveness. Our paralysis —regardless of its nature—will be destroyed as a crippling entity in our lives; our body language will be such that testimony is borne to God and his love in attitudes, in life styles, in values and in behaviour patterns.

In the name of Christ Jesus, and by the power of the Holy Spirit, let our lives be as our words and our words as our lives. God is not mocked. When we come to him in faith, willing to submit to his will and love, he gives us the power both to be genuine and to share that genuineness with others so that they too can know that we believe in a God of Love who says: "My son, your

sins are forgiven." That is the body language of Christ! That is
the body language of the Christian church! That is the body
language of the believer!

Jesus says to each of his faithful followers:

"My Son, your sins are forgiven
  Your faith has made you well
    God is at work in you
      Rise up and walk
        You shall be my witnesses

A new commandment I give to you, that you love one another;

  even as I have loved you,
    that you also love one another."

The epiphany—the revelation of God and his love in the midst
of human life is such body language. *Listen!. . . . Respond! . . .
and you shall live!* Amen.

ARNOLD D. WEIGEL,
Christ The King Lutheran Church,
Thornhill, Ontario, Canada

DON'T MISS THE POINT

The Transfiguration of Our Lord—Last Sunday after the Epiphany
Mark 9:2-9

Do you ever have the problem I often have? Someone will tell a
joke and think it is hilarious, but I miss the point. That is also
a problem many of us have with life—we miss the point. Things
just don't make sense sometimes. We have disappointment after
disappointment. We can't figure it out. And this can happen even
more easily with our life in Christ. Jesus said things like, "Give
and it shall be given unto you," or "Love your enemies," or "You
have to lose your life in order to find it." Unfortunately, we often
miss the point, or maybe lose it even though we once had it. As a
result, everything gets short circuited; the goal isn't reached; the
results don't happen. When we miss the point of a joke, we fail
to laugh and so miss out on the fun. When we miss the point in
what's happening around us, our lives can seem quite meaningless. But worst of all, and most tragic, is to find no joy in following Christ because we have failed to understand what he was
talking about; because we have completely missed the point he
was trying to make.

A Special Revelation for Peter, James, and John

Today's Gospel lesson is a good example of this. Jesus takes Peter, James, and John up on a mountain top, evidently to give these three chief disciples a special revelation of just who their teacher really is. Perhaps, it is also to confirm the confession of faith Peter had made for the other disciples just six days earlier when he had said to Jesus, "You are the Christ." This revelation would help these disciples to get the point, to understand the meaning of what is soon to happen in Christ's life—his going up to Jerusalem to offer himself as the sacrificial lamb of God whose blood would take away the sins of the world.

But They Miss the Point

But what happens on that mountain top? Peter and his friends completely miss the point! Let's tune in on the story. Suddenly, right before the disciples' eyes, the appearance of Jesus is transfigured, changed. He looks different. His face glows brightly and his clothes become dazzling white. Then Moses and Elijah are standing with Jesus. So what do we hear Peter saying? "Isn't this nice. Lord, it is well that we are here. What a show! Why, we have a ringside seat on heaven itself. Hey, there's Moses and Elijah over there. Now if ever there were great men of faith, they certainly were!" What was happening here sounds a bit like theater-in-the-round where you get right in on the action. The actors are right there. You can reach out and touch them, and at times the audience actually gets to be a part of the action. Of course, you know and everyone else knows that you aren't an actor. But still, you can go home and say, "Wasn't that great!" Well, Peter thought it was so great that he wanted to stay around awhile and enjoy it. "Lord, how about if we disciples set up some little shelters here. This is just too great." Peter, missing the point, wanted to settle down and enjoy the show.

And, Often, So Do We

Aren't we that way, too? We have all that great drama going on in the Scriptures—the stories of Noah, Abraham, the great men of faith, Isaac, Jacob, Moses, the dividing of the waters of the Red Sea, manna in the wilderness, great battles, intrigue, David and his adventures! Then there is Christ's life—the stilling of the waters, feeding of thousands, healings, even people coming back from death. Or there are the stories of Paul and the other apostles—shipwrecks, escapes, danger. Then there is the great drama of the early church—the men of faith who faced lions and gladiators and all the rest—more drama and adventure and crisis. What a thing to sit in on! Or even today—we like to hear stories about the mission fields from men home on furlough. We are enthralled with stories of excitement, adventure, trails through the forests, tribal ceremonies, tribal warfare, flying in supplies, crossing rivers, riding motorcycles over the mountain roads. Isn't that great! And, with Peter, we might want to set up a permanent theater for this ongoing drama, with comfortable box seats into which we might settle back to enjoy it all. That's what Peter seems to have had in mind and we would do the same. "Master, shall we build some shelters here?" But Jesus didn't answer Peter and he won't answer us.

The God of Glory Is Revealed in Jesus

Jesus didn't answer because greater things than these were yet to happen. Suddenly, the cloud of glory covers the mountain and the voice from heaven says, "This is my beloved Son; listen to him." What's all happening here? Moses, Elijah, Jesus transfigured! God is telling these disciples something. Think about it! Isn't this the sequence of God's revealing himself to his people? God's first revelation of himself to his chosen people was at Mt. Sinai when God called Moses up onto the mountain to receive the Ten Commandments. The mountain was covered with the fiery glory of God. Lightning flashed and thunder sounded. When Moses came back down the mountain his face glowed brightly because he had been in the presence of God's glory.

Then there was Elijah, the greatest of the prophets. We heard about his fiery entrance into heaven in today's Old Testament Lesson. Elijah also experienced God's glory on a mountain top. It was at Mt. Carmel. Remember how Elijah once thought that he was the only person left in all of Israel still worshiping the true God and that everyone else was worshiping Baal, an idol. And remember how God arranged a contest between Baal and himself. The followers of Baal set up an altar with an offering. Then they prayed to their god all day long, begging him, pleading with him, to burn up their offering, but nothing happened. Then at the end of the day Elijah set up his altar and prayed to God. And God revealed his glory. He sent down fire from heaven and burned up the offering, and the stone altar, and even the water with which Elijah had soaked his offering and the altar and the ground on which it stood.

Yes, God had revealed his glory in the past in the presence of Moses, the great law-giver and leader of God's people. He also had revealed it to his prophet Elijah. But now God's glory is revealed —not to a man—but in and through a man. Suddenly, right before the eyes of the three disciples, Jesus' face and clothes are changed into a glowing, dazzling whiteness. Next, the voice of God from heaven confirms it, "This is my beloved Son." God has come directly into the midst of his chosen people—not indirectly through the law given to Moses or in the word spoken by the prophets— but in person. What could be more fantastic? Yet, Peter seems to miss the point. "Let's sit down and enjoy this for awhile." But Jesus doesn't let that happen. God removes his glory from the mountain top. Moses and Elijah are gone. Jesus then immediately takes the disciples down the mountain to lead them into ever more experiences of God's glorious presence among men—the greatest of which is still to come.

God's Glory Transfigures the Disciples at Pentecost

In this man Jesus, the disciples are to experience their God in a most dramatic way. Yet, it isn't until much later that they finally do get the point of it all. That was on Pentecost when the same glory of God which they had seen in Jesus came to each one of them in the form of little flames of fire—and they became changed men. Suddenly, those disciples started doing the things Jesus had done. They became loving, forgiving, helping people. They even did some of the miracles he had done. But most of all they became witnesses to this God of glory who had been with them in Jesus and now was actually within them. They began telling everyone they met about this glorious God of theirs whose forgiving love had been made real for them in Jesus Christ who died and then rose again.

We Too Are to Be Transfigured

Now what's the point of all this for us? Just this. We can't do what Peter did. We can't say, "Isn't this nice. The show's great. Let's sit back and enjoy it." No, Jesus took his disciples down from that mountain and he takes us down, too, right back into life, because he has a job for us to do. Jesus transfigured his first disciples by putting God's glory, his Spirit, that burning presence, right inside of them. Jesus does the very same thing to us. He started it in baptism when he put his Spirit into us and he wants to keep that Spirit burning brightly by always coming to us again and again in his Word and in the sacrament of his body and blood. The point and goal and result is to be the same with us as it was for those disciples. Paul spells it out so well in today's

Epistle. Each of us is to reflect the glory of the Lord which we have seen in Jesus. We are to be changed into his likeness. We are to take on his glory. We are to become like Jesus—loving, forgiving, helping, healing—thus announcing to everyone we meet God's good news of salvation which Jesus made possible. Now there's something to get excited about!

That's the Point I Dare Never Miss

But I can read your minds. You're saying, "But I don't feel like that. I've tried but it doesn't seem to happen with me. I'm not like Jesus. So often I'm not loving and forgiving and kind. I feel so guilty!" But don't be discouraged! The disciples had the same failings we have, the same guilts, the same doubts. So don't be discouraged. You see, we have the same answer for failure and guilt and doubt that they had—Jesus Christ: God's answer to it all; his Good News. Jesus is not only the example we are to follow. He is also the power that makes us able to follow. And he is the forgiveness and the Renewer when we fail to follow. *That's the point I dare never miss!* I can never make it through this life on my own. My report card keeps coming out all full of F's and U's. Yet God, in that ordinary looking man named Jesus, has made it possible for all that to be changed. He has even made it possible for me to be transfigured, to become once again one of God's beloved children who are so pleasing to him. That can happen because he has given me his Son's very own life, a life filled with God's glory —and power—and spirit—if only I will accept and believe it. Yes, that's the point I dare never miss. Amen.

HAROLD KITZMANN
Our Redeemer Lutheran Church
Fayetteville, North Carolina

THE HUMANITY OF CHRIST AND OUR LIVES

First Sunday in Lent
Mark 1:12-15

Mark writes his Gospel in a vivid and urgent fashion. The action moves quickly from one event to another and the contrast between the events is often important. This is the case with our Gospel for the day. Mark 1:12 tells us, "The Spirit immediately drove him out into the wilderness and he was in the wilderness forty days, tempted by Satan. . . ." This is in striking contrast to the preceding verses. There Jesus had just been baptized by John, the heavens opened and God declared, "Thou art my beloved Son, with thee I am well pleased." It surprises us that, just when it is revealed that Jesus is God's Son, he is driven into the wilderness to be tempted. That sequence of events goes against all of our presuppositions.

It is natural for us to suppose that God, in his omnipotence, will protect his people from the pains, ills and problems that face the unbelievers. And so, if God's Son appears in the flesh, we assume that he will be exalted above the problems that beset the common run of humanity. When the revelation comes that Jesus is God's beloved Son, we expect some glorious proof of this statement. Jesus will receive some great favor or power. When, instead, the revelation is followed by Jesus being tempted, even as we are tempted, it seems to us to be incongruous.

Paul tells us in 1 Corinthians 1:23 that the preaching of Christ crucified was a "stumbling block to Jews and folly to Gentiles." And so it was. The Gentile world had many myths of gods and goddesses who, for various reasons, took on human form and spent time on earth. But in none of these did the god or goddess become truly human. The human form was always a masquerade and whenever it became convenient to the divine being the human form was discarded and divine powers were exercised. If Christians had simply said that their God had appeared in a human form it would not have seemed to be folly. But Christians claimed that God had appeared in this truly human person, Jesus of Nazareth. Furthermore, Jesus was not a conquering hero who moved through human affairs untouched by the problems of human life. He was tempted, grew tired and hungry, he was crucified, dead and buried. All of this violated everything that people expected of their gods.

Early in the history of the Christian church there appeared a heresy which denied Christ's humanity. Some people argued that the divine word of God had not really become human, it had only taken on the appearance of humanity. In other words, they tried to picture Jesus in the same way in which Greek and Roman myths had told of gods and goddesses pretending to be human beings. Other people argued that the divine word had come to the man Jesus, dwelt in him for a period of time but the Word had left Jesus before he was tempted in Gethsemane or suffered and died on the cross.

The early Christians fought this heresy for many years. They recognized that if they denied the true humanity of Jesus, they would have lost the very heart of Christian faith. With John they affirmed that the Word had become flesh (John 1:14). The word "flesh" implied that God's Word had become a full and complete human being, one who stood under divine judgment and who must perish like all flesh. When Jesus was tempted it was a real human temptation and not some kind of play acting by a divine being who could not be tempted.

When we think of Luther's Reformation we think first of his rediscovery of the doctrine of justification by grace through faith. But we should not forget that almost as important to Luther was his rediscovery of the humanity of Jesus. The medieval church had lost sight of Jesus' humanity and even some of Luther's fellow-Protestants could not really believe that God had appeared in and through the human flesh of the man, Jesus. Thus Luther never tired of emphasizing that the only God we know is the God who came to be born of a woman, suckled at her breast, grew in stature and knowledge, was tempted like as we are tempted, suffered, was dead and buried. Luther marveled that God chose to come to us precisely in and through this humanity, weakness and finiteness. God was not like the medieval lord who sat in his manor while hired hands did the dirty work. God was like a nobleman who went himself to clean out the barn.

Despite the battle of the early Christians and the Reformers, there can be no question that the church still falls into the heresy of denying Jesus' full humanity. Christian art, Sunday school literature, much theology and popular interpretations of Jesus have conspired to picture him as one who was not really a finite human being. We may say that he is human but nonetheless we always imply that Jesus had resources of divinity which protected him from the temptations, doubts, fears and problems that you and I must face.

When the movie *Jesus Christ Superstar* appeared it shocked many Christians. One of the things that most shocked them was the scene of Jesus' temptation in Gethsemane. The movie portrayed a man who was in deep trouble, torn with self-doubts and critical of God himself. We have seen many movies dealing with the life of Jesus, but in most of them Jesus was portrayed as such a divine figure that we could never get really troubled over Gethsemane. We knew that this divine being, who moved through the world without ever quite touching the dirt beneath his feet, could not really succumb to temptation. However tempted he might appear to be, we knew that it was not for real. In *Superstar*, however, we beheld one who was really tempted as we are tempted and that shocked us. And yet, *Superstar* came close to portraying the scene as our Gospels describe it. They tell of a man so sorely tempted that he sweat blood. Why were we shocked at *Superstar*'s portrayal? Was it not because we have not really taken seriously the humanity of Jesus?

I recall reading a story about a man who wanted to learn what it was like to be a hobo. He adopted the clothes and way of life of the hoboes and won their confidence and friendship. To be prepared for emergencies this man had sewn a hundred dollar bill into the lining of his ragged coat. One day one of his hobo friends fell seriously ill. The man unsewed the hundred dollar bill so that he could get medical help for his friend. This incident destroyed the relationship between the man and the hoboes. The true hoboes, who knew what real poverty is, recognized that anyone who could go around with a hundred dollar bill sewn into his coat was not really one of them. He was living a masquerade. That story illustrates what we have often done to Jesus. We have pictured him in such a way that he was divinity sewn into his coat so that he is not really up against the kind of temptations, trials and troubles that we have to face. He may have worn our clothes and seemed to have lived our way of life for a time, but he was never really one of us. When the chips are down he had resources that we do not have.

The fact that we have so much difficulty in accepting the full humanity of Jesus is revealing. It reveals first of all what we are all seeking in our religious life. We human beings are naturally religious because we seek in religion a preservation from the misfortunes, the trials and the troubles of life. We expect that it will pay us to be good and religious. If we worship God, obey him, make sacrifices for him or to him, then he will surely reward us by preserving us from the misfortunes of those who surround us. We have preached this kind of religion to the unbelievers. We have enticed them with the idea that if they will but become Christian they will be happy, healthy, wealthy and wise. Jesus, however, said that God "makes his sun rise on the evil and on the good and sends rain on the just and the unjust (Matt. 5:45). That disappoints all of our hopes about religion. If the blessings of God fall alike on the good and the evil, then it does not pay us to be good. One way that we avoid taking Jesus' statement seriously is to deny that the hot sun of temptation or the cold rain of suffering fell upon Jesus even as it falls upon us. If we admit that God did not protect his Son from temptation, suffering and death, how can we continue to hope that he will protect us?

There is another thing about the human Jesus that disturbs us. When we are strong, we do not give up our strength to become weak even if that would help the weak. When we are wise we do not seek to become ignorant even if that might help the ignorant. When we are rich we do not give away our wealth so that the poor may be fed. And so, if we were God, we would not give up our omnipotent powers to become like our creation. When we read that Christ did not grasp at equality with God but emptied himself to become a servant (Phil. 2:6-8) it stands in bold judgment over the way we live. If we were to admit that God's Word really did become flesh, that he was tempted and suffered like us, we could no longer continue in our present paths. As Christians we would have to ask ourselves some painful questions about the affluent lives that we North Americans lead. We would have to re-evaluate the patterns of success that we have set for ourselves. To save ourselves that kind of disturbance we create a Jesus with a divine hundred dollar bill sewn into his human clothes. Since Jesus did not really give up his omnipotent powers, we are not really called to take up our crosses.

Jesus was tempted for forty days but "the angels ministered to him." That is, even in the pain and the agony of his temptation there was manifest to him the love of God. In the epistle for the day Paul makes the same point (Rom. 8:31-39). Paul tells us that we shall not be separated from God's love by tribulation, distress, persecution, famine, nakedness, peril or sword. Implicitly Paul is telling Christians that they are not going to be spared from any of these ills that inflict the human race. On the contrary, the Christian will face all of these and more because they will be "regarded as sheep to be slaughtered." When we recall that God did not spare his Son from temptation but sent the angels to minister to him in the temptation we realize that we can know the wonder of God's love even in hardship and suffering. The humanity of Christ means that we can know God's love in the whole of our lives.

If we turn to religion to gain protection from the ills of life, we naturally look for and find God's love in our victories. When we are successful in achieving our goals and dreams, when illness is miraculously cured, when our church grows rapidly and increases its budget, when we are healthy, we see God's love manifest to us. When the opposite of these things happen to us we cry out in protest, "Why did this happen to me?"

At first sight, taking the humanity of Jesus seriously seems to be the final disappointment of all our religious hopes. If God did not spare his own son from the temptations, sufferings and death that life brings, we cannot expect him to spare us. But on second sight, we realize that the human Jesus is able to reveal to us God's love in precisely the unexpected places. It is when Jesus is undergoing the strain of temptation that angels ministered unto him. Similarly we find God's love becoming real to us when we fail to achieve success, when death comes, when tragedy strikes.

We are again in the season of Lent. At the end of this season there is the glorious message of the resurrection of Christ from the dead. It is natural for us to leap ahead to Christ's final victory and to forget what comes before. But our text for the day reminds us that before the first Easter morning Jesus was tempted and tried, he suffered and died. In our lives we would like to have Easter without Gethsemane or Good Friday. But we have not been promised that. What we have been promised is that when we are tempted the angels will minister to us. "I am sure that neither death, nor life, nor angels, nor principalities, nor things present, nor things to come, nor powers, nor height, nor depth, nor anything else in all creation, will be able to separate us from the love of God in Christ Jesus our Lord."

WILLIAM HORDERN, President
Lutheran Theological Seminary
Saskatoon, Saskatchewan, Canada

FINDING LIFE BY LOSING IT

Second Sunday in Lent
Mark 8:31-38

As deep an insight into the meaning of life as has ever been spoken was given by Christ on his way to the cross. Around the destiny of his own life he wrapped a teaching for every life. Concerning his own suffering death, the message reads: Take the love he brought. Concerning the believer's life, it says: Lead the life he taught.

"He began to teach them," Mark's gospel reads. It would be the hardest lesson they had ever learned. After almost three years with him, the disciples were put to their most difficult test. Could they discern the meaning of the cross? What Jesus was going to say would stagger them. It would be absolutely mind-boggling. Therefore, well ahead of time, love was preparing the beloved. Jesus was always preparing his disciples for the next step. He only began to teach them here about his cross. The teaching would never end. The Holy Spirit would continue it long after Jesus' departure from earth.

"He began to teach them that the Son of man must suffer many things." That the divine One could succumb to suffering was foreign to the thought of the day. He would be victor, not victim. The title, "Son of man," meaning the God-sent Messiah, guaranteed exemption from suffering in popular thought. Yet

Christ was saying here to his disciples that he was about to suffer "terrible things," as one translation renders it. He would experience excruciating agonies. This left the disciples speechless. They just couldn't handle such a concept. Sometime after the event they would discover that "with his stripes we are healed." Through the suffering death of the Messiah God would work out the world's reconciliation with the Father. On the way to Jerusalem, however, they were utterly baffled.

Jesus went on to share with his disciples that "the Son of man must . . . be rejected by the elders and the chief priests and the scribes." This, too, boggled the mind. Why go to Jerusalem if this was in store? Head back to Galilee while there was time. Of all people the religious leaders should accept God's Messiah. This rejection was to cut Jesus more than the whips. "He came to his own home, and his own people received him not." What a shudder must have shaken Christ's own heart as he foresaw the rejection he must experience!

He must be killed, Jesus told his disciples. The prediction was getting more fantastic with every phrase. Here was the ultimate shocker. Afterward they would learn to understand it as Paul interpreted it, "God shows his love for us in that while we were yet sinners Christ died for us." But now this never even dawned on them. They were simply appalled by what he was saying. When Jesus came to the climax, ". . . and after three days rise again," they were completely lost. That probably didn't even register because they were so bothered by what he had been saying. Their heads were going around in circles.

"And he said this plainly," Mark's gospel records. This was no parable or allegory with hidden meaning. It was frank, open, and devastating. At least they could never say he hadn't told them. This was just the first time. Other times would follow. Jesus wanted them to have a solid basis for interpreting what was to follow. When it would happen, they might remember what he told them. Meanwhile, they could start thinking about it in advance. During their whole lifetime they would not have anything more important to ponder.

The Startling Hidden Meaning

After the disciples would witness the suffering death and triumphant resurrection of their Lord, they would come to realize the earth-shaking meaning of these events. God was embracing humankind with a rapturous offer of mercy through Christ. No person ever again need feel rejected or lost or hopeless. By his cross Christ drew the sting from life and death. For those who put their trust in what he did for them, there is peace with God for the sinner and indescribable joy both now and forever. The secret hid from creation was now shouted over the earth. God totally loves every person. He did all that was necessary to settle everyone's account with him. Even when it required the torture, death, and resurrection of his only Son, he didn't hesitate. Henceforth, no catastrophe or threat, even death itself, could ever terrorize a believer or give him an anxious day. God holds us to his heart in tender mercy and pardon for the sake of Christ. This is why Christ suffered terrible things, was cruelly rejected by his own, was crucified like a criminal, and was raised to life on the third day. It made possible the priceless assurance that divine love supports human life in trial and death for the sake of Christ. God worked it all out on his own in the strangest way, defying human logic, but meeting human crisis.

All this, however, was not apparent in that plain talk on the way to Jerusalem, so Peter reacted to Jesus' stabbing prediction, taking him by the arm and beginning to rebuke him. "You shouldn't say such things," he must have protested. While Jesus was trying to draw the disciples into partnership with him in his sorrow, Peter rejected the whole concept out of hand. If even Peter completely missed the point after being in the inner circle with Jesus for three years, no one today ought to be over-confident about his understanding of the gospel, but always pray for the light and leading of the Holy Spirit. Probably all the rest thought like Peter but didn't say it.

Jesus shot back a stunning reply. First he looked into the disciple's thoughts, found them confused and disbelieving, and then ordered, "Get behind me, Satan! For you are not on the side of God, but of men." Strictly speaking, Satan, not Peter, was addressed, but Peter had allowed himself to become a mouthpiece for Satan in what he said. One translation renders Jesus' words to Peter, "You are not looking at this from God's point of view, but from man's." How often the same mistake occurs! We face our problems, meet our crises, and confront our opportunities from a human point of view instead of from God's point of view. It can save so much heartache to reflect first for a while on how God looks at the situation and what he can do with it. Jesus did not humiliate Peter in what he said. He was stern toward Satan, but loving toward Peter. For the disciple's sake some strong response had to be made; the temptation had to be firmly rejected.

Take the love he brought. The disciples would learn to read this meaning in the events Jesus predicted about himself, but Jesus wasn't finished. Lead the life he taught is the other conclusion they could draw from what he next told them. The life would be lived in the empowerment of that magnificent love. To the multitude and his disciples Jesus spoke the incisive words, "If any man would come after me, let him deny himself and take up his cross and follow me." No exceptions are possible. This is a universal principle of life. "If any man would come after me . . ."

"Let him deny himself." One translation puts it, "leave self behind." Another goes, "he must forget himself;" another, "put aside your own pleasures." Get yourself out of the center of life. Put the other person there. "The greatest gift I ever received," said a young successful attorney, "was a gift I got one Christmas when my dad gave me a small box. Inside was a note saying, 'Son, this year I will give you 365 hours, an hour every day after dinner. It's yours. We'll talk about what you want to talk about, we'll go where you want to go, play what you want to play. It will be *your* hour.' My dad not only kept his promise of that gift," said the attorney, "but every year he renewed it, and it's the greatest gift I ever had in my life." "If any man would come after me, let him deny himself." Too often we deny others instead of ourself. It doesn't work backwards.

"Let him . . . take up his cross," Christ continued. The reference is to a condemned criminal carrying his cross through the streets of Jerusalem up to the hill outside the city where he would be crucified. The cross is a burden taken upon one's self for the sake of others. It is assumed in love and carried without complaint. It may be a very heavy burden. Christ apparently staggered and stumbled under the weight of his cross up the slopes of Calvary. Today a cross might be a woman doing the food shopping for a neighbor during her illness or a student carrying books home to a fellow student with a broken leg or a worker taking time he really doesn't have to train a new worker or a parent taking time to answer patiently the many questions of small children or a teacher spending time after school hours to give individual attention to a backward learner. Whatever it is, it represents a burden voluntarily assumed in love for someone else. "Let him deny himself and take up his cross and follow me."

Life's Master Principle

Then Jesus gave life's great master principle: "For whoever would save his life will lose it; and whoever loses his life for my sake and the gospel's will save it." This is, in effect, a sacred promise of God. If one gives his life away upon others, he can't lose. He can only win. A man retires at age 55 from a high position in a corporation. Claiming that he has earned his "bundle," he plans to give himself away during the rest of his life in full-time voluntary service to church and community. He won't draw maximum retirement pay with such early retirement, but he will draw maximum joy from the greatly increased direct service that he can give to others.

Every personal relationship can be regarded as a situation from which to get or to which to give. A husband and wife can regard their marriage as a relationship from which each seeks to get everything possible from the other or to give everything possible to the other. Two neighbors with adjoining properties may seek to use each other for everything they can get or to serve each other with everything they can share. Lifestyle adaptation for the sake of the brother and sister in God's family because of what Christ has done for all is the master principle of life. Every day is a new laboratory in which to test it. Life is not to get but to give. In seeking to get from others life turns sour; in living primarily to give to others life becomes sweet.

"For what does it profit a man, to gain the whole world and forfeit his life?" Jesus asked. Today's concern is with the bottom line. After all the columns of profit and loss, what does the bottom line say? Jesus is talking here in those very terms. If a person spends his life amassing things and money but doesn't take ample time to help others in the process, what will he have to show for it in the final accounting before God when the criteria will not be money and things but spiritual values and the quality of personal relationships? In a society that worships the botttom line in terms of financial gain, a contemporary translation of Jesus' words is arresting: "What profit does a man show who gains the whole world and destroys himself in the process?"

"For what can a man give in return for his life?" Christ pressed further. What is a fair exchange? Would one trade a diamond for dirt? Or gold for fool's gold? There is no equal exchange when it comes to life, meaning life that is made up of inner peace, joy, fulfillment, and hope. Today's collect prays, "Bring back all who have erred and gone astray from your Word, and lead them again in faith to receive and hold fast to your truth."

Jesus concluded, "For whoever is ashamed of me and of my words in this adulterous and sinful generation, of him will the Son of man also be ashamed, when he comes in the glory of his Father with the holy angels." The way a Christian lives announces his shame or his pride regarding Christ. If such a one crumples under the pressures of society and constantly compromises Christian principles, he is ashamed of Christ. If, however, that person holds fast through thick and thin because of Christ's steadfastness toward him, then Christ is honored. When the Lord comes in his glory, all will be revealed. Pray God for the courage to live for Christ in this day and toward that one.

Take the love he brought. Lead the life he taught. The two are interwoven. Living solely in trust upon that radiant love for us, we can be motivated to live the life he taught. Living that life will turn us back time and again for strength to that love he brought. The master love and the master life go together. In Christ, the Savior, we find the source of both.

ROBERT W. STACKEL, Director
Love Compels Action/World Hunger Appeal
LCA—New York

GENUINE WORSHIP

Third Sunday in Lent
John 2:13-22

"Destroy this temple, and in three days I will raise it up again." This was the sign which Jesus gave when asked why he had the audacity to overthrow the money changers' tables and drive out those who were buying and selling with all their sheep and oxen. Jesus had entered the outer court of the temple. He saw the Passover pilgrims paying to exchange their money for the coins accepted in payment of the temple tax. He watched them purchasing sheep and oxen for sacrifices. The longer he watched, the more furious he became. He took cords, made a whip and drove them out of the temple—sheep, oxen and all. He overturned the money changers' tables and sent them scrambling after their scattered coins. Evidently he had a soft spot in his heart for those who had pigeons in cages. Pigeons were all that the poor could afford for sacrifice. He merely told those who sold pigeons to take them and get out.

This story is usually called the cleansing of the temple. John places it at the beginning of Jesus' ministry and during the first of three visits to Jerusalem to observe the Passover there. The other three evangelists concentrate on the Galilean ministry of Jesus and tell of only one Passover visit to Jerusalem. They place this event during the Holy Week, shortly after Jesus entered Jerusalem on Palm Sunday. It appears that this was one of the incidents which triggered the decision of the leaders of the people that Jesus had to go. In retrospect the disciples recalled a verse from Psalm 69: "Zeal for thy house will consume me," that is, destroy me. And zeal for the Lord's house did indeed lead to his crucifixion.

You can imagine the tension which this daring action of Jesus created. Like the great prophets of old, Jesus protested against profaning the house of God. He left everything in complete disarray. "How dare you?" Jesus was asked. "What sign or miraculous proof do you have which clearly authorizes you to do this?" Jesus answered, "Destroy this temple and in three days I will raise it up." The people, quite naturally, thought that he had reference to the temple in which they were standing. For forty-six years the building of the temple had been in progress, and it was not even completed. And Jesus will raise it in three days! "Preposterous," they thought. Later, however, it was this very charge which was brought against Jesus before the high priest. Under the cross they taunted him: "You who would destroy the temple and rebuild it in three days, save yourself. If you are the Christ, come down from the cross."

Old Worship Abolished

Preposterous or not, the cleansing of the temple had messianic overtones. This was exactly what the Messiah was to do. But Jesus came not merely to protest the profaning of the temple. He came not merely to reform the worship of the temple. He came to abolish old forms of worship so that a new form might arise and take its place. The mission of Jesus was far from being merely destructive. He came to institute the worship of God in spirit and in genuine reality. He acted to put an end to the sacrifices of sheep and oxen and pigeons as if these could atone for sin. There was always a corps of prophets telling men that no sacrifice of men could ever put a man right with God. Jesus here alluded to another sacrifice that could. "All right, if you want a sign, I'll give you a sign. Destroy this temple. You do this and see what happens. In three days I will raise it up again." And the whole world will have a temple where all people may worship in spirit and truth. After his resurrection it dawned on the disciples that Jesus was speaking of the temple of his body. And they believed the Scripture, for the Scriptures testified of him.

Temples in Need of Cleansing

Are there temples in need of cleansing today? Certainly not in the senses of abolishing sacrifices of animals. But how do men attempt to be right with God? What is the purpose of worship?

Basically there are two kinds of religion or worship. One is based on man achieving a satisfactory relationship with God by doing something to win God's favor. Do something. Be good. Believe in the right doctrine. Help the poor. This is the religion of righteousness by the law. Moses wrote that "The man who practices the righteousness which is based on the law will have to find life by it," that is, be saved by the law.

God Acts—We React

There is another kind of religion. It does not begin with man's righteousness. It does not even begin with any action of man. It begins with God's action—God's action in Christ. God was in Christ reconciling the world to himself and he has forgiven us all our sins. He who believes in him shall be saved. Genuine worship begins with God's action. We react in response to God.

It is not a case of us acting and God reacting to our action. Rather God acts in Christ, and we respond to God's grace with faith, love, obedience and service. In his first epistle John writes, "Beloved, we are now the sons of God." We do good not because we are trying to become children of God. We are God's children, and therefore, we do. If we act because we are trying to become the children of God, we live in fear—the fear of rejection, the fear of never doing enough or being good enough.

It is interesting to note that in Exodus 20 the prologue to the Ten Commandments reads: "I am the Lord thy God, who brought you out of the land of Egypt." This is the covenant Lord who made an agreement with Abraham, Isaac, and Jacob and who in remembrance of this covenant acted to fulfill his promise and to deliver them from the bondage of Pharoah's slavery. He is the God who acts in man's behalf. Then the text continues, "Therefore, you shall have no other gods before me. You shall not take the name of the Lord your God in vain. Remember the Sabbath day to keep it holy. Honor your father and mother. You shall not kill. You shall not steal. You shall not commit adultery. You shall not bear false witness. You shall not covet."

For us, the temple has been cleansed. The old form of law worship is abolished. We worship in the glorious liberty of the children of God who are freed to bring voluntary and spontaneous sacrifices of thanksgiving, hymns of adoration and devotion and deeds of love and service to him who has graciously called us to be his own. We have a temple where we can serve God in the reality of God's grace in Christ. "For freedom Christ has set us free; stand fast, therefore, and do not submit to the yoke of slavery" (Gal. 5:1). Thanks be to God for his inexpressible gift.

CLARENCE W. KNIPPA
Grace Lutheran Church
Tulsa, Oklahoma

CRAVING FOR SAVING

Fourth Sunday in Lent
John 3:14-21

To all of God's beloved called to be saints, grace to you and peace from God our Father and the Lord Jesus Christ. Amen.

During the Lenten season, I like to find a book that really puts my faith to the test. If Jesus Christ is the truth for us, we should not be afraid to do mental combat with authors who propose challenging ideas. This year I happened upon a book entitled *Rabbi J*, a best seller by Johannes Lehmann. It is his point that the real life of Jesus is hidden behind a camouflage which results in a distorted story and a misinformed church. I had to face the prospect that the Christ I preach and teach is riddled with fabrication and the religion of which I am a priest is not based upon divine revelation but merely human reflection.

Lehmann's RABBI J

When I read such a book, I like to place myself within the heart and mind of the author, so that both of us are testing the mettle of my belief. The big question that *Rabbi J* forced me to ask is, "Who is Jesus?"

Lehmann says the real Jesus is quite a different man from the one propagated by his biographers and created by his worshippers. Our images of Jesus have come to us through two filters. The first is the New Testament writers. They purposely obscured the life of Jesus because they didn't dare to reveal his true motive. The evangelists drew a one-sidedly devout picture, concealing the political aspects of his life. The second filter is the theologians, especially Paul. Like a magnifying glass, they explained and expanded upon the teachings of Jesus. The teachers of the church enlarged upon the death of Jesus, for example, and made it an act of atonement for the benefit of everybody. They set aside everything about Jesus the Jew and made him into a Christ, a savior of all mankind. The first Christians bought this scheme, transferring their lost hope in Jesus into a living hope in Christ, a spiritual Messiah.

A Man After My Heart

So who is Jesus? Who is the figure that emerges as we reflect upon the passage, "For God so loved the world, that he gave his only begotten Son, that whosoever believes in him should not perish but have everlasting life." Well, for one thing, Rabbi J was a real man. We can and must hang on to that. One of the earliest heresies of the church was to deny this fact. A fact not obscured by the evangelists. Nor have our church theologians been guilty of making Jesus into a heavenly titan who merely masqueraded as a man.

Jesus knew the burdens of physical exhaustion. He came and followed the conditions of humanity to their inevitable conclusion. He died. He died alone—as all of us must die. It's very important for me to know that Jesus was a genuine human being. If I can be sure that he was a real person, then I can understand how he can be with me in my sinning and in my suffering. He came in weakness, humility, and humanity. He woos me instead of overpowering me. He wins me by his love, not by his dazzling authority.

A Real Lover of a Man

So when I tell you that "Jesus loves you," I mean love of a deeply passionate kind, like two lovers give and receive. Perhaps you have suffered a terrible loss in your family. Can Jesus help you accept it and learn to live with it? Does he understand the vacuum, the emptiness, the excruciating agony? Yes, he loves you. You can trust him to help you resolve your bitterness and endure your pain. Someone in the audience this morning is losing his or her love. Before your very eyes, your loved one is dying and you can't do anything about it. Or, the person you have vowed to live with forever is slipping away from you and your enthusiasm for divorce is zero. If it helps, I know someone who loves you. Whose love for you can partly fill the empty place in your life. Perhaps you've just lost your job. It's like having the rug pulled out from under you, or falling down a well. You are anxious, you are fearful, you don't know where to turn. It's easy for others to say that it is only a step towards something better. But you wonder what could be better than having a job and having material security. Is there a love that will never let you go? That can catch you when the bottom falls out? Indeed there is. When you've had it, my dear Christian sisters and brothers, when you've come to the end of your rope or when your own capacity to love has been drained, when your well is dry, when you must face important decisions, remember, Jesus loves you. This I know. How do I know it? Because of who he is, a real lover of a man.

Craving for Saving

One of the lessons of psychology is that minds continually subjected to an appeal or warning they don't wish to heed develop a fatal immunity to truth. Jesus warned about the soil so hardened by the traffic of familiar ideas it was impenetrable to fruitful change. Too much exposure to any one thing sickens, bores, or disgusts, as many a "pro football widow" on Sunday afternoon will attest.

John 3:16 is a verse that, because it is so well known, might have lost its power to convey the intended meaning. And the subject with which it deals—salvation—to use the language of finance today, probably has suffered a devaluation of purchasing power.

Yes, everyone remembers John 3:16. But can anyone remember with whom Jesus is speaking when he concludes his conversation with "God so loved the world that he gave his only Son. . . ."? It is not, after all, a verse that is fenced off and standing alone. John 3:16 has a context, it happens in a real life situation. The person Jesus is engaging in dialog is Nicodemus. The two of them are talking about religion. They're discussing salvation.

J. Robert Nelson writes an article in *Religion in Life*, (Winter 1974) in which he states that everybody wants to be saved. This desire is a universal human experience. We may describe our searches differently, but the quest, the craving for saving is irrepressible for all mankind. It shapes not only our religious life but our social and political life as well.

Yearnings of the Human Spirit

Nelson says salvation is concerned with three things: (1) the need to improve oneself, (2) the longing for true happiness, and (3) the hope that good will endure. The human spirit has always been drawn to these basic yearnings. In spite of the diffidence and tastelessness of the media hucksters who profit without conscience from these universal human desires, and in spite of all the "Jesus Saves" signs, and in spite of the manipulation through electronic revivalism, salvation is still a very alive and throbbing thing. We reflect on our existence. Our search is unsatisfied. Our hunger unfulfilled. Everyone is craving for saving. The need to improve. The longing for happiness. The hope that good will ultimately triumph.

And such a variety of ingenious things that human beings have done to realize these spiritual goals. Altars have been built on which to burn animals, and even other people. Beautiful and frightening costumes are worn and people dance themselves into a frenzy. Incense is offered, prayer wheels spun, songs are sung. Pyramids are built, bodies are starved—all in hopes of satisfying a deep-felt craving for saving. Rich men have built temples and the poor spent their pennies to secure safe passage from suffering to health, from ignorance to knowledge, guilt to forgiveness, mortality to immortality.

The Essential Difference

And Nicodemus, too. He is one in the long line of humanity who has counted his good deeds in anticipation of a just reward and tranquil eternity. His conversation with Jesus vividly portrays the essential difference between the saving way of the Heavenly Father and the vast array of noble means of seeking protection from temptation, death, and the devil.

Nicodemus is confused, understandably so. There is no doubt in his mind Jesus is a teacher sent from God. This country needs good rabbis. How else are we to keep the law and further the purposes of God? But what else is this you say? "Unless one is born anew, he cannot see the kingdom." How is it possible to be born again? And what is this new theology? "Unless one is born of water and the spirit he cannot enter the kingdom." How can this be?

Now here is the difference. For Nicodemus salvation depends upon what he does. He keeps the commandments. By living the obedient life he furthers God's kingdom. But for Jesus, salvation centers upon what God does, the new life he gives, the power and presence of the divine that his Spirit activates in us. "Nicodemus, it is *not* the offering you burn, the dances you do, the indulgences you buy, the religious rent you pay, the church colleges you support. The initiative is with God."

A Gift in Search of Recipients

But how? demands Nicodemus. How does God do this? It is one thing to repudiate all that is called religion, but it is quite another thing to say what is left. What of man's craving for saving? How does God go about saving? The answer is: John 3:16. The message of the Bible distilled into one little verse. God so loved the world, that's how. He sent Jesus, that's how. An astonishing gift. Salvation is free.

We can picture Nicodemus turning away, muttering in deep disappointment: "How can this be? It won't sell. He won't even be able to give it away. A man could get himself killed." And Jesus knowing he must identify himself with God's searching, saving love for the world, sets his course for Jerusalem, aware of a bitter end.

Dear brothers and sisters in Christ, God loves you. His love goes searching for your response. His salvation is continuing through your faith.

JACK HUSTAD
First Lutheran Church
Fergus Falls, Minnesota

WHAT DO YOU SING FOR?
WHAT DO YOU LONG FOR?

Fifth Sunday in Lent
John 12:20-33

The dean of a New York seminary has said that when he interviews a candidate for a teaching position he first asks him two questions, "What do you sing for?" and "What do you long for?" Then, after they have discussed these questions, he goes on to discuss his academic qualifications.

On this Sunday morning, as we near the peak of our Lenten season, let me ask the same questions: "What do you sing for? What do you long for?" Your answer to these questions will in some degree, perhaps even to a large extent, determine what will happen to you as you look toward Holy Week and enter into the experience of Easter.

What Do You Sing For?

"What do you sing for?" What is it that you celebrate in your life? What is it that really makes your heart sing? Or don't you ever sing? What are those aspects of your life that you can affirm and say "yes" to?

This is a very personal question; so personal, in fact, that you might never speak an answer to another living soul. Is it a person? Is there a person in your life who loves you and makes you sing? Is it a memory? A time which recaptures the fun moments? Perhaps it was a time when a depth and richness and compassion and surge of strength came out of those memories with a strength you did not know you had?

A mysterious question, really. When we sing we sing for all that life has given us, we do it with an insight into the mystery of ourselves, the mystery of a relationship where there is giving and receiving and sacrifice, the mystery of loss and breaking and healing . . . somehow the mystery that is "you" becomes even greater. What do you sing for?

What Do You Long For?

Now the second question: "What do you long for?" Where is your discontent? What change do you want? What kind of difference do you want to make in life? What do you agonize for? Our longings for the future arise out of the songs of the present. Our songs show the affirmations we make in life.

So what do you long for? More money or more meaning? More comfort or more sacrifice? More drifting or more purpose? More getting your way or more being used by a purpose or a person?

We are approaching a major celebration for our nation. A major question is what do we long for in our national life? What is it that we sing for in this year of the bi-centennial? In profound ways we find ourselves in an uneasy lull. As we look at our nation and world, how and for what reasons do we move ahead?

In this morning's Gospel we hear of the account of some Greeks who come to Philip and state, "we wish to see Jesus." Philip joins with Andrew and they go to Jesus with the report. Our Lord responds with an affirmation of his world-wide mission, one which presupposes his death and glorification. The way to life lies in the renunciation of life. As with a grain of wheat, unless it falls into the ground and dies, it remains solitary.

What do we sing for? What do we long for? These are perennial questions. Gentiles came and told the disciples that they would see Jesus. His answer is the same today. He will draw all men to himself. He will be lifted up from earth. From death will come his life. To see Jesus we must see life rising from death.

These questions are universal—not only for seminary presidents or pastors. They are asked by people who sing about and long for people. People who love and are loved. People who rejoice in the relationships that give meaning—those loves, those sacrifices, those deaths—in them people are in touch with a bedrock reality, where life comes as a grace and we know that we are safe and loved. All people who sing of love and long for love . . . people like us who realize that love itself asks the questions and love itself gives the answers.

We sing for love and long for love. Jesus said that the man who loves himself is lost but he who hates himself will be kept safe for eternal life. There is a love which breaks through the paralysis of the solitary, one which we can share and experience forever.

The love that Jesus spoke about, the love which would lift men up, was a love which rose out of death.

From Death ...

Physically, death closes in upon each of us. What each of us does with our years, during the time that we live and move and have our being, reflects our being swallowed up in death or discovering a new dimension of life. There is the death that comes to loved ones or friends who move away and are lost . . . the dying of old images and trusted allegiances and dependable ways of doing things. There is a dying when naive and childlike faith in allegiance to people in places of leadership is questioned. Our nation has emerged from a nightmare of disillusionment and anger that reflects this kind of death.

It's a dying time whenever patterns change and familiar ways are left behind. Death is in the air when we realize that our land of plenty is running dry, when we realize that we don't have as much room in which to move or air to breathe or energy to use as we desire. When old certainties die and we are unsure—that's a dying time. It was a dying time as Greeks, coming to worship at the festival, told the disciples that they would see Jesus.

It was a dying time for a culture, a society, a religion . . . they wanted something to sing for, something to long for which promised life.

More than forty years ago, one of the great dramas of our century began with the kidnapping of the 20 month old son of Charles Lindbergh. "I will write everything as I would like it to be told me," Anne Morrow Lindbergh wrote to her mother-in-law. "At 7:30 Betty (the nurse) and I were putting the baby to bed. We closed and bolted all the shutters except one on the window where the shutters are warped and won't close. At 10 Betty went into the baby, shut the window first, then lit the electric stove, then turned to the bed. It was empty and the sides were still up. No blankets taken. You know the rest. . . ."

Then the awful waiting. Finally, Anne Morrow Lindbergh wrote in her diary: "The baby's body was found in the woods on Hopewell-Mount Rose Road. Killed by a blow on the head. I feel strangely a sense of peace—not peace, but an end to restlessness, a finality, as though I were sleeping in a grave."

In recalling the months and years that followed, she writes: "I do not believe that suffering teaches. If suffering alone taught, all the world would be wise, since everyone suffers. To suffering must be added mourning, understanding, patience, love, openness, and the willingness to remain vulnerable."

That is a story about a woman afflicted by a devastating kind of sadness and death and loss and how she survived it by first building a wall of self-control and that way getting by and getting done what had to be done. When the end came, hurt and fragile, she entered into a kind of sleeping in the grave that numbs and deadens feeling but allows people like us to keep going and not just stop.

. . . to Life

But surviving the agony, she knows that suffering alone does not teach. Living demands a willingness to remain vulnerable. Life can be lived as a stone. We can spend our lives numbly sleeping in the grave. We all do our share of that kind of dying. But there is an alternative. Out of death a new power and strength . . . a new self, a new mysterious "you." Something to sing for . . . something to long for.

Jesus' words are plain. He said that the man who loves himself is lost . . . if anyone serves me he must follow me . . . I will draw everyone to myself when I am lifted up from earth. What do you sing for? . . . what do you long for? . . . important questions. Jesus calls us out of our graves toward new life, beyond the numbness of sleeping in graves. He calls us toward a glorious new creation born out of griefs, war, disappointments, sorrow, betrayals, broken dreams.

What do you sing for—What do you long for? We can sing for love . . . we can long for love. If we follow him, we take the gamble of letting the gravestone be rolled away and risk giving up our hold on death. Then we not only sing for love and long for love . . . by grace we decide for love.

RALPH EDWARD PETERSON
Saint Peter's Church
New York, New York

THE HEART OF THE GOSPEL

Sunday of the Passion—Palm Sunday
Mark 15:1-39

The Church Year Calendar and Lectionary (*Contemporary Worship 6*) *provides a preliminary service with processional for this day, developing the theme of Palm Sunday, with the Gospel Mark 11:1-10. This text emphasizes the Passion of our Lord and traverses the same ground as the parallel from the Gospel of St. John for Good Friday.*

Mark begins his book: "The beginning of the gospel of Jesus Christ the Son of God." "Gospel" means the proclamation of good news. One conclusion which the early church provided for Mark's book reads: "After this (namely after his resurrection) Jesus himself sent out by means of them from east to west the sacred and imperishable proclamation of eternal salvation." For anybody who heard our text today for the first time it would seem like anything but good news. For it is the account of the suffering and death of Jesus Christ, the object of the church's contemplation through the whole week before Easter Sunday. Let us remember why we are doing this. We ponder that work of Jesus Christ not only in one week of the year, but in all preaching of the Good News, in the sacrament of the body and blood of our Lord, in the signs and symbols of the church. For that cross of Jesus Christ is the climax of his ministry to the world, through it he is the one source and power for our life with God. As we ponder it in this hour, may it help us to reach out to God for rescue from death, for faith and life, for closeness to our Heavenly Father.

We Confront Squalor, Hatred, Death

On the surface we see nothing supernatural or mystic about this story. Here we face human nature at its worst. Criminals are being executed, and Jesus is being framed, as we call it, railroaded into dreadful crucifixion. The executioners are hardened and cold. The jeering throng of bystanders boils with venom. The government official in charge of the execution sees no guilt in Jesus but gives in for political reasons, "wishing to satisfy the crowd." We are familiar with such things: surface piety, false religion, justice surrendered to expediency, cruelty, hatred. This is real. This is the kind of world we live in.

This story is, first of all, about Jesus Christ. But it does not show him as the benign healer or powerful wonder-worker or stirring preacher. He is here the victim of suffering, pain, and death. He even refuses to defend himself, and he had told his disciples not to employ arms against his opponents. There's one thing even more dreadful, for the climax of his suffering is that his God, as he calls him, has himself forsaken him. Here we have death in its most profound dimension: not simply the stoppage of breath in the body, but the stoppage of God, the separation from God which is loss of life in its most exact sense. This, too, we know something about. We have our pains and handicaps; we face death around the corner day by day. And the life of God in our hearts? Behind the surface of our lives and even of our worship and churchgoing, how are we thinking of God? Is he there to pray to? Are we satisfied that he is present within us? Are we sure not simply of the precepts and formulas of our faith and doctrine, but of the presence of God with us in this life and in the life to come?

We Confront God's Own Action

In today's Epistle, Paul sees through the action of Jesus Christ on the cross. He sees it as an act by which Jesus identified himself with our own life and death, as action which he did on our behalf, and at the behest of God. At one and the same moment he found himself forsaken by God, and obedient to the mandate and fulfilling the task which God had sent him into the world to do. It is as though the Heavenly Father reads our minds at the distance of nearly two thousand years from the first Good Friday, and sees how shallow religion and empty worship and apathy about God tend to infect our lives, and so he devises a way by which he reaches into our lives at their homeliest and most sensitive level to penetrate our minds and reach our hearts with his concern. He gives up his own Son as a servant to rescue us from sin by being a shareholder in it, by experiencing the sum total of its shame and squalor and rancor and separation from God. He has his Son to experience our distance from God so that he might draw close to us again.

This is the heart of the gospel, the meaning of the Passion of our Lord. This dreadful scene of the cross drives to the core of human need, namely its distance from God. It responds to that need in the cry of our Lord, *Eloi, eloi, lama sabachthani,* My God, my God, why hast thou forsaken me? For here Jesus shares the distance of humankind from God, in order himself to be the bridge by which God reaches out to us all.

It makes little difference whether we feel that distance a thing of our own making, sense guilt over our sin and rebellion and antipathy against God; or whether it is simply that we are in sorrow and anxiety and perplexity and despair and feel that God doesn't care. In this act of Christ on the cross we see the basic problem of us all, the distance from God, and the basic answer to the problem, that God gives his own Son into the death that is in itself separation from God, so that we might have life. "He has made him who knew no sin," Paul tells the Corinthians, "to be sin for us, that we might be made the righteousness of God in him."

Mark records an incident of the Passion story that shows the effort of God to reach into the lives of his people: The veil of the

temple was torn in two from top to bottom. That veil pictured the
distance between God and man. It was drawn aside only once a
year, on the great Day of Atonement, as the priest entered the
Holy of Holies with the incense depicting the prayers of the
people, and the slain beast picturing the offering that had to be
made for the sins both of the priest and the people. Today's lesson from the prophet Zechariah describes that blood as the rescue
from captivity of prisoners and exiles because it portrayed the
mercy of God. This time, says the writer to the Hebrews, in the
death of Jesus Christ the priest did not have to make an offering
for himself; he was the offering. This time God completes the
story prefigured by the Exodus of his people from Egypt and the
establishment in the Holy Land, by the restoration to Jerusalem,
by the ceremonies in the tabernacle and the temple for the gathering of the chosen people. Now the veil has been drawn aside once
and for all time, now the distance between God and man is
bridged by God's giving his Son into death for the sins of the
world.

We Share God's Saving Act

Do you still feel a distance from it all? Perhaps not so much
from God to whom you pray daily and especially when you are in
trouble, as from this event of Christ on the cross and what it may
possibly have to do with you? How can we make this scene on
Calvary our own?

To begin with, we need to realize that God is really doing everything for us, everything that he can do. He is giving up his
own Son. Imagine a parent with a desperately sick child. It needs
surgery. All the preparations are made. "What can I do?" says
the parent with anguish and concern. "Let me hold your instruments; let me blow into the child's lungs; let me guide your
hand, doctor"—is that what the parent says? Probably not. Perhaps the doctor in kindness will say, "You can go up into the
operating theater and you can watch me, and when I'm done you
can be happy with me and your child that all is over." And so all
that we can do about our own peace with God is to stand and see
what he has done through his Son, stand and look over and over
again. We hear this story not only on Passion Sunday or Good
Friday but in various forms over and over again. We receive the
body and blood of our Lord, the blood of the covenant and of the
New Testament in his blood, in remembrance of this act of his
dying on the cross for us. God is doing the really great thing for
us; he is erasing the distance between himself and us, as he gives
up his Son. Our task is to look and see, to remember with thanks.

At the same time we can realize that if we really concentrate on what God is doing in Christ, we shall face up more completely to Christ himself. Even though he came into the world to share our lives, our birth and our living and our death, we tend to idealize him, separate him from our everyday life, bypass him when it comes to finding the power for our everyday life and need. The pagan captain of the guard in the story can teach us something. As he witnessed the jeering crowd and the patient sufferer dying with a strong cry on his lips, he said, "Truly this man was a Son of God." He saw that this person had a connection for us between God and ourselves, that he was about God's business and not at the end of a career of brigandage.

This means that as we remember and hear this story we do so with the realization that this hearing is more like eating. We begin to realize what Jesus meant when he said that he was the bread of life. His act on the cross is food for our life. When we eat food we are not making it, growing it, cooking, talking about it; we are consuming it, taking it. So it is that we have to practice over and over again the simple taking of the story, taking it as food, taking it for our use and growth. We call that the act of faith, faith that God has given his Son to be our redeemer and re-uniter with himself

One thing we can do a little better than the first disciples. Perhaps it will help us to review the story of Christ's Passion on the Sunday before it took place. For we have been merging the account of the suffering and death of Jesus with our rejoicing that on the first Palm Sunday he came to do it. On the first Good Friday the disciples were a gloomy group, along with the women who had followed Jesus as special helpers. Even on Easter morning they didn't understand what had happened and they were concentrating on his physical death rather than on the gift of life to us all through his death from God. Right in the hearing of this somber story we can be filled with the thankfulness that Jesus died for us all and rose again. That thankfulness need not have practices of jollity or escape, but it can have the quality of insight into God's unspeakably great gift for us all. On Pentecost Peter told the crowd: "You killed the Author of Life"—a dreadful act of cruelty, but the way by which God himself could give his own kind of life to them and to us for all time.

Thus our receiving of this story today is not just a religious exercise of devotion scheduled for the day called the Sunday of the Passion. Least of all is it a revival of a myth out of the ancient past with religious overtones. But it is God at this moment reaching down into our lives with the plea that we be not distant from him, however unseen he may be, but that we be reunited with him and together with him through the gift of his Son, Jesus Christ our Lord, who has shared our sin and death that he might draw us back to God again for this world and for the life to come. For Jesus was not just a broken victim of human hate, there on the cross. He was God's way of tearing apart the veil between ourselves and him, God's way of giving us his kind of life, God at work within us now and forever. View it with thanksgiving, tell it with joy, cling to it with faith and trust always.

RICHARD R. CAEMMERER SR.
Concordia Seminary in Exile
St. Louis, Missouri

THE SACRAMENTAL MEAL

Maundy Thursday
Mark 14:12-26

It really isn't much of a room—the one they show you to when you make the pilgrimage to Jerusalem. You find it after being led through a maze-like route of passageways which supposedly are streets; then up stair treads of smooth stone, worn round by centuries of feet. The room is plain, its walls of white limestone slabs clean-cut and pure with straightforward simplicity. You wonder whether Jesus and his disciples actually did eat the "Last Supper" there. No one can say with certainty, but visiting the room, walking the canyon-like winding streets of his Jerusalem puts you in the spirit of joining him and the disciples in that last meal. Just as does reading once again the story of how it first happened according to Mark.

It wasn't much of a meal either. Not really a banquet as we might think of it—more like a kind of anniversary celebration and as often happens with anniversary meals foods with many symbolic meanings. In our house at Christmastime the central family gathering, almost the heart of our family Christmas has come to be Christmas Eve dinner with herring salad, which we all have helped to make. Begun when the children were small it has taken on even richer symbolic meaning now that they are grown with their own families.

So the Passover meal had become for Israel: What started out as a farewell to slavery in Egypt of a tribal group in which the remarkable deliverance arranged by Jehovah was celebrated now was the annual celebration of deliverance, of Exodus. So we understand the concern of the disciples "Where will you have us go and prepare for you to eat the Passover?" and the order "Go into the city and follow a man carrying a jar of water and wherever he enters say to the householder 'where is my guest room where I am to eat the Passover with my disciples?' and he will show you a large upper room furnished and ready; there prepare for us." It is urgent that they share together this *sacramental meal*.

"I Give You Myself"

Rituals of fellowship surrounding eating are very common in almost all cultures. Among most of the people of the Middle East, to dine in the tent or home of the family is to be received as one of them—in extending you hospitality in food and drink they are giving themselves and the protection of their home and family circles to you, you are really "taken in."

Unfortunately we have lost most of these ancient and meaningful understandings and rituals around hospitality and eating but one remains—the sacramental meal. Here in Holy Communion these deep meanings of eating and drinking, are gathered together first in the Passover meal itself and then in the covenant meal which we celebrate (this evening). Paul writes of it "The cup of blessing which we bless is a communion"—a fusion, a sacramental union of bread and wine and the body and blood of Christ.

This is troublesome language. Do we mean to suggest that the wine literally becomes blood so that like the Masai of Kenya we find ourselves sustained literally by blood? The bread actually flesh—muscle, fat, tissue? Hardly.

We remember how in scriptural language body, *soma* meant not only flesh, head, arms, legs, but really the whole of a person— his being. And so with blood; it was the belief of the ancient Jews that the seat of life, the "soul" resided in the bloodstream—a dramatic way of saying that the soul is all of a person. So in these words "This is my body—my blood" Christ means not to say that he gives us these literal elements, but rather a dramatic and vivid way of saying—I give you myself!

So, in deep symbolic language in the elements of this meal, bread and wine, Christ gives us himself in a manner similar to, but much deeper than a host gives himself to his friends in a meal, a mother gives her life to the child in feeding it, a friend gives himself to a friend in handclasp, or a groom gives himself to the bride in marriage.

To Live in Christ

In the nordic sagas, drinking and eating is by no means simply a matter of thirst or hunger. The Minne (a sort of wine) is regarded as a bond of friendship between the drinker and those that have given him the beverage. Every drink bewitches, renders the past forgiven, and binds a new relationship.

Christ gives not only himself to us in this sacramental meal, but he takes us into himself and makes us a part of himself even as he has given himself, to become a part of us.

Luther vividly describes this in the terms of a betrothal or marriage, in which a rich prince marries a poor cinderella. In the marriage the prince gives all his wealth, his heritage, his royal blood to his poor wife and she becomes the queen. He takes her commonness, her poverty, into himself and becomes a "commoner." This is the second sense in which we can understand the word communion in this sacramental meal. Christ not only enters into communion with us but wants to lift us up into communion, oneness, with himself so that we become a part of his being, his body.

It is out of this background then that we can understand an even deeper significance to the idea of church as "the body of Christ." For it is indeed the organism of those Christians who are now a part of Christ through this sacrament. When those disciples ate that first sacramental meal together with Christ in the upper room they were remembering and declaring that they were a part of the ancient family of Israel, the family of Abraham and Moses. The family of those who had been led to freedom out of bondage from Egypt, a part of the body of Israel. So we remember, become, and declare ourselves part of the body of Christ.

The only other human experience besides eating where this deep intimacy is actualized is in the sexual/spiritual aspects of the marriage relationship. This has some rather profound implications for our own life and action. We are no longer "just our own person" or "our own man" or, "our own woman." We are "in Christ." As Paul declares: "I live, but yet not I. Christ lives in me," and we could add, "I live in Christ."

Christ and I have become a part of each other in communion. My actions in the world then are a part of his acting for good or ill. He does his work in the world through me: a part, an organ, perhaps only a cell in his body. Paul reminds us of this in his parish letter to the Corinthian Christians: "Do you not know that your body is a temple of the Holy Spirit within you, which you have from God? You are not your own; you were bought with a price—so glorify God in your body."

So the current slogan, "do your own thing" really can't apply to Christians any more than it can to husband and wife or even friends and lovers who are bound together in commitment, affection and love.

But this communion between me and Christ which is established and constantly renewed by this sacrament meal, this eating of bread and wine, his body, his life blood, his being, is not a kind of "private love affair between Christ and me." There is a third communion that happens in this sacramental meal.

A Worldwide Communion

One of the most moving celebrations of the Sacrament of Holy Communion for me which I shall never forget, took place in a little country chapel built of rough cement blocks roughly plastered and whitewashed inside and out, with a corrugated tin roof that had more holes in it than the ceiling of a planetarium.

Most of the people came to the church barefoot in what to us looked like clothing gotten at bargain prices in a rummage sale.

I can remember as Betty and I somewhat hesitantly entered the church already filled, so that some of the women were sitting on the floor in the aisle. We spoke a strange tongue, our clothing was so rich by comparison it was embarrassing. We were the only whites. Every head turned, they seemed to stare, as we entered to take our place, especially when we chose not to follow their custom of the men on one side and the women on the other. We tried to join in the hymns they sang which had familiar tunes, but strange words. We were strangers

Then it came time for the sacrament. We could follow along by the actions of the liturgy so we knew what was happening. Group after group knelt around the altar to receive the broken bread and the common cup. Finally it came our turn to join them and we could feel their wonder whether we would actually kneel beside them.

We knelt along side those brothers and sisters in the body of Christ and ate with them of the bread and took the common cup from the native pastor. As we rose to turn and walk back to our seats down the aisle, we could feel the transformation. No more the hostile gaze but friendly smiles. We had become one of them. We, a part of their family in Christ. White men, too. Europeans. In a land where only rarely would Europeans consent to recognize Zulus as brothers, we had joined them at the altar. A communion took place. And it was actualized by their action. We were no longer strangers.

Never had I felt such warm handshakes and smiles of welcome

in the church yard after a service. Never was I more proud to be accepted as a member of a family.

As Christ joins us to himself, by that action, whether we want it or not, whether we do anything about it or not, we are joined into a Holy Communion of saints by this eating and drinking.

We can renounce that fellowship, we can deny it, we can even ignore it, as Judas attempted to do, but we cannot prevent it from happening; nor can we prevent accepting the consequences for our life and action of that communion.

We here too are bound together and that bond is renewed by this eating and drinking and we become what we are, one body in Christ. Not just a duet, Christ and me—but a choir, an orchestra, with many gifts and talents and needs which we are now bound to share with each other in some way, bound to share with the world in some service.

Not only are we here in this church bound together into a kind of fellowship within this congregation. We are also bound by Christ into communion with that congregation in Natal, in Nigeria, in Columbus, in India, Germany, Alaska, and across the world. We are grafted into one worldwide communion of saints, the body of Christ.

We are now bound to do his work in the world and we are strengthened for that work by this renewed communion which takes place, Christ giving of himself to us, his grafting us into himself, and his binding all of us as brothers and sisters, farflung families, into his body, the communion of saints. Amen.

ARTHUR H. BECKER
Lutheran Theological Seminary
Columbus, Ohio

HE DIED FOR YOU AND ME

Good Friday
John 19:17-30

It is not pleasant to watch someone die—particularly if that someone is dear to you.

Let me tell you about Ida. Ida was ninety-five years old. I had been calling on her for over eight years, as a shut-in. We would have long talks together as she sat in the home of her niece, alone most of the day. She was withered and bent. Sometimes she would doze off as I read the service of private communion; at other times she was most alert, moving her lips with every word of the confession and the Lord's Prayer. The days were long for her and she was weary of life, expressing her desire to "be called home." But life was tenacious. At last, the day came when she could no longer sit up. Her niece was having increased difficulty caring for her and yet felt a very keen love for her aunt. I suggested that she be placed in the hospital when the burden became too great. This she did. It appeared that she was dying of cancer, but it was very slow. The first night at the hospital, Ida wanted to see or talk to several of her relatives to say "good-bye." But she didn't die. Day after day she lay bent over in her bed waiting for death to come. After three weeks, the niece had to place her in a convalescent home because she was running out of funds. After about a week there, I got a phone call from the niece—Ida was dying at last. Getting into my car, I went out to the home and, when I asked about Ida, the nurse said that she had just died; the mortician was on the way. Ida had gotten her wish; she was gone.

Jesus' death was even more difficult for those who loved him: he was a young man, not old. His was a tragic death, not a welcome termination. His was a violent death, not a quiet sleeping away. His was an agonizing death-throe, not a comfortable end eased by medication. Difficult and unpleasant as it is, it is nevertheless important to take a long, hard look at Jesus' death, because we are involved; you see—as we have heard so many times before—"He died for you and me."

The Scene of Crucifixion

John, the Evangelist, portrays the crucifixion of Jesus in brief, declarative words:

> So they took Jesus, and he went out, bearing his own cross, to the place called the place of a skull, which is called in Hebrew Golgotha. There they crucified him, and with him two others, one on either side, and Jesus between them.

John does not mention Simon of Cyrene, the spectator pressed into service to carry the cross—as mentioned by Mark and Luke. Nor does John report the conversation with the thieves who hung on either side—as the other three Gospels include. The cry of despair is also missing in John, as is Matthew's dramatic stroke about the rending of the curtain of the temple at the moment of Jesus' death. We have here the simple, stark scene, of a young criminal bent under the load of an instrument of execution, plodding between a file of people toward a hill where he will die. "There they crucified him," that is, they stretched him out on a beam of wood, impaling his hands with spikes and raising his suspended body upright, above ground-level. There he was to hang until death mercifully ended the agony.

But where John is unique in his reporting of the scene is the emphasis and interpretation he makes on the sign that was placed above his head on the cross. The inscription, at Pilate's order, was "Jesus of Nazareth, the King of the Jews." And not only that, but it was written tri-lingually on the placard—in Hebrew, in Latin and in Greek—as the languages which would assure the broadest awareness of the name and ascription. A report is even given of Pilate's insistence upon this title in the face of official protestations by those in high religious authority.

This is a point of reflection upon the name of Jesus which Johann Sebastian Bach includes in his "St. John Passion." Thinking about the name of Jesus in the context of the cross, Bach has the chorus sing, as though it was the confessional response of the fellowship of believers:

> In the depths of my heart,
> Your name and cross
> Shine at all times and in every hour.
> Because of these I can be happy.
> Let this picture appear to me
> As comfort in my time of stress,
> As you, Lord Christ, so freely
> Have sacrificed your life for me.

The Importance of Relationships

There is supposed to be something highly significant about what a person says when he is about to die. I remember finding in the library one time a book which was a collection of such quotations on the part of famous people. We place high importance on such words as though they epitomize the individual's life. Perhaps they represent, rather, our tenacious clinging to a relationship with that person. John has recorded three such statements on the part of Jesus before "he bowed his head and gave up his spirit." Let us look at each one for what it may be saying to us.

The first of these deals with the importance of relationships. It springs from that poignant vignette where ". . . standing by the cross of Jesus were his mother, and his mother's sister, Mary the wife of Clopas, and Mary Magdalene." These are the three women who were most closely related to Jesus in their life. They are standing there heart-broken and grief-stricken by the scene of despair and failure. The love-bond is that of a mother, an aunt and a reborn profligate, respectively, drawn by this image of perfection in the midst of his humiliation. The intensity and nature of their feelings can only be conjectured. But then Jesus' attention is drawn to his mother in the floating sensation of his agony:

> When Jesus saw his mother, and the disciple whom he loved standing near, he said to his mother, "Woman, behold, your son!" Then he said to the disciple, "Behold, your mother!" And from that hour the disciple took her to his own home.

Even under such circumstances—or, perhaps, in the face of such circumstances—relationships—loving relationships—human relationships are paramount to Jesus.

I think it can be accurately said that the bond of loving relationships we have with certain specific people is the most powerful force at work in our lives. It is the termination of such a relationship which produces grief; it is the absence of such relationships which inflicts loneliness; it is the estrangement of such relationships which generates suffering, frustration, emotional injury and overt "acting-out." It is the free enjoyment of such relationships which produce contentment, peace, fulfillment and meaning to life.

This word from the cross exhibits the fact that loving relationships, responsible relationships, caring relationships are most important to Jesus. It was for these relationships that Jesus became man and entered history. It was to these relationships that Jesus extended his invitation to "follow me." It was in these relationships that his followers found their greatest joy and purpose. It was for the continuation of these relationships beyond death that Jesus died. Christianity is not joining something; it is not giving intellectual assent to a number of beliefs. Christianity is entering into a personal relationship with a personal Lord; it is in the possibility of inter-personal relationships that Christ comes to us and seeks to establish such a confessional relationship with us as the nexus of our life.

A Cry of Humiliation

The second word from the cross, which John includes in his narrative, is a cry of humiliation:

> After this Jesus . . . said . . . , "I thirst." A bowl full of vinegar stood there; so they put a sponge full of the vinegar on hyssop and held it to his mouth.

Søren Kierkegaard, the Danish theologian of the 19th century, says that humiliation is an essential characteristic of the ministry of Jesus. It demonstrates the fact that he was heterogeneous to the world. He declares that the awful picture of Jesus hanging from the cross is the image of perfect love expressing itself in the world. This is to say that the world takes offense at the pattern of perfect love, so imposing suffering upon the one who will perfectly represent it. This is why it can be said that the entire life and ministry of Jesus is one of humiliation. The "exaltation" does not begin until he has passed the test of his obedience unto death.

For the follower of Christ—you and I who claim to be his disciples—this means that 'suffering for the doctrine' is the name of the game of being a witness for the truth. When we see in Christ the perfect image of love, we are drawn to resemble that image in our own life. Suffering, then, becomes imposed—not because we seek suffering for its own sake (that is sick)—but because the image of perfect love itself is offensive to the world. This is hard to accept, for we are trained and equipped and inclined to avoid suffering at all costs in the pursuit of the comfortable life. But we are to share his humiliation before we share his exaltation if we are truly his followers.

The Ministry Is Completed

The final word which John includes from the cross is a declaration that the ministry of Jesus is completed:

> When Jesus had received the vinegar, he said, "It is finished"; and he bowed his head and gave up his spirit.

The Greek word used here signifies that something has been accomplished, completed or finished. The *telos* of anything is its aim or purpose—the objective toward which it is directed. The verb form signifies that such a goal has been achieved or ended successfully. Jesus is speaking here about the ministry to which he was called—the reason why he was born in Bethlehem, raised in Nazareth, baptized by John;—the reason why he called the disciples, healed the sick and taught about the kingdom of God. This was the confirmation of his question along the road to Caesarea Philippi, "Who do you think that I am?", and the transfiguration; this was the reason why he said, "Behold, we go up to Jerusalem where all those things about the Son of man will be fulfilled." This is the reason why he celebrated the Lord's Supper with his disciples, why he prayed in the Garden, why he met the soldiers who came to arrest him, why he was silent before the chief priest, and Pilate. The ministry was now fulfilled in the terms which John has previously described in the intimacy of Jesus' "high-priestly" prayer with his Heavenly Father. Jesus has passed the test of his obedience; the atoning work for fallen man is done; death will henceforth be swallowed up by life, and the estrangement of man with God will be healed by forgiveness. "It is finished!" You and I are involved in this because "He died for you and me." Again, Bach in his "St. John Passion" finds this application:

> My true Saviour, let me ask you,
> Exalted in your crucifixion,
> You yourself have said: "It is finished!"
> Have I been made free from death?
> Can I, through your pain and death,
> Inherit the Kingdom of Heaven?
> Is the whole world redeemed because of this?
> In your suffering
> You can, indeed, say nothing.
> But look, you bow your head
> and answer silently: Yes! ...
> It is finished!
> O comfort for sick souls;
> The night of mourning
> Atones for me in your last hour;
> The lion of Judah triumphs with power
> And wins the battle.
> It is finished!

INGOLF B. KINDEM
Mount Zion Lutheran Church
Wauwatosa, Wisconsin

LEFT HANGING ON THE RESURRECTION

The Resurrection of Our Lord—Easter Day
Mark 16:1-8

Christ is risen! He is risen, indeed! And that's where we are left to hang! The entire Christian faith is left to hang on that!

There is no careful theory or calculation we can use to prove it, no pragmatic evidence, no scientific data to support it. No one saw it happen when it happened, and there's not a man alive today who can be summoned as key witness in the case for Jesus Christ. There is nothing but the resurrection sermon of the angel, "Do not be amazed. You seek Jesus of Nazareth, who was crucified. He has risen; he is not here; see the place where they laid him." There is nothing but the faith—the witness of the faithful hearts through 20 centuries whose echo of the angel's sermon brings us to this celebration where we blend our witness into theirs. We have nothing but the word, the promise, Christ himself. He is risen! That's where we are left to hang.

"Now I would remind you, brethren, in what terms I preached the gospel to you, which you received, in which you stand, and by which you are saved." These are the facts concerning Jesus, in accordance with the Scriptures—that he lived and that he died and that he rose again. Jesus Christ is Lord. And that's where we are left to hang.

There is more to it than that, of course. He lived the perfect life of love. He died for our offenses. He rose again for our salvation. He gave himself for us to set things right with God and bring us back where we belong—inside the family of God who made us for his very own. He gave his life to pay the price of sin. He destroyed the power of death that slaps an iron chain around the world. He crushed the head of him who holds the power of death. He reclaimed the title of his own creation which had enthroned false lords, oppressive masters, and the terrors of the tyrants. These are the claims of faith—fantastic claims! How do we know? The resurrection—Christ is risen! That's where we are left to hang. That's where faith hangs—not on a set of proofs incontrovertible, but on the promise and the word.

There is more to it than that, of course. The resurrection is the anchor of the Christian faith. Without it we are set adrift to toss like flotsam on a sea of speculation—testing this and tasting that to find some answer somewhere to the problems that perplex us, and the Christian answer, then, becomes no more than one of many—another avenue of searching for the blind who lead the blind—searching, searching, searching, never finding. Jesus Christ has given us himself, and speculation ends right there with him. He died. He rose again. And that's where we are left to hang. Faith hangs on Christ, the risen Lord, and nothing else!

Easter is a day of faith. The resurrection of our Lord is an event of faith. The gospel of a risen and triumphant Christ sustains the faith. And be assured, faith is no formula that fits the facts of life, no logic that establishes the rules. For just about the time we think it is, something unpredictable turns up and God has broken all our rules again and smashed our air-tight, water-tight, fool-proof dogmatics. Someone close at hand is snatched by death. Christ hasn't mastered it at all. Everything goes wrong in life. There is no living Lord at all who is available to get the general circumstances squared away. The world is full of evil, and all that we can do is shake our heads about it. Where are the signs of his new age, or the signs that anything worthwhile at all was accomplished by his coming long years ago. But in the teeth of all objections from the facts of life, faith hurls the word, "He is Risen!" That's where we hang our faith, and that's where we are left to hang. Easter is a day to celebrate. Easter is a *faith* to celebrate!

Mark Is Different

I hope you noticed that Mark is the inspired writer from whose pen the resurrection gospel is proclaimed today. Not Matthew, Luke, or John, but Mark whose Gospel is the oldest of the four available in our New Testament, the first one written. That makes it different and unique. And the preacher should be honest with the word he reads and preaches—recognize the difference and uniqueness of Mark in contrast to the others, who have also given us their witness to the resurrection.

Did you note that this is where Mark's Gospel ends—suddenly, abruptly, and almost as though he had been interrupted at this point and never had the chance to finish? As the final punctuation point is put in place, we are left hanging on the resurrection, and the Gospel closes on a note of fear. The women who had come on resurrection morning to anoint the body of the Master in his tomb found the stone rolled back, and in the tomb a young man dressed in white who spoke the unexpected word, "You seek Jesus who was crucified. He has risen. He is not here." And we read they fled the tomb, for trembling and astonishment had come upon them . . . and they were afraid. That's where the Gospel ends—hanging on the word of resurrection, and they were afraid.

Strange, Isn't It?

Strange, isn't it, that Mark should end with loose ends lying all around. Strange, isn't it, that he should close his Gospel on a note of fear. Strange, isn't it, that we're left hanging on the resurrection—nothing more. No record of the witnesses who saw the Lord alive again, no story of the doubter Thomas to support our faith in time of doubt, no great commission to the little church to break loose in the world and preach and teach and make disciples of the nations. There was someone in the second century who also thought it strange. Mark's Gospel sounded incomplete with so abrupt an ending, and he took it on himself to finish it, adding on those verses 9 to 20 that are in fine print there in your Bibles.

What happened anyway? Did Mark intend to end as suddenly as this? Did he intend to tell us that the resurrection of our Lord is not the joyous victory and reversal of disaster we have made of it, but that it was and is a frightening experience? Is it possible that he took ill, or that he was arrested, or that he died before he had a chance to finish? Or did he really mean to leave us hanging on the resurrection—nothing more?

We will never know, of course, but let's accept the Word just as it is—that this is where Mark stops. For isn't this where we are stopped, and isn't this the end of faith—this utterly fantastic, unreal claim the Christian faith hurls at us. Walk that long mile in the sandals of the women who approached the tomb that morning with love's burden on their hearts and spices in their hands. Where would you expect to find the crucified who had been dead and buried? In the grave, of course, for death is final, death is certain, death marks the end, and when a man is buried in his grave, he's in the grave. No one expects to find him strolling through the shrubbery of the cemetery. It simply doesn't happen. It started in the days described in Genesis when sin began collecting wages and humanity's existence became a death march to the grave.

It has always been that way—a man is born, he lives a while, he raises children, and he dies, and that's the end of him except for memories. It's where the kingdom he had spent a lifetime building crashes and his heirs go scrambling for the leavings. We ignore it, we disguise it, we deny it, but death remains the fact of life. A fact of life, I said—not several decades down the road, but here today and all through life, for we are always in its shadow as we live and work and strive to get the most before our time runs out. Death is public enemy No. 1. It's the most important, pressing problem that we have to deal with, and the way we deal with this one will determine what we do about the other one, the problem that is life. But resurrection! Is that the way to deal with it? Are we prepared for that? Can we be left hanging on the resurrection as our hope for life? If the grave is empty and the word goes forth, "He is risen!," isn't that a frightening experience? And isn't that a problem worse than death itself?

If that word is true, if God is God of life and death, and if we hang on that, what does that have to say about these so-small lives of ours and how they will be overhauled by him and set on pathways we had never dreamed of. "They were afraid,"—that's Mark's last sentence of the Gospel. They were afraid! Afraid of what—afraid of death? Afraid of life? Left hanging on the resurrection—that and nothing more, but surely nothing less—doesn't life take on dimensions, then, that we are not entirely prepared for? More to be afraid of than the quiet peace of death's oblivion?

Left Hanging—by Faith

That's exactly where we're at, left hanging on the resurrection. Maybe Mark intends to leave us there, for that's precisely what the Easter gospel is about—not death, but life—the life that's ours in Christ right now which jettisons the small life we have clung to and confronts us with an overhaul of all our values, loyalties, priorities and turns our little worlds completely upside down. It throws us into an entirely new world where it's no longer possible to spend and be spent in a search for temporary comforts or in nurturing delightful prejudice and judgments that will make us feel a little bigger than the other dirty fellow, or in playing God at the controls of life with all the anxious moments that game brings when we suspect that we may not be big enough. The resurrection gospel strips us of our carefully designed defenses and it lays the hand of God upon us for a life much bigger than the one we carve out for ourselves. He is risen . . . and they were afraid . . . left hanging on the resurrection.

That's precisely where we are—left hanging on the resurrection. And perhaps we wish there could be more than that. Our Christian faith is built on this. The resurrection of our Lord is central in the scaffold of the Christian creed, for if Christ be not raised . . . well, who can dare describe the tragedy? But can we risk our faith and life and hope on this? Isn't it a little shaky? This bare word and promise of our Lord, "I am the resurrection and the life," and this assertion of a young man dressed in white that Christ is risen, is this enough? We could use a few supports to prop this shaky scaffold, like someone coming from the dead today to tell us that it's really true. He really lives. Or like a long parade of witnesses, perhaps, who had a first hand view of Christ alive and who could walk on water to secure and prove their testimony.

But our demand for sign and proof is unbelief, not faith, and it will not be satisfied. There is no computer to determine the probability quotient, no grave to search for clues and fingerprints and evidence to satisfy the curious. This is precisely where we are—left hanging on the resurrection. The company of Jesus Christ is not a company of those who have been satisfied with evidence. It's a company of faith, the faith that dares and risks the promise of our Lord and hurls that faith at all the contradicting evidence with one bold, "I believe!" He died, he rose again! He lives. His word and promise is secure.

That's precisely where we are—left hanging on the resurrection. Everything that makes the difference hangs on that. The guilt you carry in your heart as you remember wasted years— the resurrection says our Lord has paid for that. He has removed it. We need no longer nurse it. The chains of evil habit, the cesspool of the heart with thick, green scum of envy, greed, lust, hatred, jealousy, and selfishness—the resurrection says our Lord has cleansed us. The hungry yearning burning inside of us, the empty void, the dark despair of grief when someone close and dear has been removed from earthly scenes—the resurrection says that Christ has filled that void with hope. The fear of aging, accident, disease, and death, the clicking of the clock—the resurrection tells us that our Lord has made it possible for us to live triumphantly with purpose and determined goal. The uncertainty about tomorrow and the anxious waiting for the medical report, the outcome of a college entrance interview, the application for a job, the fear of failure—the resurrection says our Lord has wrapped tomorrow into his concern and we are free to live today. That's where we're left to hang, and life can never be the same again. Someone has us by the hand from here on out to all eternity, and he will never let us go. How can he let us go? His name is Jesus. He has given us himself, and all we need to know is that his word is sure.

ALTON F. WEDEL
Mount Olive Lutheran Church
Minneapolis, Minnesota

DOUBT AND FAITH

Second Sunday of Easter
John 20:19-31

Often a person finds it the hardest to believe that which he most eagerly wants to believe. If you care a lot about someone or something, doubts may suddenly crowd into your mind like a plague of locusts.

Who is a more tormented person than a lover who cries, "It can't be possible that she loves me. How could she ever love a person like me?" You see, he is allowing his doubts to overwhelm the actual fact and faith that a person could love him. Or a mother whose son is reported safe after being missing in action, when she is told he is returning home, suddenly says, "I simply can't believe it until I hold him in my arms." Her doubt has to be proved before she can really believe.

For Thomas, Doubt and Faith Went Together

Doubt and faith do belong together. Our Gospel text for today shows us how they do belong together, not only in Thomas' life, but in the life of every single person.

It was that way with Thomas. He doubted before he had faith. But his doubt had not destroyed his faith. His doubt simply drove him to reaffirm the faith that was such an important part of his life. But he had to struggle.

To Thomas, the cross was only what he had expected all along. When Jesus was proposing to go to Bethany, and when the news of the illness of Lazarus had come Thomas' reaction had been, "Let us also go that we may die with him" (John 11:16). Thomas never lacked courage. But in so many ways Thomas was a natural pessimist. There can never be any doubt that Thomas loved Jesus. He loved him enough to go to Jerusalem and to die with him when the other disciples had been hesitant and afraid.

What Thomas had expected really happened. Christ had died and Thomas was broken-hearted. So broken-hearted that he could not meet the eyes of people, so he went away. He wanted to be alone with his grief. King George V used to say that one of his rules of life was, "If I have to suffer, let me be like a well bred animal, and let me go and suffer alone."

Thomas had to face his suffering and his sorrow alone. And so it happened that when Jesus did return to the disciples, Thomas was not there. The news that Jesus had come back seemed to him far too good to be true and he refused to believe it. He became angry in his pessimism. He said he would never believe that Jesus had risen from the dead until he had seen and handled the prints of the nails in Jesus' hands and thrust his own hand into the wounds that the spear had made in Jesus' side.

Thomas' doubt had begun to smother his faith. In his aloneness, his doubt was turning him bitter.

Another week passed and then Jesus came back. This time Thomas was there. Maybe he was starting to come out of his grief a little bit. Maybe he had begun to realize that the place to find an answer to doubt was not holding up within himself, but rather, to be with other people.

Jesus knew Thomas' heart. He repeated Thomas' own words and then he invited Thomas to make the test that he had demanded.

Thomas' heart must have broken at the same time that it rejoiced. He fell down on his knees in love and devotion, and all that he could say was, "My Lord and my God!" Jesus said to him,

"Have you believed because you have seen me? Blessed are those who have not seen and yet believe."

Jesus is really saying to Thomas, "Look, Thomas, you've been looking in the wrong places. You've had all kinds of doubts. But when you've had those doubts you should have kept looking and then you could have believed. Thomas, all things in life can't be seen, sometimes, Thomas, we have to believe. Thomas, seeing is not believing."

The tragedy of Thomas was not in his lack of love or faithfulness. The pity for this good man was that for eight days he lived in the anguish of uncertainty and doubt. The reason he failed to have his Easter hopes realized was simply that he was looking in the wrong place. He was looking in the place other than the place where Jesus was. The disciples were all together, but Thomas was not with them. He was alone.

We Can't Find the Answers Alone

In the battle for understanding between doubt and faith, one of the greatest things that we have to learn from Thomas is that we can never find the answers if we are alone. Rather, we can only find the answers of faith in fellowship.

This was the one big mistake that Thomas made. He withdrew from the Christian fellowship. He sought loneliness rather than togetherness and because he was not there with his fellow Christians he missed the coming of Jesus again.

We miss a great deal when we separate ourselves from Christian fellowship. Things can happen to us within the fellowship of Christ's church which could never happen to us when we are alone.

When Jesus spoke to them and breathed the Holy Spirit on them, it gave them the power to forgive sins and to find forgiveness in each other's life. It gave them an understanding of what it meant to be together as fellow Christians, and to seek, and to search, to console, and to sorrow with one another as well as to rejoice with one another.

On this second Sunday after Easter, the question I suppose every pastor asks is "Where are all the people who were here on Easter Sunday? Why would they come to proclaim the Lord's resurrection with all of its power, and the confession of faith that he lives and rules in each and every life, and then this Sunday, just a few days later, not be here."

At least when Thomas missed the Lord the first time, he discovered that he couldn't find him alone if he was going to stay home somewhere and feel sorry for himself. He wouldn't discover the meaning of his faith if he sat at home. The second time Jesus

Christ appeared Thomas found himself among the fellowship of believers. He found himself in relationship to others who were looking, waiting, and praying for the Lord, and so he did discover Jesus Christ.

Doubts always breed doubts. But faith breeds faith. The fellowship of believers means that we come together with those who confess and believe like we do so that we can share concerns. So that we can share an understanding of what God is trying to say to us. So that we can share one another's burdens and sorrows and questions.

This doesn't mean that there is no room for doubt. It means exactly the opposite. It means that this is the arena in which we can voice our doubts. The arena in which we can ask questions that relate to our faith because this is where we gain understanding of what God's Word says for each of us.

Our Doubts Drive Us to Seek Answers

Our doubts should drive us to find answers. Our whole technical civilization has been built on doubt. It has been built on the drive of men and women who were dissatisfied with the old answers, so they began to push into new frontiers of knowledge.

Copernicus doubted that the world was flat, and so he set the stage for the space age. Columbus ventured out believing that the world was round, not knowing for sure, but gambling against the chance that he might sail right off the edge of the earth into a bottomless abyss, which was what people thought the earth was like at that time.

Robert Fulton and James Watt doubted that power and locomotion were limited to men and horses and the wind, and so, with a steam engine they began a parade that now includes jet planes, rockets and atomic energy.

Someone has said that these doubters were all too lazy to do things the old, hard way, so they therefore thought up the new ways. In any event, we owe them all very much.

Think how lucky we are that there were people who doubted in witchcraft and ghosts. Many years ago people lived in a kind of constant fear because they thought that there were mischievous spirits that went roaming about haunting and taunting people. Whole communities were sent into panic and people were imprisoned or killed all because people believed in the wrong things. Again, it was the doubters who saved the day. But they saved the day because they searched for answers.

Doubting is good. But it's good only when it leads a person on a search for the truth and for knowledge in a way that he might find the answers.

It was the doubt of Thomas that made him separate from his fellowmen. But it was also the doubt of Thomas that lead him to seek the right answers. That drove him back into the fellowship of other people, and there he made his great confession of faith as he gave himself to Jesus Christ again.

It was important for Thomas to doubt. It was important for him to say, "I don't believe it. I won't believe it until I see it." It was important for him to say that because he was very honest with himself, but he didn't leave it there. He went out to search for the answers. Doubts should lead to answers.

Some doubts are good. Some are not good. Doubts should drive us to seek the answers. They should drive us to a deeper commitment to Jesus Christ, just as they did for Thomas.

We Confess Our Faith to Become Stronger

Doubts should be like weightlifting. You may walk up to a set of barbells and see that there is 200 pounds on it and say, "I can never lift that." But if you take that same set of barbells and put on 25 pounds, and then 50, and then 100, and then 150, and then 200, ultimately you would be strengthened by the doubts that you originally had and by the struggles that were a part of your life and your existence.

This is what the Christian faith is all about. The doubts do come, and yet we find the answers in Jesus Christ, and in relationship to other people. Then we move out to lift those weights and to help other people lift weights, and we lose ourselves in giving ourselves to other people.

Doubt should always be linked to faith, and faith must always be linked to other people. Faith in Jesus Christ is always a proclamation and a moving out and a great commission of going and doing as Jesus Christ would go and do. There is a power in the gospel, but the power has to be used.

There is a chain of five Great Lakes in the northern part of our country. Some days they're as placid and still as a mirror. Yet that same water, when it's channeled into the Niagara River and tumbles over Niagara Falls becomes a boiling, roaring torrent. In doing this it creates electricity that provides light, heat, and energy for thousands of homes and factories. But that power is left in the water unless it starts moving into the channel where it can become harnessed for a purpose.

The power of God is still here. It's like the Niagara River.

Wherever lives are open channels through which that power can go, there is proof they have the miraculous workings of God. It means that as we struggle through doubts in our lives our faith will drive us out to tell the good news. If Christ means anything to us we cannot help but tell someone else. We are bound to make an impression on others. And they, in turn, will be assured that they too can come to the place where they will receive that power and that strength so that we can together confess as Thomas did, "My Lord and my God!"

REUBEN GROEHLER
Roseville Lutheran Church
St. Paul, Minnesota

THE ROAD OF SALVATION

Third Sunday of Easter
Luke 24:36-49

Jesus, says Luke, "opened their minds to understand the scriptures," so that they could comprehend his suffering, death, and resurrection; and so that they could undertake their resultant mission. What was it Jesus said to them? From Luke's perspective it may have been something like this:

Why do you wonder, my brothers? And why do strange thoughts arise in your hearts? Is it so incomprehensible to you that I should suffer, and rise from the dead on the third day? Consider the story of our people, Israel, and you will see and understand.

In the Beginning

In the beginning God created the heavens and the earth, the sea, and all that is in them. Then he created man and woman, and said to them, "Till the earth, and make it fruitful; multiply and fill the earth." And it was so.

And out of all the peoples of the earth God chose Abraham to be the father of his own people, and God set his seal on them—not because they were more in number than any other people on the earth, for they were the fewest, but because the Lord loved them. And he said to them, "I will be your God, and you shall be my people."

Yet Israel was not always God's holy people. For like all peoples of the earth Israel knew times of faithfulness and unfaithfulness, obedience and disobedience, haughtiness and humility, purity of heart and perversity. It was not because they were better than any other nation on the face of the earth that God chose them, but because the Lord loved them. And he sent them to be a light to the nations, and to be a blessing by which all the families of the earth would bless themselves.

The Lord gave them teachers and wise men to instruct them; prophets to warn and awaken them; priests to help them remember and to praise the Lord. When they cried to him in distress he sent them deliverers.

With a strong hand he led them out of Egypt and gave them the promised land. With a mighty arm he brought them back from captivity in Babylon. "Remember these things, O Jacob," he said, "for you are my servant. I formed you, you are my servant; O Israel you will not be forgotten by me. I have swept away your transgressions like a cloud, and your sins like mist; return to me, for I have redeemed you" (Isa. 44:21-22).

The Road of Salvation

The Lord was leading Israel along the road of salvation. Yet it seemed to Israel a hard road, and they murmured against it, saying, "My way is hid from the Lord, and my right is disregarded by my God" (Isa. 40:27). But some prophets and seers began to understand the road, and through Israel's long history—through times of slavery and freedom, subjugation and independence—an understanding began to grow which gave new hope.

The understanding was this: *life can be attained only through death.*

Sometimes this was literally true: A whole generation had to die in the wilderness in order that Israel could cease being Egyptian slaves and become inheritors of the promised land; several generations had to pass away in Exile in Babylon in order that a purified people could begin again.

Sometimes it was true in a profounder way: Abraham died to the security of his homeland in order to go to the land and the destiny God would show him, and so became a blessing; Jacob through agony became Israel; David plunged into remorse when confronted by Nathan of his sin against Uriah, and became a humbler and wiser king.

This understanding was given voice in varying ways. The Psalmist said,

For thou, O God, hast tested us;
  thou hast tried us as silver is tried.
Thou didst bring us into the net;

> thou didst lay affliction on our loins;
> thou didst let men ride over our heads;
> we went through fire and through water;
> yet thou hast brought us forth to a spacious place.
>   (Ps. 66:10-12)

And Isaiah, speaking of the Servant of the Lord who is one and yet many, said,

> He was wounded for our transgressions,
>   he was buried for our iniquities;
> upon him was the chastisement that made us whole,
>   and with his stripes we are healed.
>   (Isa. 53:5)

Life can come only through dying.

Along with this understanding there grew up another: *Life can come only through dying because God himself is present in the dying to bring forth life.*

> Isaiah saw this most clearly. He said,
> Fear not, for I have redeemed you;
>   I have called you by name, you are mine.
> When you pass through the waters I will be with you;
>   and through the rivers, they shall not overwhelm you;
> when you walk through fire you shall not be burned,
>   and the flame shall not consume you.
> For I am the Lord your God,
>   the Holy One of Israel, your Savior.
>   (Isa. 43:1-3)

And the Psalmist sang praise to the Lord who was present with Israel in the deep waters:

> Give thanks to him who smote the first-born of Egypt . . .
>   and brought Israel out from among them . . .
> who divided the Red Sea in sunder . . .
> and made Israel pass through the midst of it . . .
> who led his people through the wilderness . . .
> who smote great kings . . .
> and gave their land as a heritage . . . to Israel his
>   servant. . . . (Ps. 136:10-22)

God did those things; he was present in these mighty events in the history of his people Israel. He is present to save: he is present in the dying, bringing forth life.

A Hard Road?

But only a few understood. It is hard to die. It is harder to believe that that is the way God brings life and salvation. It is hardest of all to believe and see the hand of God in death! I know—I suffered, and felt forsaken of God, and cried out to him in the darkness. Yet I committed myself to him, for when the darkness comes there is no other refuge.

Yet we think of God as our enemy, as One set against us. So the people murmured while death stalked them in the wilderness, accusing God of leading them into the desert to die. How right they were, though they did not know it! For only by dying to Egypt and their slavishness could they become free! So they cried out from Babylon, accusing God of having deserted them to perish in a foreign land. How right they were, though they did not know it! For only by dying to Babylon and compromising alliances could they become free again.

My friends, hear me! "Weeping may tarry for the night, but joy comes with the morning" (Ps. 30:5b). For God is in the night, bringing the morning.

When the Time Had Come

And so, when the time had come, God determined to make fully known his presence in the night. I was born in the night—and it was a hard birth, there, in Bethlehem. My mother did not often speak of it. And I was named Immanuel, "God with us."

But people do not want God-with-them—do not want a God so near at hand—except the poor in spirit who are open to the unexpected presence; those who mourn, who cannot hope in anything but God; the meek, who make no claim of rights for themselves; the righteous, who cannot abide deceit; the merciful, who refuse to enter into competition; the pure in heart, who refrain from judgment; the peacemakers, who have no vested interests; the persecuted, who know the way of life through death!

Immanuel—God with us—bringing life out of death!

And you, my brothers, stumbled often. You could not receive my words that the Son of man must go to Jerusalem, and be mocked and crucified, and rise on the third day. Yet this is the fulfillment of God's way of redemption. It is the full demonstration that the road of salvation is God walking with you on your road, bringing the dawn out of the darkness, the new out of the old, life out of death.

But I must go.

And you must go. Go and speak to the peoples of the earth. Call them to repentance—for that is the dying to the old; and promise them forgiveness—which is the finding of the new.

Do it in the power of my Spirit.

Do it in my name; for I am Israel—the one and the many; I am Everyman—you will find your story in my story; I am Immanuel—"God with us."

EDUARD RICHARD RIEGERT
Waterloo Lutheran Seminary
Waterloo, Ontario, Canada

JESUS' CLAIM AND CALL

Fourth Sunday of Easter
John 10:11-18

A Familiar Picture: The Good Shepherd

One of the most familiar pictures the Bible uses to teach us about our relationship to God is that of a shepherd and his sheep. It has its roots deep in the Old Testament. In the most popular psalm, Psalm 23, the author declares, "The Lord is my shepherd." He describes his Lord as a good shepherd who takes care of his faithful believers who are his sheep.

Jesus uses this same picture in the Gospel for this Fourth Sunday of Easter when he says, "I am the good shepherd. The good shepherd lays down his life for the sheep" (John 10:11). His listeners knew that a real shepherd is concerned first and foremost with the welfare of his flock. He would provide it the necessities of life such as food and drink. When a wild animal attacked, he would risk his life for the sheep. He would put his own life in jeopardy to protect his flock.

Jesus Claims Us as His Own

But Jesus is doing much more than telling pretty stories about heroic shepherds who rescue lovable little lambs from the mouths of hungry lions. He is claiming us as his own. He is saying, "I am the Lord to whom the psalmist looked in all his needs. I am the One who leads and provides. I am the One who goes with you through the valley of the shadow of death. I prepare a banquet table before you in the presence of your enemies. I fill your life with goodness and mercy and lead you to dwell in my house forever."

He says even more: "I am the good shepherd. The good shepherd lays down his life for the sheep." He sees what he will do so that his flock, you and I, may live for him now and with him forever. The lessons of Lent and Easter are still fresh in our minds. We know how he fulfilled this prophecy with his death on Calvary. In the Gospel we hear him declare: "No one can kill me without my consent—I lay down my life voluntarily. For I have the right and the power to lay it down when I want to and also the right and power to take it again." We believe that this claim was validated with his glorious resurrection from the dead. We accept his claim to be the psalmist's Lord—and yours and mine. We say with the writer of today's first lesson, "We are already God's children, right now!" (1 John 3:2). We confess with Peter in the second lesson, "There is salvation in no one else" (Acts 4:12).

But We Reject That Claim

Our problem is that we reject that claim. It is not by accident that the Lord compares us to sheep. "I am the good shepherd and know my own sheep." Indeed he knows sheep; we are like sheep. I learned something about sheep as a boy on a farm in Minnesota. My father raised a small flock of sheep more as a hobby than as a serious sheep farmer. Our little flock grew to about thirty in number when it was attacked by packs of roving dogs. Instead of staying together or fleeing to the shelter of the barnyard, they would panic and scatter in every direction. The swift-footed dogs could outrun them and destroyed them, one by one.

Jesus knows us with our weaknesses and fears. He knows how the human family still loves to wander and stray. He wants us to be one flock gathered around him. He wants to be the Lord of our life, but what happens? We have our own wills. We decide to do what we please without regard for the Lord's will or the consequences of our actions. Some of us are carried away by our greed and selfishness; sometimes we are ruined by our lusts and desires. It may be our temper or lack of self-control which leads us to deny his claim. Each of us must confess with Isaiah that in some way, we are the ones who strayed away like sheep.

Jesus Calls Us Back for a Purpose

But Jesus calls us back. Jesus told the story of the shepherd who brought his flock of one hundred sheep into shelter out of the storm on the mountain. He counted them and found one missing. He left the ninety-nine and went out after the one sheep lost in the night and the storm. When he found the lost sheep, he picked him up, brought him home, and rejoiced with his neighbors.

So also the Good Shepherd will not let us go. He calls us back through the pangs of our conscience and the witness of the church. He picks us up in his grace and love. He forgives us all our sins. And he brings us back home, home to himself and his love. But for a purpose. When the risen Lord stood with his disciples in the Upper Room the week after the first Easter, he said, "As the Father has sent me, even so I send you" (John 20:21). He sends us out to continue the work which he began. He asks us to follow his example of shepherding so that his blessings are conveyed to others.

Not to Use Him

First, Jesus points to a negative example, that of the hired man. The hired man is not a true shepherd. He represents the kind of life which seeks to use Jesus and his church. He is content to stop with the picture of the Good Shepherd as a picture of consolation which permits him to cuddle safely in the Lord's arms. This is the kind of life which rejoices at the story of the resurrection, but never "goes and tells." It is a life which "uses" the church for the socially accepted traditions of baptism, confirmation, marriage, and funerals, but carefully avoids commitment or responsibility for the life of the parish community. It is a life which faults the establishment for its failures or the youth for its rebellions, but fails to offer its love, its loyalty, or even sympathetic understanding. The church today is in trouble—as much as any flock of sheep which is being attacked by wolves. A hired man will run when he sees the wolf coming and will leave the sheep, for they aren't his and he isn't their shepherd. The hired man runs because he is a hired man and has no real concern for the sheep. The church will not be a blessing to those who use it for what they can get out of it. Nor will they be a blessing to the church, to the flock of the Good Shepherd.

But to Follow Him

In contrast to the negative example of the hired man, the Lord Jesus calls our attention to himself as the Good Shepherd. Even as the Father sent him to lay down his life for the sheep, so he calls us to follow that example. He calls us to commit ourselves to the task of shepherding one another. Today, as always, the flock is in danger of letting the weaker ones wander away. There exists in every age the danger that the flock may be divided by the wolves of dissension and distrust, the body of Christ, his church, dissected into many denominations. Indeed church bodies and congregations frequently find themselves on the verge of schism over one issue or another.

In such a time as this it is necessary for everyone who calls Jesus his Good Shepherd to follow the example of the Master: to lay down personal preferences and prejudices for the sake of the unity of the flock. This will mean the kind of struggle which the Good Shepherd experienced in Gethsemane. It means that we resolve to do, not what we want, but what must be done for the sake of the kingdom. It is our risen Lord who has shown us that when we lay down our lives for others, he gives them back to us. He enables us to rise above our weaknesses as we seek to be shepherds of each other.

This is the day we pay tribute to the mothers of the land and reflect on the meaning and importance of family living. The first opportunity which most of us have to be shepherds to each other is in the setting of the family. I was reminded of this by a motto suggested for Christian fathers. It said, "The best thing a father can do for his children is to love their mother." I am sure that we can reverse that on this Mother's Day. The point would be the same. We do most of our learning by personal experience rather than by reading books or listening to pious lectures and sermons. This is especially true of attitudes and values.

As children see our response to the people around us—the way we treat our mates, our neighbors, the clerks at the store; the way we talk about our family, friends, and fellow church members —they are being taught how to respond to people around them. I notice, for example, that there is nothing which makes my children so angry as my anger toward them. I suspect they are learning from their father. When children see what is important to their parents and elders, they set their own values along the same lines. Whether husband or wife, parent or child, brother or sister, our first opportunities to follow the example of the Good Shepherd are usually in the home.

Jesus goes on, "I have other sheep, that are not of this fold; I must bring them also, and they will heed my voice. So there will be one flock, one shepherd" (John 10:16). These words do not let us snuggle comfortably like a lamb in the shepherd's arms on a cold night. The reason he has called us is to reach out to others who are not yet a part of his flock, who are not yet in his fold. We have referred to the shepherd who left the ninty-nine in the fold to go out after the lost one. Thus this gospel is a missionary and evangelistic text. The Good Shepherd leads us out of our family and congregation, out of our city and synod into the world which he came to claim for himself. The path is not an easy one. It is a path which leads to criticism when we seek to stand up for what our Good Shepherd taught. It is not easy to live the kind of life demonstrated by the Good Shepherd in a world which is hostile to him and to his ways. But the Good Shepherd leads us out so he can lead others in.

The wonderful thing is that the Good Shepherd has not only left us a path to follow; he goes with us at our side. He is ready to help and to lead. A small boy once followed his father around the barnyard as he did the chores. It was winter and the yard was covered with a deep blanket of snow. The little boy wandered around and around, back and forth, through the deep snow, until he wore himself out. He was unable to go any further. "I can't walk any more," he cried to his father. His father replied, "Follow my steps." The boy followed his father's steps. The path was broken for him and he was able to follow easily.

My friends, following the steps of Jesus, being shepherds to each other in our families and in our congregation, going out into the world after the other sheep, is much more difficult than following someone through deep snow. But of this we can be sure: no matter what struggle or challenge we may face, Jesus has already gone ahead to make a path for us. He is the Good Shepherd who leads us, lifts us when we fall, carrys us when we can't go on. He claims us and he calls us. He will see us through until we see his word fulfilled, "There will be one flock, one shepherd." It is this claim and call which he seals to us again this morning in his Holy Supper. It is a foretaste of the celebration which he will set before us then. And he lets us begin to enjoy it now.

PALMER G. H. RUSCHKE
Jehovah Lutheran Church
St. Paul, Minnesota

ABIDING IN CHRIST

Fifth Sunday of Easter
John 15:1-8
(A Confirmation Sermon)

Baptism marks the beginning of the Christian life. God reaches down and adopts us as his children, heirs to all the blessings he gives his own. At that moment, we receive the forgiveness of sins and the gift of the Holy Spirit. Parents and sponsors promise to nurture us in our new spiritual life and to be God's channels to guide us to that time when we become personally responsible.

All of life is a growth process; the work of the Holy Spirit is not complete in us until we reach glory. We are in the process of becoming, never arriving at full spiritual maturity in this world. Confirmation Day is a point on that line from baptism to glory that is a significant milestone, but not the end of the process.

It is a time when the young person assumes personal responsibility for continued growth. It is a time when he or she personally says: I believe in Jesus Christ as my personal Lord and Savior, and I want to go on.

Abiding in Christ

The Gospel for today compares the mystical relationship between Christ and the believer to the vine and its branches. The concept of vine and vineyard has its roots in the Old Testament where Israel is likened to a vine. (Compare Isaiah 5:1-7; Jeremiah 2:21; Ezekiel 15.) The vine is symbolic of the nation, imperfect, running wild, and often failing to bear fruit.

Jesus Christ claims to be the New Testament counterpart to the Old Testament vine. "I am the true vine," he claims; "you are the branches." Only as the branch is grafted onto the vine can there be life and growth and fruit. Only as there is a personal, vital, living relationship with Jesus Christ can there be spiritual life, growth, and fruit-bearing. Ten times the idea of "abiding in Christ" as the branch is related to the vine is used in the text.

Application of the text to the practical day-by-day Christian life is as varied as the imagination. We are grafted to Christ. We are related mystically to him. We need to be cultivated, watered, pruned, and disciplined. We must bear fruits of faith, and careful nurture is essential for maximum fruitbearing. First, let us consider the

Mystery of Abiding

Abiding in Christ describes the intimate relationship of Jesus and the believer. Christ is in us, and we are in him. Involved is knowing him personally as friend and companion, not just knowing about him. Involved is letting him become the center of your life, dethroning the ego and allowing Jesus to take control of one's life. Paul said, "It is no longer I who live, but Christ living in me."

I interviewed each member of the confirmation class about his personal relationship with Jesus Christ, and I discovered that each person is at a different level of spiritual growth. Not all have had a conscious, dramatic change they can point to. Several have had deep, moving, spiritual experiences. Some are concerned that this has not happened. Among peers they hear personal testimonies of that known moment of decision and wonder why this has not happened to them. Some feel inferior and inadequate in their Christian growth and are hoping Confirmation Day may bring that moment.

I tried to share with each confirmand that there was no single way the Holy Spirit works. We cannot box him in; he comes in a variety of forms and gives a variety of gifts. For some of you, confirmation may be a moment of increased awareness of the presence and power of the Holy Spirit. I trust for none of you, confirmation will mark the end of the growth process. Too often a young person who successfully completes the catechetical requirements imitates his elders, decides he knows enough, and disappears from the life and work of the church. Often it takes a personal crisis or responsibility of his own family to be drawn back to his basic need for God, implanted by faithful parents, pastors, and Sunday school teachers and by the Holy Spirit during those formative years.

For those of you for whom Christ has become real in a dramatic way, we praise him and rejoice. For those of you who have never known when you were not abiding in Christ and who trust in the promises of God, we praise the Lord and rejoice. For those of you who still are not quite sure of the mystery of this new life in Christ, begun at Baptism and being confirmed today, perhaps this day may bring the moment of decision when you make that "leap of faith" and say, "Lord Jesus, I don't understand, but I want to believe. Help me overcome my doubts and put my trust and confidence in you." And for you who have a firm intellectual knowledge of the way of salvation as revealed in God's Word, and are secure in the facts of the Scriptures and promises of God, and who have not experienced the ecstasy of a mountain-top experience, we praise the Lord and rejoice. Most of us are not mystics—probably a majority of us—and for us a personal relationship with Jesus Christ, abiding in him, is as real as if we had a special vision or revelation of his coming into our lives. For those of us who have not experienced that moment of decision, there are ways of looking at our relationship with Jesus that are real and reassuring.

Consider two human examples: In counselling with a married couple, it soon became evident that the husband was totally dependent upon his wife for support at nearly every level of their relationship. His abnormal behavior had finally driven his wife to the decision to leave. His impassioned plea in the final meeting of the three of us was to point to a tree in a nearby garden where a bottom branch, laden with fruit, was being supported by a board due to the weight of the fruit. "Leaving me, my wife of many years, will be like pushing the prop out from under the branch of the tree. The branch will collapse and break under the strain; and so will I. I will not be able to survive without you." It was a tender moment. The wife was aware of the potential consequences of her decision; I could not dissuade her. Subsequent events proved the husband's fear of the future without his wife to be a valid concern. Similarly, Jesus Christ is that prop on whom we are dependent. But he promises never to forsake us; and he keeps his promises. He will be by our side forever. Abiding in Christ means leaning on the presence and power and grace of Christ which he promises will be sufficient for all our needs.

Another example is the alcoholic who came to the end of the rope and made the confession, "I am powerless in overcoming my weakness; I admit I need help. I have lost control over my life; I need a power beyond myself." Referral to the local Alcoholics Anonymous chapter meeting in our church was followed by his personal contact of the chairman of the local group. He was assigned to a member of the chapter, a reformed alcoholic. The key to a life of sobriety is following the ten steps, meeting regularly with the group, keeping contact with the friend who understands the pitfalls of withdrawal, and the necessity of remaining a teetotaler. A basic principle of AA is mutual support and encouragement of one another. Jesus Christ is like that reformed friend. Abiding in Christ means he is always there, more willing to help than we are to seek his counsel. If abiding in Christ is real for you, by whatever route you have come to this relationship, it will produce fruits of the Christian life. If the branch does not bear fruit, it is cast into the fire and burned.

Pruning and Abiding

In order to maximize the fruit, pruning is necessary. Observation of the vineyards of California through the eyes of an experienced farmer made me aware of how necessary pruning is to increase the fruit and minimize non-productive growth. To develop a strong vine, a new vine is pruned three years before grapes are permitted to grow. Each year thereafter the fruit-bearing vine is pruned to guarantee that the life energy of the plant will be directed to the development of healthy fruit.

Often the vine or plant that is pruned looks ugly and barren. In the pruning periods of our lives, we know things are not going well. We may suffer humiliation and depression. We show few results in our daily lives at times like this. We may become resentful and blame God. We may even be tempted to give up our faith. But when we become aware that the cutting, trimming, and retraining is a loving action of our Vinedresser Father, who wants us to be healthy and vital branches, then we can submit to the pruning knife, no matter how much it hurts. Often a car needs a realignment to insure its continued efficient operation. So do we need this refinement so that Christ's life-giving energy can flow through us and produce fruit.

A warning is also sounded about trying to produce an effective Christian life without this close relationship with Christ. Followers of Jesus, as branches, are part of him, and to be effective must completely depend upon him. Failure to do so means the branches wither and die. Such Christians, by severing themselves from the source of spiritual life, have condemned themselves. On the other hand, remaining in constant union with Christ will produce fruits of the Christian life.

Fruits of Abiding

With Christ in command and pruning and cleansing accepted, more effective discipleship will follow as fruits of faith as naturally as for a grapevine to produce grapes. For the newly confirmed this will mean a growing life of prayer. Note that a special fruit of abiding in Christ is a productive prayer life. Jesus makes a staggering promise. "If you live in union with me and let my teachings guide your lives, your prayers cannot fail!" They cannot fail because if—and note this important requirement—you live in union with Christ, you will ask nothing contrary to the will of God. Fruits of abiding will involve a hunger and thirsting for the living Christ that will be satisfied only through worship and Bible study. Fruits of abiding will include a change of attitudes and behavior toward people and situations. It will mean more acts of loving service to others; it will bring a sense of wholeness to our life, getting it all together. It will mean an increased awareness and appreciation of God's direction and blessing; it will mean having new peace and joy. All these fruits add up to the spirit-filled life (cf. Gal. 5:22) : "Fruits of the spirit" will increase toward a fullness of the spirit" in all who are abiding in Christ.

Two special blessings will result from increased fruit-bearing. First, your own life will be enriched; and secondly, you will bring glory to God. Your example will cause others to sit up and take notice and ask, "What do you have that I lack?" This opens doors for witnessing to the power of the gospel.

Our reliance upon Christ can be likened to Christ's dependence on his Father; the secret of Jesus' life was his constant contact with his Father. Often he would withdraw from the crowds to communicate with his Father and renew his strength. So, the secret of our life is abiding in Christ—keeping contact with him. Like the alcoholic, we must admit our need—want help—seek a friend—and maintain contact with that friend. Jesus is that friend with whom we can communicate in prayer and who promises never to forsake us but to be with us all the days of our lives. Jesus says his followers are like that. Some are lovely fruit-bearing branches; others are useless and bear no fruit. What kind of a branch are you?

FRED BERNLOHR
Christ Lutheran Church
Columbus, Ohio

CHOSEN IN LOVE TO LOVE
Sixth Sunday of Easter
John 15:9-17

Not so very many years ago in one of the national presidential campaigns, one of the candidates tried to bring a complex and difficult public issue into focus by asking the question, Can love be commanded? Or, as another form of the same question asked, is it not in the very nature of love that it must be given voluntarily, or not at all?

Those are good questions! Most of us are not political analysts by trade and it is therefore difficult for us to know all we should about political campaigning. Nonetheless, it is possible for us to have some insight into why some candidates win elections and others lose. So, somewhere in the background of the reasons why a politician eventually lost a particular election may be the innocent suggestion that his political advisors never should have permitted him to ask such provocative questions as "Can love be commanded?" of the electorate. Perhaps the explanation for his loss is as simple as this: the psychology of electioneering does not let a candidate ask voters to consider the fundamentally selfish nature of human beings! Sound political strategy, in most instances, regards those in the running for political office as wise who do not compel voters to reflect upon the moral implications of love and charity and respect for others.

You see, as shrewd as political wisdom may be, it is not the highest form of wisdom, nor does the world turn ultimately on the axis of the political process. Important matters in life and love usually are not decided by counting votes. Rather, for us, wisdom is revealed in the course of living. It is in the very midst of trying to live as we know we ought that we are challenged to testify by giving faithful response to those tough questions, Can love be commanded? or is it not in the very nature of love that it must be given voluntarily, or not at all?

What do you think?

Well, what do you think? Can love be triggered by a command to love? "Of course not," most answer almost immediately. "True love comes from within a person and no human being can command another's love."

Then, a simple and direct order to love will not bring forth love, especially if the person is unwilling to love? "Again, of course not—and if it ever does happen in that way, it happens very rarely."

So you are saying, then, that your control over your capacity to love is absolute, total, untouchable by another? "Practically so, at least some of the time, perhaps even most of the time."

"Of course," someone else might add, "there is another perspective to consider. There is the question of how much of one's love is not really given voluntarily so much as it is drawn out of a person by the object of that love." Think of how often we have heard that illustrated as people say: "I just love the way he sings . . . I love her for her smile . . . I love him because he is always so helpful and friendly. . . . She is so beautiful when she is angry that I cannot help but love her."

Therefore, on second thought, perhaps in some subtle way love is commanded. Maybe we should answer these questions by admitting that love is sometimes purely given but at other times it is pulled out of us. Sometimes I can love freely, and sometimes another commands it from me.

"So in answer to your question whether the two ideas of commandment and love can go together, at the very least I would have to say that it definitely gives one something to think about."

The debate takes place—sometimes

As a result of putting the question, people do give much thought to the matter. It is one of the tough questions in life. The debate takes place, and it goes on and on. In marathon sessions aimed at marriage enrichment, into the early morning hours in college dormitories, around the bridge table, in the seminary classroom, and even in the setting of an Adult Sunday School Class the discussion takes place whether love is the result of an internal push or an external pull. Indeed, wherever people have the time and the inclination to debate the ancient question, there it is to be heard: Can love be commanded?

But to certain chosen ones, something revolutionary happens on the way to the debate site. They hear a clear word from the Lord.

And his word is this: "This is my commandment, that you love one another as I have loved you." And just in case the hearing of that word was overcast by the feverish activity of the brain already at work pondering the tough question, again the word is spoken: "This I command you, to love one another."

While some delight in speculating whether it is at all possible to regulate public conscience and an individual's emotions, others —called by God in Christ to be his servants and friends—learn that their membership in the "Nature of Love" debating club has been withdrawn for them. They are told, "No longer are you mere servants. You are now my friends, because I have revealed to you the love of the Father. In our friendship, there is no need for shyness or secretiveness, for speculation or superficiality."

The friendship between Jesus Christ and the redeemed means that the whole question of the possibility of a coming together of love and commandment has been transcended. Mere obedience to a commandment does not make for friendship. Real friendship signifies a kinship of spirit, a drawing together of two persons—and unending talk of commandments and obedience to commands and legislating emotions will never begin to comprehend that truth.

Perhaps that is the reason why Jesus and the New Testament writers are so restrained in speaking about the true nature of love. Do you recall the words our Lord used to define and describe love? "A man was going down from Jerusalem to Jericho, and he fell among robbers, who stripped him and beat him, and departed, leaving him half dead. But a Samaritan, when he saw him, he had compassion."

And in another setting, Jesus spoke of love to Simon, saying, "Do you see this woman? I entered your house, you gave me no water for my feet, but she has wet my feet with her tears and wiped them with her hair. You gave me no kiss, but from the time I came in she has not ceased to kiss my feet. You did not anoint my head with oil, but she has anointed my feet with ointment. Therefore I tell you, her sins, which are many, are forgiven, for she loved much; but he who is forgiven little, loves little."

On yet another occasion, our Lord chooses these words to begin his discourse on love: "What man of you, having a hundred sheep, if he has lost one of them, does not leave the ninety-nine in the wilderness, and go after the one which is lost, until he finds it?"

Paul's well-known chapter to the Corinthians on the "more excellent way" is scarcely more helpful for those who would insist upon a more elaborate treatise. No, to speak of love (as does Paul) as being "not" this and "not" that puts the scholastic at a disadvantage and compels the searcher for the nature of love to take seriously the admonition to "make love your aim," or as the Today's English Version translates the verse, "It is love [and not the definition of the nature of love], then, that you should strive for." That's good advice! Heed it and it will put you into closer touch with the giver of the commandment than will all your investigation into the reasons why people do care about others, and why they help them, and honor them, and serve them. In short, in loving we learn what love is all about.

The Christian experience—after the debate has been ended

At least that has been the experience of Christians through the centuries. You see, seldom are those who name the name of Jesus as Lord and Savior given the luxury of being able to sit back for a time of careful consideration of all the philosophical and psychological nuances of love and loving. For us, more often than not loving implies a spontaneous action, not endless discussion. For Christians, loving means impassioned touching another's life, and not debate on the interrelatedness of the human will and human action. And while some continue to find delight in speculation, those who are Jesus' friends become more and more convinced by the Holy Spirit that the Lord's way is the lovely way which brings us together into a fellowship marked by love. Something has happened to us on the way to the debate. No longer does the debate seem relevant. Questions about love have become lost in the action of loving. Something good has happened to us!

What has happened?

That something good is that God in Christ has called us into a very select group. "You did not choose me," he says, "but I chose you and appointed you that you should go and bear fruit and that your fruit should abide." He has chosen us to be branches on God's own vine! "I have chosen you." The loving power of the almighty God himself is given to you through Jesus Christ. *You have been chosen in love to love!* That is truly good news!

It all may sound incredible, but it is true. In reality it is God's own love which through the Christian seeks its way to the neighbor. Through you God reaches out in love. Through you he wills to reveal his loving heart and through you he hands on the power of holy love. It's beyond our comprehension—but it happens!

And for that, thank God! Thank him for choosing you to be in

154

that loving fellowship of those who have heard the commandment
to love. Thank him for giving you the power to love. Amen.

J. Peter Pelkonen
Faith Lutheran Church
Akron, Ohio

CHRIST THE KING

The Ascension of Our Lord
Luke 24:44-53

Is that glow of Easter still around you? I *really* hope so! I
hope your life has a refreshing spirit because of Easter. I hope
you are shining bright!

The holy history we celebrate today is part of Easter. He is
risen and today he is rising! Rising so that we will always know
for sure that he is always with us as Lord and King. Lord and
King with full power.

That "Preacher Imp" Inside

Preachers are tempted to make slightly sarcastic remarks about
the great number of worshipers on Easter Sunday. "We'll see you
back here again at Christmas," the little "preacher imp" inside
would like to say. Well, we preachers usually don't have to be concerned about that when it comes to the church's celebration of
Ascension Day. The number of Christians who come together for
Thursday Ascension Day festival worship is usually quite small
when compared to Easter. We're here and we're still hearing the
trumpet echoes of "Jesus Christ Is Risen Today!!" and "I Know
That My Redeemer Lives!!" I'm so happy you're here in the warm
glow of Ascension Day.

Our Lord's Coronation Day

Today we celebrate our Lord's Coronation Day. He ascended
into heaven. No longer the Suffering Servant of Isaiah 53. Now
King of Kings and Lord of Lords. The songs are different, too.
No longer "Stricken, Smitten, and Afflicted." Now it's "Crown
Him With Many Crowns!" The colors are different, from peni-
tent purple to victory white. Now we look at the biblical narrative.
It seems too short. Too simple for such a cataclysmic event. And
the response of the followers of Jesus—too pedestrian. They just

"worshiped him and returned to Jerusalem with great joy, and were continually in the temple, praising and blessing God." That's what you expect biblical, religious people to do! And that's what they do!

Jesus—Friend of Sinners and Disciples

The Gospel according to Luke is perhaps the most beautiful of all the Gospels because Luke portrays Christ as God, Savior, and Friend of Sinners. In his Acts of the Apostles, Luke records the disciples' "must-have-been-exasperating" question: "Lord, is this the time when you are to establish once again the sovereignty of Israel?" They were still looking for power. Jesus responds by telling them that they would have the Spirit's power to carry out the mission.

What impresses me about Jesus just before his ascension into heaven is his loving treatment of the men he chose as his disciples. He doesn't say, "Men, we've been through all this before." Jesus simply informs them that the power of the Spirit of God would be theirs.

"He opened their minds to understand the Scriptures." He referred them to the entire Old Testament, "the law of Moses, the prophets, and the psalms." Jesus wanted his disciples to get it straight. His last will and testament does not begin with the words: "Being of sound mind. . . ." He just repeats again for his disciples the whole of his life and mission, that the Christ is to suffer death and to rise from the dead on the third day, and that in his name repentance bringing the forgiveness of sins is to be proclaimed to all nations." Today the church is tellingly reminded that the death and resurrection of Jesus are the basis for all Christian proclamation. The heart of it all.

Jesus Remembers

Do you ever wonder what Jesus thought about just before his ascension? He looked down on Bethany, on the Garden, on the city of Jerusalem. Perhaps his thoughts flashed by the events of just a month and a half earlier. Pilate taking a basin of water and saying, "See, I am washing my hands of this whole affair." And hearing again the roar of the crowd, "Crucify him! Crucify him!" Pilate asking, "What is truth?" And Peter. He knew Peter would be okay now. He knew that Peter and God's Spirit would be an unbeatable combination. Judas. A special sadness must have touched Jesus' heart when he thought about Judas. Wondering what the disciples were doing when he was hanging on the cross.

Thomas. He loved that man and all the men he called to be his disciples. Then he reviewed in his mind his contacts with the disciples and the other believers after coming alive again.

Ascension Commission

It was a very special moment now. And Luke nearly low-profiles the glory of the event. "Then he led them out as far as Bethany, and blessed them with uplifted hands; and in the act of blessing he parted from them. And they returned to Jerusalem with great joy, and spent all their time in the temple praising God." And ringing in their ears was the challenge they were beginning to understand at this point: "You shall be witness unto me in Jerusalem, Judea, and Samaria, and to the uttermost parts of the world." And he had said, "Go therefore, and teach all nations, baptizing them in the name of the Father and of the Son and of the Holy Ghost, teaching them to observe whatsoever I have commanded you. And, lo, I am with you always, to the end of the world." That was enough for the disciples. I will be with you, he said. They knew he would. They would be more than disciples. They would be apostles. A whole new job description would be theirs. And now comes the disciples' excitement. They returned to the city with great joy, headed straight for the temple, praised and blessed God all the way, and waited for a Pentecost they knew would come. They were getting the Spirit!

How About You?

One of the great problems of the church today, as I see it, is the lack of enthusiasm among God's people. Not enough punch. Not enough drive. Not enough excitement. Not when you know and believe that God has gotten his act together for you. Not when you know and believe God's loving forgiveness in Jesus Christ. Halford Luccock once said, "That is the trouble with the religion of many people. There is never any ecstasy, no hop, skip, and jump, just a dutiful trudge. Pick out a good minor ecstasy before you petrify." I would like to shout that to the whole church: PICK OUT A GOOD MINOR ECSTASY BEFORE YOU PETRIFY! Paul was like that. His enthusiasm and joy jump out all over the place in his letter to the Christians at Philippi. He writes: "I thank my God for you all every time I think of you; and every time I pray for you, I pray with joy, because of the way you have helped me in the work of the gospel, from the very first day until now (Phil. 1:3-5). And Paul is anything but funereal when he talks about cemeteries and death. "O death, where is thy sting? O death, where is thy victory? But thanks be to God who gives us the victory through our Lord Jesus Christ!" (1 Cor. 15:55, 57).

You Can't Lose

No way you can lose. No way! Christ makes everything new! He said: "Because I live, you shall live also!" Romans 6 leaps into our minds. "We were buried therefore with him by baptism into death, so that as Christ was raised from the dead by the glory of the Father, we too might walk in newness of life" (Rom. 6:4). That's the stuff that courage is made of. That's the sure hope. Christ lives. Christ reigns. We win. Christ's victory is ours.

This Ascension Day as individual Christians and people of the Christian community we confess our lagging ways, our dull words, our slowness to pick up on the great things God has in store for us. We admit that we have held back from joining in the great march of victory led by our Lord and Master. We confess that we have been too cautious, too preoccupied, too "religious," too empty, too careful.

I like what John Arthur Gossip says: "If we would help people to be valiant in their Christian living, we should be ringing out over the world that Christ has won, that evil is toppling, that the end is sure, that nothing can for long resist our mighty and victorious Lord. That is the tonic that we need to keep us healthy, the trumpet blast to fire our blood, and send us crowding in behind the Master, swinging happily upon our way, ready and eager to face anything, laughing and singing and recklessly unafraid, because the feel of victory is in the air, as our hearts thrill to it."

Today God leads us onward, upward. His Spirit comes to fire us up, to move us out, to proclaim in words and actions of love that Jesus Christ is our living Savior. Today he says to you and me, "Behold, I make all things new." That's us.

NATHAN O. LOESCH
Bethany Lutheran Church
Long Beach, California

SANCTIFY US IN THE TRUTH

Seventh Sunday of Easter
John 17:17b-19

Goodbye and Farewell

"Sanctify them in the truth." The text is the climax of that section of John's gospel known as the "farewell discourse" of

Jesus. The words are those of Jesus which the church has come to know as the High Priestly prayer. The setting in which John has placed the prayer is that of the last hours of Jesus' life. The words are last words—the words of a man who knew that his hour had come—the last words of a man about to die. And because last words are precious to us, it is helpful to our understanding of these last words to briefly sketch the situation which preceded them as John relates it in his gospel.

It was the day before the Feast of the Passover. Earlier in the week there had been a quiet visit with friends at Bethany—a quiet hour or two followed by the stir and noise that accompanied his entrance into Jerusalem. But time was growing short. Judas was already about his work. There remained still much to be said, much to be done. As if to capitalize on the shortness of the time and provide a capsule statement of his entire ministry, Jesus gathered his closest friends to share a last meal. As he did so, he gave them the dramatic instruction that was to serve as their guide after he was gone. Taking a towel and basin, he washed their feet and said, "I have given you an example that you also should do as I have done to you." It was the menial task of a servant, but it vividly reinforced the nature of his ministry and the scope of their discipleship lest they forget the purpose for which he had come and the cause to which they had been called.

And so, he prayed . . .

"Sanctify them in the truth; thy word is truth."

The Truth: Two Views

The truth . . . a bit later Pilate would ask him about that. He was not the first, nor would he be the last. For mankind—so wonderfully made, fashioned in the very likeness of God, created above all other creatures with the capacity to think and reason—has always been fascinated by that illusive concept. And in their fascination men have approached the matter of truth in at least two different ways: that of an arrogant dogmatism on the one hand, and a hopeless cynicism on the other.

The first goes like this: if you would know and possess the truth then you must come to know and possess my philosophical method, or my political and economic system, or my concept of government, or my style of life, or my understanding of the universe, or my mode of religious thought. Simply think as I think, understand as I understand, be governed as I am governed, live as I live, believe as I believe, and truth will be yours! It's a way of saying that only the experiences and institutions of my life have validity. If the world and its people would kindly begin to march in step with me, then, at last, peace and tranquility would envelop the earth. For truth is bounded by the limits of my experience and culture and tradition.

Negatively, it's a bit like the grandmother who, after watching the landing of the astronauts on the moon, declared, "There's no truth in it. It's only a trick the television people are playing on us." For one who had traveled to this country by steamer seventy years before, who had given birth to her babies unattended in a sod house, who had watched her husband first till the land of their homestead with ox and a plow, there could be no truth in the announcement that men were on the moon. We do much the same thing whenever we threaten and coerce people of differing races and cultures and traditions to lock step with the experiences and traditions of our lives in order to know and possess the truth. As if we had an exclusive corner on the market. It's the sin of man's first parents repeated again—the sin of claiming for ourselves the role and place of God.

Men have also approached the matter of truth with hopeless cynicism. It goes like this: since life is filled with a mixture of many truths and half-truths and outright falsehoods, there really is not much point in getting too worked up about it. After all, when you put it all together, life is just one great contradiction in which there is nothing that is of ultimate truth anyway. Ernest Hemingway, in his short story, "A Clean, Well Lighted Place," illustrates the despair of that cynicism well in the scene of two waiters discussing the suicide attempt of an old man in despair "about nothing." One of them, musing about life and his own fears and the contradictions in the world about him, concludes that everything is really nothing and man is nothing too. Using the Spanish word for nothing he rambles through the language of the Lord's Prayer: "Our nada who art in nada, nada be thy name . . . thy will be nada . . . give us our daily nada . . . deliver us from nada." Everything—the world, life, man, God—everything is nothing but nothing! It's the classic cry of the nihilist in our day—the whimpering, intangible pain of despair in which truth is an illusion and hope is gone and God, if there is a god, seems nowhere to be found.

And from time to time, we know that feeling too. There's the daily anxiety about our children: how will they turn out, what kind of world will they inherit, can they really expect a future? There's the nagging feeling of being trapped. The years flit by, you're suddenly forty or fifty years old, the working years are reduced to fifteen or twenty-five, and you begin to feel imprisoned—imprisoned by your job or your wife or your family— trapped in a world you didn't make and over which you have no control. There's the haunting feeling of being alone and lonely. Not that you have no friends or that your family no longer loves you; but rather that kind of loneliness in which contact with other people is like touching a shadow—in which there is no depth of human relationship. And in that brooding emptiness, riddled with contradiction, the echo of our Lord at prayer is heard again.

I Am the Truth

"Sanctify them in the truth; thy word is truth."

The truth ... not as the arrogant exclusiveness which separates men from each other, nor as the hopeless cynicism that drives men to despair of any truth, nor even as some middle ground between the two which men must somehow walk in order to insure that they will not be trapped by either. But rather, that which is wholly new—that which breaks down the walls and barriers behind which men hide from each other—that which brings life and hope and promise and a future to men's lives—that which liberates and sets men free! It's the recurring theme that John returns to again and again. Listen ...

- And the Word became flesh and dwelt among us, full of grace and truth; we beheld his glory, glory as of the only Son of the Father.

- You sent to John, and he has borne witness to the truth.

- If you continue in my word, you are truly my disciples, and you will know the truth, and the truth will make you free.

- I am the way, and the truth, and the life.

- For this I have come into the world, to bear witness to the truth.

The truth ... not an argument to be won or a doctrine to be pondered or a contradiction to be overcome—but a person! Jesus of Nazareth—born of Mary by the power of the Spirit of God—in baptism, confirmed by the Spirit to be the chosen and anointed of God—by the Spirit announced that the purposes of God in the world of men are fulfilled in his person. "I am the truth," he said. Not that he is the truth because his teaching is true, his teaching is true because he is in himself the truth. It was a way of saying that the whole counsel of God and the aspirations and hopes of all people everywhere are met in him. Freedom in the face of captivity, justice in the face of oppression, forgiveness in the face of guilt, brotherhood in the face of prejudice, love in the face of hatred begin and end in him. The full and complete counsel of God and the longing of mankind in every generation and circumstance of history are fulfilled in this one in whom the spirit of God was pleased to dwell.

The Truth Is for Doing

We call this prayer the High Priestly prayer because in it Jesus consecrates—sanctifies, sets apart—the church to its life and task in the world. And it is clear that this consecration takes place not by means of any single word or prayer of the historical Jesus, but it takes place by means of his total life and ministry, by his suffering and death. And it does not come to an end there, but rather by the spirit of God who raised him from the dead, it continues throughout the whole life and history of the church.

That's the unseen reality in which the Christian community stands. For the truth in which it was consecrated was not and is not a static doctrine to be contemplated, but rather an event and activity to be done. Not removed from the world, the community had actually been sent by Christ into the world to proclaim and do the truth that he himself had revealed. Consecrated in him, they would taste the same wholeness, the same oneness with God and with each other, the same unconquerable joy—and yet not quite the same, for they were men and not God. There would remain and continue to remain down through the centuries a resistance to the truth. Yet they were men upon whom God had poured out the offer of freedom and truth, of life and hope, in such measure that they were compelled to use every opportunity to share something of that freedom and truth and life with others. It was not the offer of another religion, nor the offer of another moral code —it was the offer of the life that had been intended for men by their creator from the beginning. Empowered by the Spirit, their ministry was the ministry of Jesus. They were to preach the same gospel of the kingdom that he had preached; they were to proclaim the forgiveness of sin to men as he had done; they were to be the prophetic voice of God "setting at liberty those who were oppressed" just as he had been that prophetic voice.

To be consecrated in Jesus is to do the truth. We need to be reminded of that often. For as the holders of the legacy of the Augsburg Confession we've taken seriously the matter of grace and faith and word alone. But truth is not merely the recital of a creed or the statement of a confession. And the world into which we are sent cares very little about how we say it, but it watches very carefully to see how we do it, how we live it in the context of our lives with others. For the truth is something to be done.

And how does one do the truth? Consecrated through the death and resurrection of Jesus, the truth is done wherever and whenever the people of God share his ministry in the world. The Letter to Diognetus, an anonymous writing of the second century Christian community describes it like this:

> Christians cannot be distinguished from the rest of the human race by country or language or customs. They do not live in cities of their own; they do not use a peculiar form of speech; they do not follow an eccentric manner of life. They live in their own countries, but only as aliens. They have a share in everything as citizens, and endure everything as foreigners. They busy themselves on earth, but their citizenship is in heaven. They love all men, and by all men are persecuted. They are unknown, and still they are condemned; they are put to death, and yet they are brought to life. They are poor, and yet they make many rich; they are destitute, and yet they enjoy abundance. They are dishonored, and in their very dishonor are glorified.

Within our own century the same thing is expressed in the life of the Japanese saint, Toyohiko Kagawa. Living in the slums of Kobe, he ministered to people. He preached, he wrote books, he made money, and it was all done to change the conditions of the people living there. He was stabbed and beaten, burned and stomped upon, by drunks and pimps and pushers. But he had read of Jesus and his love, and that they might know something of that love he would give all he had. "Penniless and without food I can live," he said, "Penniless I can share my rags. But I cannot bear to hear hungry children cry."

How does one do the truth? As Jesus shared a last meal and a last word with his friends he said it like this: "I have given you an example that you also should do as I have done to you. A new commandment I give to you, that you love one another; even as I have loved you, that you also love one another.

Sanctify them in the truth . . . not as a concept for idle speculation, but as the will and purpose of God revealed in Jesus Christ which we are called to do in the world of men . . . thy word is truth. Amen.

WADE E. DAVICK
First Lutheran Church
Minot, North Dakota

GIVE ME A RIVER!

The Day of Pentecost
John 7:37-39a

When anyone talks about rivers coming out of his heart, he must be using picture language. But just what was it that Jesus wanted to illustrate with those rivers when he talked about the Spirit of God? If we had been there on a dusty day in the dry season, it wouldn't have been so hard to understand. After everyone had finished with his prayers for rain, Jesus was describing the Spirit as an inexhaustible supply of what you and I need just as much as dry land needs water. And then he extends us the offer, the invitation, to call upon him, *"Give me a river."* When water is what you need, a river would be ideal. For God to give our parched souls a river of his Spirit would also be ideal, for it would provide us with *a reservoir for satisfaction.*

When you're thirsty, water means life. And that's the kind of water Jesus offered, the water of life. To the woman at the well he described it as "a spring of water welling up to eternal life." Here he talks about a river in order to make it clear that with him there are no shortages, no dry seasons. In a rain-poor land like Palestine every year could be a disaster if the needed rain didn't fall, and so the whole nation joined in prayer for rain at this festival, the Feast of Tabernacles. But Jesus calls out that anyone that comes to him can drink from a river, an inexhaustible supply, a reservoir for satisfaction. God's water supply is ample for our whole lives; from the few drops splashed on a baby's head in Baptism to the last sip through a glass straw that wets the lips of the dying, there is no shortage of the water of life with the God who offers us a river.

Of course, water is only one kind of symbol for what we need, just as Jesus spoke of himself elsewhere as the bread of life or the light of life. In all these ways he is saying that he is all that we need, that he is a reservoir for satisfaction. And this abundant supply he wants to give us, if only we ask, "Give me a river." And yet, it is also true that he only gives us what we need for *now.* He grants no advance supply, for he wants to train us to depend on him everyday. He doesn't want to equip us so that we won't have to come back to him each day to ask for our daily bread and for our daily supply of the water of life. He grants us his Spirit that same way, not according to the measure of our selfish greed, so that we might be able to outdo one another in our possession of his gifts, but in a supply that varies according to our need and his purpose. Through that he teaches us to trust him. God wants us to know, as Paul says, that if he gave us his own

Son because of our need, how could we possibly fear that he would hold anything else back from us that we might need. Oh, indeed he does give us a river, but only one day at a time.

But to ask "Give me a river," means to ask for more than a reservoir for satisfaction. It also means to ask for *a resource for strength*. To us a river represents a power source. While in Jesus' time there were no generators or dynamos, they still thought in a somewhat similar way; for them too spirit meant strength or power. In today's Old Testament Lesson it was spirit that made the difference between death and life. It was the force that empowered dry bones to stand up and live. When Jacob was an old man and his sons brought him word that Joseph was still alive in Egypt, the book of Genesis tells us that Jacob's spirit revived. We would say "he began hitting on all four again." In just the opposite way, when the Queen of Sheba listened to Solomon's wisdom and saw all his splendor, she was so overwhelmed that it says there was no more spirit left in her. Today's word for that kind of spirit would be "energy," and when we pray "Give me a river" we're using it that way too, we're asking for energy from God, a resource for strength.

In view of all the confusion about the gift of the Spirit today, it would be well for us to ask, "Strength for what?" The way to approach that question in the Bible's own way of speaking would be to ask, "The spirit of what?" Since the river Jesus talks about comes from his own heart, it must be his Spirit, the Spirit of Jesus Christ, the Spirit of God that is meant. But then that also means he's talking about the spirit of holiness, of love, of joy, and of peace. And those things do mean strength! To live that kind of life calls for power. Sin is easy, holiness is hard; hate comes naturally, love and peace require hard work. For these things I need a river. I need to pray, "God, give me a river."

We can penetrate further into what kind of strength Jesus offers us here by noticing where this strength comes from. It isn't physical strength; it is heart power. The river Jesus talks about flows from his heart. Heart, we are reminded in our worship almost every Sunday, is in many ways the same as spirit. When we sing the offertory, "Create in me a clean heart, O God; and renew a right spirit within me," we are singing twice over, "Give me a new heart." In the chapter before today's Old Testament Lesson Ezekiel promised God's people a new spirit and a new heart. And they both are really the same; they are the resource for strength that new life needs. And they are what Jesus Christ offers us. He offered it to his apostles, and they took him seriously. They caught his Spirit, and they lived with that power.

Kierkegaard told a parable about a king who had some horses.

He had a coachman to train the horses and drive them regularly, but in an economy move the king decided to dismiss the coachman and drive the horses himself. However, because the king used his coach only rarely, the horses, which the coachman had kept in top-notch shape, soon became sadly out of condition. They could not make even the shortest trip without becoming winded. And so, the king decided to give the horses back to the coachman that he might drive them regularly. Kierkegaard observed that this is what God does with his saints. His apostles and saints were just ordinary men and women, but they were driven. Oh, how they were driven! They were driven by the Spirit of God.

I don't like to admit it, but I need to be driven. Perhaps you do too. Even though God has given us a river as a resource for strength, it seems that our need requires that he keep after us each day to use that strength. So it looks like we have to pray each day, "Give me a river today."

But in some ways that's a dangerous thing to ask for. Because to have the Spirit of God is to have *a reason for sorrow*. A reservoir for satisfaction sounds great; a resource for strength would always be welcome; but who wants a reason for sorrow? The whole idea of praying for a reason for sorrow seems weird. Especially if we are praying for the river of God's Spirit, how can the spirit of love, joy, and peace possibly fit with sorrow? You simply can't be both happy and sad at the same time. And yet God is! According to the 15th chapter of Luke, God gets his joy when one sinner repents. But in that chapter the joy of finding is always presented over against the background of the pain of losing. If God's joy comes when he gets back the lost, he can't have that joy without the pain of having lost.

The best way I know to describe God's sorrow is to call it frustration, frustrated love. You see, God wants us all, and he wants each one of us all the way as his own. You can see that's a recipe for grief. You just can't win 'em all! But who wants frustration? Who needs it? We've got enough of that already. Think of the farmer who wants and needs higher prices in order to meet his own expenses. He doesn't want to starve poor people, and yet he knows that's exactly what will result from the higher prices he needs. That's frustration. That's it exactly! Frustration is a part of life, an inescapable part of human life, and thereby an inescapable part of the heart of the God who has chosen to love human beings. Not to feel that kind of frustration is to be partly dead.

There is an old movie in which Fredric March plays the part of an elderly widower who falls in love with young Kim Novak. But along with the joy of love he discovers the pain of jealousy, and he breaks off the romance, telling the girl he just can't stand this kind of pain. But after a brief return to his lonely room he realizes that to be able to feel pain is a sign of life, and that while he had been dead in his loneliness, now he was beginning to come alive again. He comes back to try to pick up the pieces of his romance knowing that he has to expect and accept the pain that goes with being alive.

We are called to share in God's sorrow, and we must—if we share his love. What other choice is there? Would you tell the evangelism committee not to try to reach all people? I'd sooner tell the treasurer not to pay all the bills. Which one of you will tell the shepherd to settle for the 99 sheep and forget the one that is lost? Which one of you will tell the woman to be content with her 9 coins and not to bother about the one that is lost? And which one of you will tell the father to be content with his one son and not to grieve over the one that is lost? No, if you ask God to give you the river that is his Spirit, this sorrow goes with it.

And really, it wouldn't do any good even for us to refuse to pray, "Give me a river." For this text speaks about a time before Pentecost. It ends by saying, "This he said about the Spirit, which those who believe in him were to receive." But the very next words say, "For as yet the Spirit had not been given." On this anniversary of Pentecost we are celebrating that the Spirit has been given—and given, and given! God hasn't held back or been stingy. To everyone who has cried, "Give me a river," he has opened up his heart and "out of his heart have flowed rivers of living water." And even if it never occurred to us what it meant to share our Father's heart, he gave us a share in his heart when he made us his sons. He has given us a river. And because it comes from his heart, it is a very special kind of river. To all of us he has given all that is in his heart. And now we have it, we have all the satisfaction, all the strength, and all the sorrow that lives in the heart of God. Amen.

RONALD HALS
Ev. Lutheran Theological Seminary
Columbus, Ohio

BORN OF THE SPIRIT

The Holy Trinity—First Sunday after Pentecost
John 3:1-17

I suspect there is some of Nicodemus in most of us.

He seems to me to belong as much to our age as to his own.

He is open to new ideas and possibilities and independent enough
to give Jesus a hearing for himself. He is sceptical enough to
want straight answers before he commits himself to anything. He
is willing to take the risk of breaking step with his colleagues in
the Sanhedrin and make up his own mind about Jesus and his
movement. He is cautious enough to do so alone and by night. He
likes a theological discussion and prides himself in his sensible-
ness and logic. He likes to keep the stakes low; he is reluctant to
put his reputation or career on the line.

His question is fundamental. His question, too, belongs to our
age as well as to his. Somewhere deep within he seems to yearn
for a faith that is both vital and certain. He yearns for some sign
that God *really* exists. My hunch is that the rituals of prayer and
fasting, of liturgy and sacrifice had become meaningless and un-
satisfying. The politics and formalities of institutional religion
were draining his faith of its spirit and power. He wanted more
than a secure place in the religious establishment; he wanted a
taste of God.

Testing a Prophet

Nicodemus was not going to be taken in easily by the popular
rabbi and his motley crew of followers. Jesus was called a Nazarene
(a sort of "hick" in contemporary parlance), a friend of drunks
and sinners, a fraud and blasphemer. He also knew something of
the fear and jealousy of his detractors. And he was impressed by
Jesus' mighty signs. Not simply showy magic, but healing, the
kind of response to the hurts of people that God would offer.

So combining boldness and caution, faith and doubt, confidence
and trembling, he meets Jesus in the dark of night. He comes
with neither a question nor a commitment. He shares his logical
and yet tentative conclusion about Jesus: "Rabbi, your miracles
make it obvious that God has sent you." I suspect he expects an
enthusiastic response. After all, a Pharisee and member of the
Sanhedrin would give prestige and credibility to Jesus and his un-
washed followers.

But, in Nicodemus' mind, it would be up to Jesus to sell himself
and his cause. I don't know just what Nicodemus wanted from
Jesus. I doubt if he knew. He certainly did not need Jesus to con-
vince him to believe in God. He was already something of a religious fanatic.

If Nicodemus were like some churchmen of our times, I suspect he might have wanted to discuss doctrine. He might have
wanted to test Jesus' orthodoxy. Did Jesus support the heresies

of the Zealots? Did he cop out with the compromises of the Sadducees? Was he supporting subversive political movements? Or leading one of his own? How did he relate his religion to politics? And so forth. You know the kind of questions with which modern day prophets are stoned.

No, I think Nicodemus had grown weary of an institutionalized and bureaucratized religion which "kept the form of religion while denying its power." I see him as a religious man in search of God. Have you ever felt that way? Has your involvement in the machinery of churchly activity—organizations, budgets, programming, etc.—ever seemed to choke the life and spirit and joy and freedom of faith? Maybe it would be helpful for many of us to slip away for a quiet night's encounter with our living Lord.

The God Question

Many modern Americans, it seems to me, both inside and outside of the church stand with Nicodemus on the question of God. The issue is not whether God exists. Ninety-six percent of all Americans, Gallup tells us, believe in God in some sense or another. More than sixty percent are involved in institutional religion of some kind. The question is not so much whether God exists, but who or what God is for us and what relevance he may have for our lives.

Luther stated it more broadly. He contended that *everyone* has a god. There is simply no such thing as a person without a god! The question of faith, then, is not whether or not we believe in a god, but who or what is *really* god for us.

Luther gives us some help. He says that whatever we fear, love and trust above all else, that is our god. If Luther is right, then I won't discover my *real* god by checking out the creeds of my church. I will discover my god by asking where I find my security, what is it that I hope for, what do I prize most highly in life? Viewed from this perspective, the false gods of our age do not come from doctrinal heresies and alien religious ideas but from inverted loyalties. What is it that our age trusts and loves most? Military power and national glory? Family pride? Financial or social security? Status and popularity? What do you trust and love most?

Tillich said it much the same way. He spoke of "God" as that for which we have an "ultimate concern." Simply put, whatever matters—*really* matters—for us, *that* is our god. Seen in this light, our struggle for a faith in God has to do with tension over what is at the center of our lives that gives direction and meaning to everything else we do.

Tailor-Made Gods

This does not mean that when we trust and love money, status, social acceptance or other things most of all that we give up our formal affirmation of God in a more religious sense. No, we have a way of tailor-making our sense of God to suit our needs and aid us in achieving what really matters to us.

J. B. Phillips describes such do-it-yourself god-making in his durable and popular little book, *Your God Is Too Small*. He helps us understand how a person with a need for emotional support might develop a concept of God as a "Cosmic Psychic Crutch." People who crave law and order to give stability to their world, may conceive of God much like a "Cosmic Cop." Those who want to escape from the jarring reality of a harsh world may project for themselves a soft and warm "Heavenly Marshmallow." God might be conceived in the image of a "Universal Computer" for those who find security in precision and consistency.

You can play this game yourself—matching life values with concepts of God. More important, you can do it for yourself. How do you shape your thinking about God to harmonize with what you fear, trust and love most in the world around you?

The God I Don't Believe In

Such gods are created in the image of man. They are not the God who created man in his image. They get in the way of God's claim on our lives.

I find myself agreeing with atheistic minded people at times. One such friend of mine contends that faith in God is an emotional crutch for people who can't hack it alone in the real world. He argues with Freud that people search for God because they crave an all-wise and all-powerful father who can take the responsibility of living from their shoulders. People create God, he says, because they outgrow their parents.

Now I think most of us do have this sort of need for a caring Father; and God does in fact look after the needs of his people. Yet at this point I agree with the atheist: I *don't* believe in the same God he *doesn't* believe in. I don't believe in the gods people create for themselves whether for noble or selfish ends. Idols are carved out of human wants and needs as well as wood and stone.

The Limits of Logic

Is this what Nicodemus needed to learn? His religion, piety, logic, religious establishment and ritual could get between himself and God. Nor could his logic or wit unravel the mysteries of the kingdom of God.

In effect, Jesus by-passed Nicodemus' initial observation that God must be with him or he would not be able to do his healing wonders. Such logic will not lead to faith. Nicodemus will not find God by getting answers to his questions.

Jesus' response seems at once more simple and much more profound than Nicodemus could have expected: "I tell you the truth, no one can see the kingdom of God unless he is born again." No clarifying footnotes. Nicodemus will simply have to wrestle with that statement. So will we.

"Can't happen," he protests, "physically impossible! A grown man cannot return to and from the shape and place of his matrix." Jesus does not rescue him from his puzzlement. What is needed for faith, Nicodemus will have to learn, is not old logic but new birth. He may search for God in the rituals and writings and theology of his tradition, but it will be God who does the finding. He may try to fit God into his box of religious categories, but the new-life giving Spirit, Jesus says, blows as free as the wind and Nicodemus' logic will not be able to catch it or even know where it comes from or where it goes.

Born of the Spirit

Let us, too, learn with Nicodemus. The God who creates the universe and holds all things in the palm of his hand cannot be confined in the structures and rituals and architecture of formal religion. The God who comes offering himself in human flesh in Jesus to make us whole is less understood in the wonder of his miracles than in his suffering servanthood. The Spirit that generates new life and new relationships for the kingdom cannot be confined to our logic, predictions or institutions.

So let the Spirit blow. Sense him blowing in the good news we share that we are accepted and loved and given eternal life in Christ. Sense the Spirit blowing as we celebrate the unity we share with one another in the kingdom and family of our Father. Sense the Spirit blow as we search out together day by day the new meanings and new directions God gives to us.

Let the Spirit blow!

DAVID L. LUECKE
Interfaith Center
Columbia, Maryland

THE LORD OF THE SABBATH

Second Sunday after Pentecost
Mark 2:23-28

When I was a few years younger, I was simply enthralled with the book entitled *Gulliver's Travels*. It never ceased to start those fantasy juices flowing in my system when I read about Gulliver. His experience of being shipwrecked in the middle of the ocean and being thrust on an island in the middle of nowhere always found me on the edge of my chair.

And I suppose that's because there isn't anything more exciting to a young boy than some story of being shipwrecked on an island, whether it be *Robinson Crusoe, Swiss Family Robinson, Gulliver's Travels,* or that great classic of modern day television, *Gilligan's Island.*

I never saw the movie of Gulliver, so all of this fantasy had to take place in my mind. And I could just see him lying there on the ground with thousands of small threads rendering him completely helpless. I don't really know if there were thousands of strings in the story, but that was how I imagined it.

There were threads around his arms and legs, each of his fingers were tied securely to the ground, and there were even strings tied around the strands of his hair. With thousands and thousands of those tiny Lilliputians running around tying the strings, Gulliver was as helpless as a baby.

As I read this text from Mark 2, I was struck with the fact that exactly the same thing happened to people in the first century as happened to Gulliver, and this centered in the observance of the Sabbath. If you will recall, the Sabbath day was given by God as recorded in Genesis 1 as a time for rest, a time to use this time as a gift from God for rest and recuperation and worship.

It was not a time in which people were to tie themselves in knots, but to be freed from all the chains and duties that came to them during the week. It was meant to be a time of celebration and fellowship and sharing and singing and hoping about the future. It was a great idea that God had come up with, and of course it still is.

But something had gone wrong. Like the thousands of tiny, little threads which subdued the vitality of Gulliver, so the Sabbath day and all of its regulations sometimes tied people into knots and destroyed their freedom.

Jesus was terribly disturbed about the misuse of the Sabbath, and he wades right in to the issue with no holds barred. First he heals a man on the Sabbath, and all chaos breaks loose. "You can't do that, Jesus," the Pharisees rail at him. But they haven't seen anything yet."

Soon Jesus and his disciples are walking through the grainfields on their journey between towns, and lunchtime comes around. So in the custom of the day, they pick some grain from the field and sit down to eat. But the Pharisees are at his throat immediately for it is forbidden to pick food on the Sabbath. "Don't you know the law, Jesus? You can't go around doing these things on the Sabbath, you are undermining the whole fabric of our faith."

But Jesus' anger rises steadily throughout these confrontations, as he sees how many people are in prison because of these laws, and how they have taken to majoring in declaration. People, you've got this all turned around. The Sabbath day is made for man, not man for the Sabbath. In other words, the kingdom of God is here to set people free, to be good news, not to find new ways of tying people in knots.

And this was a bombshell. But it was not the first nor the last, because this was the way Jesus treated many of the traditions. Do they serve the spiritual and physical needs of the people, he would ask. If they don't, get rid of them. What is a tradition worth if it distorts the gospel? Nothing, says Jesus, let's get rid of them and recapture the grace of God.

It's no accident that this text in Mark follows right after the words Jesus says about old and new wineskins. According to that very familiar parable, Jesus talks about the folly of trying to put new wine into old wineskins. New wine will expand and will burst the skin, for new wine demands new skins.

The gospel of Christ also does not fit in the old traditions of Pharasaic Judaism. The Sabbath was meant to be a time of celebration, of joy and peace and love and hope, not a time for new bondage. You can't put the new life of Christ into the old life of careful and obsolete tradition.

And I find this text to be particularly relevant to the church in our time. And the question we must ask of ourselves is this: How are we celebrating the Sabbath, or our day of worship? Is a time of new freedom, or rejoicing, or is it simply a new kind of prison? How many of you are here today because you felt you had to come, not because you wanted to come? If your answer has something to do with coercion, then the Sabbath has not been made for you at all.

I heard a story of a black woman who had raised her son in the midst of a very exciting and free black church in one of our cities. But when the boy reached college age, he went off to a college in a white setting, and had a complete immersion in the white culture, and white church.

On one of his college breaks, he came home for a few days, and while he was visiting he and his mother went to church. It was a great celebration that day, with much singing and shouting and hallelujahs and amens and arms raised. After the service, as they were driving home, the boy said to his mother, "The pastor today wasn't very good, was he?" Well, said his mother, maybe not, but weren't we in the congregation good today.

Beautiful. Worship is much more than just a monologue by the pastor, and a couple of hymns. The Sabbath is made to fulfill the spiritual and psychological and emotional needs of people, not the other way around. And I think this really says something to Lutherans as we look forward to the future. There has got to be more participation by people in the congregation.

We have come out of a tradition that is almost completely authority centered; authority vested in the clergy or their appointed spokesmen. But the gospel today it seems is ready to burst these old skins, and we need constantly new skins to contain that gospel. Jesus Christ is the same today as he ever was, but the way in which we worship him must change to meet the people where they are.

Jesus' words, however, apply to more than just the Sabbath. He was talking also about persons like you and me finding freedom in every area of our lives. He was talking about life becoming that joyful pilgrimage that it was meant to be. He put every institution on notice that it was made for people, not people for the institution.

Marriage, he said, was made for the persons in it, not the other way around. Government was made for people, to serve the social and physical and psychological needs of people, not the other way around. Schools were made for the young people in them, not the other way around. Every institution rises and falls as it is able to serve the needs of people.

Much of our problem has come from our understanding or lack of it about God, which in many ways is not a Christian understanding. Most of us have grown up with a picture of God in our minds that describes him as powerful, authoritarian, unchanging, judgmental, angry, and arbitrary. Its kind of the approach, "Lord, if I do anything wrong, strike me down."

And because we have seen God in this way, we have tended to make our institutions this way. Many of our homes are like this, many of our churches, and governments and schools. They are authoritarian, judgmental, all knowing, never admitting any fallibility or mistakes, defensive about their authority and resistant to all forms of change.

But the moment we look at the life of Jesus Christ, our picture of God changes drastically. Jesus came to throw out obsolete traditions and to pump new life into relevant ones. He came to live a life of love. And he said in many different ways, "If you have seen me, you have seen the Father."

God is a God of love and compassion and suffering on behalf of others. The Spirit of Christ is never one which is heavy handed and arbitrary, but a Spirit which loved and cared and gave itself even unto death. And Jesus told us that we share in his life if we are his disciples, I came, he said, "that you might have life and might have it more abundantly." That doesn't sound at all like a new prison.

The pastor who comes across as all knowing or authoritarian or resistant to change is not true to the gospel. The church which is more concerned about right doctrine than about the love and Spirit of Jesus Christ is in opposition to the Jesus of the New Testament.

A people which is more concerned about its own congregation, than about the community or about the hurting in our world has tried to put new wine into old skins. You and I, if we are more concerned with receiving than with giving, more interested in our rights than our responsibilities, more turned on by being loved than in loving, have missed the whole impact of the gospel.

I'll never forget the time when this truth was burned into me like a fire. When I received my first job as a youth director, I knew next to nothing about ministry. I was afraid, uncertain and defensive. The first week of my new job, the pastor of that church went on a vacation, leaving the whole store to me, which was really leaving it all alone.

At that time there was an old lady in the parish dying of cancer at the local hospital, and it was understood that I should go and visit her. I didn't want to go, because I didn't know what I would do when I got there. But about the time I was ready to find an excuse for not going, the secretary of the congregation, who had been there for about thirty years, volunteered to go with me. I quickly accepted her offer.

When we arrived in the room, I was very concerned that I appear as an authority on the Christian faith, that I would be able to give that old lady some faith, and hope. I began by asking the lady how she felt, but there was no response. Everything I said to her, she did not respond. I became more and more uneasy.

Finally, when all else failed, I thought I should read some Scripture for her, but when I reached for my Testament, it was in another coat. So I told her I would recite the 23rd Psalm for her, but as I went through it, I forgot most of it. I knew she must be crying inside about my inability to help her, and I just knew that the church secretary would go back to the council and tell them I was completely worthless.

But just as I was about to fall apart in despair, the secretary went over to the bed, and took both hands of the dying woman. Jane, she said, we love you, we love you very much. God loves you, and all of your friends are praying for you. And then she bent over and gave her a kiss on the cheek. And with that the old lady broke out into a smile and shook her head affirmatively as if now it was okay.

A day later, she died. But she had seen the love of God in Jesus Christ in her friends. We are called not to be an authority or one with all the answers, but to love. Jesus has set us free to love, he has cut the strings and set us free.

MERVIN E. THOMPSON
Prince of Peace Lutheran Church
Burnsville, Minnesota

BINDING UP THE STRONG MAN

Third Sunday after Pentecost
Mark 3:20-35

In a time when we Christians are becoming increasingly aware of our weaknesses in the world, when we are reconciling ourselves to our minority status and resigning ourselves to the limit powers we possess to effect wide-spread spiritual or social change, the Gospel for the day comes as a reminder and a rescuer. It contains an image that Jesus used to defend his ministry against his accusers. That same image carries us to the heart of the New Testament message of hope.

In the Gospel lesson Jesus refers to a strong man whose house is entered, who is over-powered and bound by someone who is stronger than he and whose goods and possessions are then plundered. The implication is surely that Jesus is that mysterious someone who is stronger than the strong man, stronger than all the demonic forces of evil that possess human beings. That certain claim is good and encouraging news for us to hear.

All this power-charged imagery took place in an emotionally-charged episode. Jesus' popularity was building and broadening through the country side. And no wonder, because his preaching had an element of radical newness and excitement about it. He was calling people to repentance; to a life change which challenged them to live the future now; to a life style in which the hopes and promises traditionally reserved for a new distant age were made certain and sure. His message was mind blowing. His presence was the sign that the kingdom of God had come.

Such a message had dangerous ramifications for the religious establishment, of course. So a delegation of the usual officials came from Jerusalem, allegedly to investigate Jesus. Actually, however, their mission was to infiltrate the ranks of his followers and to discredit him by labeling him. They made it clear that according to the official position, Jesus was a heretic. They labeled him a sorcerer possessed by demonic power. It was the usual way to deal with religious innovators.

There apparently was no question that what Jesus was doing was having a good effect. People were being liberated. The blind were seeing new meaning in life, the deaf were hearing good news, and the cripples of life were jumping for joy. But what was actually happening to people was of no consequence. What mattered was whether or not the proper forms and practices were being preserved.

It is interesting that Jesus does not need to resort to any special spiritual interpretation in his own defense, as his accusers did in making their claims against him. He simply points out the ridiculousness of their accusation. How could he be doing good things and at the same time, be motivated by the powers of evil? If that were the case, then Satan himself would be embroiled in a civil war and his power rendered ineffective, which is obviously not the case. "But, there is another possibility," replies Jesus. "I could be the one who is stronger than the evil one. I am the one who bound the strong man and I am the one who liberates those whom he possesses."

That bold and certain sound of confidence is what makes the Jesus story good news. Every part of it echoes this note of fulfillment. Joachim Jeremias concludes his book on The Parables of Jesus with this summary of the New Testament message. "The strong man is disarmed, the forces of evil are in retreat, the physician has come to the sick, the lepers are cleansed, the heavy burden of guilt is removed, the lost sheep has been brought home, the door of the Father's house stands open, the poor and the beggars are summoned to the banquet, a master whose grace is undeserved pays his wages in full, a great joy fills all hearts."

Yet, while that confidence and certainty is derived from the image of Jesus as the one who binds the strong man, how well that same image preserves the struggle we experience in our attempts to live that certain faith.

For example, the image makes it clear that the strong man does indeed possess and lay first claim to us in life. Our freedom must be wrestled from him. The strong man takes many forms: fear, insecurity, guilt and greed are some of the more characteristic disguises he wears when he stands guard over us.

Nor does the image say that the strong man is destroyed and done away with. He is still there and still strong. He is bound, but even so the implication is that he can at any time slip from his bindings and repossess those who have been taken from his control. At least such an implication speaks to the experience of faith in the world.

And from the extended story of Jesus' own life we know that binding the strongest man and setting free what he possesses means wrestling all the way to the death and beyond death to life and freedom.

Nevertheless, the word remains clear and sharp, confronting and welcome. In this world where the strong man rules, someone has come and keeps coming who is "stronger than he."

We hear this word today, however, with different ears, in a vastly different situation, with different conclusions and consequences. We are not defending our ministry as Jesus was. The whole idea of one who is stronger than the evil about us is not so much a fact to be argued as it is a faith to be embraced. The strong man of our world is taking new and grotesque forms. In addition to all the personal forms his possession can take, we now find ourselves locked into a world of famine and starvation, economic imbalance and limited resources.

We are told on the one hand that our own civilization is in the throes of decline and indeed the signs about us are ominous. But even more critical than that is the growing skepticism about our corporate human future. Robert Heilbronner writes in his book *The Human Prospect*, "The outlook for humanity, I believe, is painful, difficult, perhaps desperate, and the hope that can be held out for their future prospect seems very slim indeed."

It is in this milieu that we hear the claim of Jesus in the gospel, that he is the one who is stronger than the evil one. Suddenly it is all quite different and a quite critical matter. It is a matter of believing and in that believing to take a radical stance toward the world and the future. God calls his people to believe and in believing to strike a stance of hope in the world. The Christ who claims to be the one who binds the strong man is calling his church today to be a people of hope especially in all those human situations where there is little or no hope at all. This is our uniqueness and this is our gift to the world.

The critical difference that Christian hope can make is illustrated by a story told about the East Harlem Protestant Parish, an experimental ministry in a section of New York City once called America's most complete ghetto.

In mid 1950s, the East Harlem Protestant Parish led the church in the discovery of its urban mission. The innovative approaches to ministry and the excitement they generated began to capture the interest and imagination of many people. Then the parish became the subject of a network TV documentary. Camera crews were hauled into the slums to record this new thing that had come to pass. One of the pastors seemed pleased and commented on the sensitivity of the technicians to the people and to the mission of the parish. Then one day, just a few weeks before the program was to be aired, the pastor discovered that the program had been entitled "One Square Mile of Hell." In anger he called the producer demanding that the title be changed or the program cancelled. The label was a total misinterpretation of the whole meaning and mission of the parish. Immediately, the producer saw the critical difference and in moments the title was changed to "One Square Mile of Hope."

Christian hope is a stance in the midst of the hopelessness of life. It is not blinders to spare us from reality or tinted glasses to soften the view. Christian hope is a decision we make, a conclusion we reach, a stance we strike to believe in Jesus and in his claim to be the one who is stronger than he.

Such a conclusion has consequences.

The text from Mark's Gospel centers on the image of the one who is strong enough to bind up the strong man. But then it quickly moves on to the consequences. First to follow is a saying from Jesus about forgiveness; who will receive it and who will not. Then, there is an incident added when Jesus appears to be downright crude to his mother and brothers. Both the saying and the incident have a positive and a negative thrust.

In the saying, Jesus openly announces that all the sins of the people will be forgiven including all their slanderous and sacrilegious talk except those, who like his accusers, are trying to destroy the work of God's spirit in the world. Needless to say, most of the effort of biblical scholarship and most biblical discussions on this passage focus on the narrow restriction at the end rather than the gracious declaration of divine grace at the beginning.

Likewise with the incident that ends the episode. Jesus' mother and brothers come looking for him. Word is sent to Jesus through the crowd that they are here and asking for him. For a moment, Jesus freezes the situation. The crowd is on the inside. His mother and brothers are on the outside. Then he uses it to illustrate that his concept of family is not narrowly genetic, but broadly missional. His brothers and sisters and mother are all those who join him in the family of God. Again, more energy is spent questioning Jesus' rejection of an exclusive family claim than celebrating the inclusiveness of his relationships.

We hear these words and see these images with eyes and ears that are full of the sights and sounds of our own time. Often, those sights and sounds are filled with plight and pessimism. For example, serious proposals are being made by people in high places that the human family should be genetically defined and separated so that we can decide in this world of shortages who will eat and live and who will not. Some of the most passionate and pessimistic prophets of the future plead for a renewal of a vision and meaning big enough to include the whole human family.

With eyes and ears full of these kinds of sights and sounds, our Gospel lesson for today presents us with an image of Jesus. It is a savior image, of one who overcomes the strong man, binds him and releases all those held in his possession. Then we hear a word of forgiveness broad enough to reach out and encompass almost everyone. And we hear a story that tells us about our real ancestoral roots in the family of God. These are the universal images that the gospel holds out to us and calls us to represent in a time full of plight and pessimism. We, too, must confront the living Christ, draw some conclusions and face some consequences of believing his word in our world.

That word calls Christian communities to be islands of hope, openness and human unity. The more seriously we take that calling, of course, the more chance there is that we will find ourselves accused as Jesus was. Now, instead of demon possession, the charge is more likely to be traitor or un-American or communist. The charge is different but the intent to discredit remains the same. The strong man is still very much in control.

At the very least, those of us who take the stance of hope and try to live out its consequences, can expect to be dubbed simpleminded fools. Of course, the Christian community already has a long and noble reputation in this area. The rumor started with Jesus himself. Our Gospel lesson begins with the observation of some people who said, "He is beside himself." That's another way the world has tried to relativize the message of Jesus.

Of course, we know how foolish and simplistic a stance of hope sounds to sophisticated ears, even our own. We know the odds against the possibility that our stance of hope, our prayers and our actions, with and on behalf of the whole family of God, can have any significant influence on our world.

But that's alright. We are not out to influence the world finally.

We are answering the call of the gospel to obedience. That's the difference that makes us free to be fools.

On the other hand, God did take one person's obedience and use it to bind up the strong man forever. Who knows how he might use ours?

WILLIAM E. LESHER, President
Pacific Lutheran Theological Seminary
Berkeley, California

GOD IS THE KING

Fourth Sunday after Pentecost
Mark 4:26-34

God always has been and always will be the king. The good news of Jesus Christ is that he wants to be our king and that he chooses to use us to let his kingdom come.

God Is a Very Special King

God is the king because he is God and Creator whether people happen to like it or not. Men cannot by their vote overthrow God or dethrone him.

But God is a very special kind of king. He wants to be a king for men not because he is stronger than they are or can control their lives. He wants them to want him—and that, not because he's some neurotic who needs people always to want him and tell him how great he is. Rather he wants people to want him because it is only when they know him and want him as their Savior and king, that they can grow and mature as human beings and become all they were meant to be.

God has always been such a king and he has always been active to establish his good kingdom. That's what he was doing when he created the world, when he called his people of the Old Covenant into existence and when he sent them the prophets. But especially in Jesus Christ was, and is, this true. Jesus' first words in Mark's gospel are: "The time is fulfilled and the kingdom of God is at hand; repent and believe in the gospel."

When you look at Jesus Christ, what do you see? You see someone loving and caring, healing the sick, accepting the outcasts, preaching the good news, casting out the evil spirits and finally giving his life for men. And you see people responding to him, wanting to be where he was, wanting to be a part of what he was doing, wanting him to be their king and Lord. In him particularly was this very special king establishing his kingdom.

When we can say, "God, I want you to be my king," that king and his kingdom have come to us and then we have become a part of God's great activity to have all men be a part of his kingdom and share in his love and goodness.

The King Cares About the Whole World

For the other thing we must say about this very special king is that he cares about his whole world—rich and poor, black and white, strong and weak, healthy and sick, young and old. He wants them all to know he's alive, that he loves and cares about them. He wants all of them to have a part of all his good things, both in this world and the next. He wants them to know they are forgiven, to be sure; but he also wants them to have enough food.

The King Uses Us

And he wants to use us in this work of sharing his love. It is to that particularly that these two parables speak. And what they say is really great good news. For they say that God will use what may seem to be our insignificant efforts to make his kingdom come.

That's good news because the task seems very difficult and complex—perhaps impossible. You think of how you might share the love of God with some friend or relative or the family next door and you really don't see how you can do it. Or you think of how you can help in a world where people are starving or where they are so poor they're living on dog food or cat food. Or you wonder how you can make a difference in the incredibly difficult racial problem in America.

The King Makes It Happen

What these parables are both saying is that our work is to scatter the seeds, our acts of faith, hope and love. It is God who will make things happen.

Look at that first parable again. When you plant a field or garden, you don't hover over the seeds as if by your presence and power to make them sprout and grow. You plant them and go about your life—sleeping and rising day by day. And one day there is the sprout and then a plant and then the harvest, "you know not how." It wasn't you. It was something outside you.

So it is with the coming of the kingdom. You scatter the seed— take care of your family, teach a Sunday school class, serve on a committee in the community, do your job in faith and love. God makes something happen so that his kingdom comes.

The second parable says something like it. A mustard seed is a tiny little thing but when it is planted a big bush grows out of it, big enough to provide shelter for the birds.

The word is: God takes what we do and brings good out of it, all out of proportion to the original act. When the problem looks so big that you feel your contribution won't make any difference, go ahead and do it anyway. Plant that little mustard seed of love and faith and then step back, because things are going to happen. You never know what great good God might make happen through it.

In his book, *Race Against Time,* Andrew Schulze tells of one such incident. It was September, at the end of World War I and he'd come to Springfield, Illinois, to enroll at Concordia Seminary. He was tired and dirty after an un-airconditioned train ride. He was on a street car in Springfield and asked the conductor how to get to Concordia Seminary. A black man overheard the question and answer, and just before he got off, he leaned over to give Schulze better directions and then added an invitation to him to come and worship with them in their little frame church. That was all he did. That was the mustard seed!

God did the rest. Schulze did go to that little church the next Sunday evening and that event changed his whole life. He became concerned about the situation of being black in a white society and ultimately gave his life to working at that problem. Later in his life he came to see that brief invitation as the voice of God calling him. And all the black man did was give him some directions and invite him to church.

And you all know the story of the black woman who one day decided she was tired of sitting in the back of a bus and sat up front. A little thing! But in a sense you might date an important part of the whole modern civil rights movement to that event.

So the good word is: your life counts. The same king who has caught you up in his love will use your deeds of faith and love to make his kingdom come. You plant the seeds. He'll do the rest.

ROBERT G. HECKMANN
Our Redeemer Lutheran Church
Newark, Delaware

WHEN YOU ARE IN A STORM

Fifth Sunday after Pentecost
Mark 4:35-41

We all know what it's like to be in a storm. A storm is when events "let loose," when the usual steady way of things goes topsy-turvy, when forces of immense power overwhelm what you are or can do, and the possibility of control disappears. "The wind arose—the waves beat into the boat—the boat was about to sink."

And we all know that storms come in two ways—usually together: the storm without, and the storm within. There are winds and waves of fear and guilt, anger and pride, belief and unbelief in wild commotion.

And we all know that in the stress of the storm we tend to cry out in some kind of accusation against anyone near—sometimes against the nearest ones. And we also cry out in some kind of acknowledgement of God. "Oh God!"

And we also know that when the storm is over, we tend to have a lot to say about it. We are something like the man who survived the Johnstown Flood of a couple generations ago. He told and told how he had been in the water—and how he had grabbed hold of that tree—until he was simply tiresome to everyone. Then, so the story goes, he died and came to the Pearly Gates. There he was asked what he would like most to happen in heaven. "Oh," he said, "could I tell about the Johnstown Flood?" "Yes," was the answer, "but remember, you'll have Noah in the audience."

Maybe we should all of us listen to the giant experiences of storm rather than tell one another about our small experiences.

In the Scriptures there are four great archetypes of storms in human experience. They are reported in the first eleven chapters of Genesis—and maybe they *are* the four main kinds of storms any of us ever know.

I. The Storm of Doubt that leads to Disobedience.

It started small enough. Eve heard the voice of the tempter, "Did God say you could not eat of *any* tree in the garden?" And in her mind, Eve began to turn that suggestion of doubting God around and around. Could God be unfair? Could God be that small?

The thought grew. When she next said what she thought that God had said, she distorted God's word. Then the tempter denied that God's word would have the effect it declared it would have. And he deceived her into thinking that the effect of a disobedience would be beneficial to her. Eve was in the storm of "shall I do it or shall I not?" But when her perceptions were all on the side of desiring the fruit and its hoped-for effects, she took and she ate; she disobeyed. And it ended with the storm-tossed pair being expelled from the garden—refugees. It was the Fall.

Do you know that storm? Have you been in that storm?

Oh, yes, I think you have. We all have. Like the disciples in the text, we have experienced that the wind of the storm arose— the wind of the question that doubts God. And then the storm within began to come up. And we distorted God's word—implied that God was not fair.

With the disciples in the boat, we accused the Lord: "Don't you care if we perish?" Impudent, foolish question! He who left heaven to take on our mean estate! He who went to the cross for us! He who gave himself for us!—"Don't you care?" But that's the way of us humans when the storm is raging. Our fear and our guilt set us to accusing the one who loves us most.

Let us here note, too, that being with Jesus does not mean exemption from storms. You and I are in the same boat as the disciples. We are with Jesus—but the storm can arise.

II. The Storm of Disappointment that becomes Jealousy.

This is the storm that came upon Cain, who finally killed his brother Abel.

Things went poorly for Cain, and he was disappointed. "My brother has it better than I do.—Why should God have a greater regard for my brother than for me?" (Oh, that is a corrosive thought!) And Cain was angry—and his countenance fell.

He was warned. The word of the Lord came to him: "Sin is couching at the door. Its desire is for you. But you must master it. Take hold of yourself, Cain. Rebuke that corrosive, jealous mood. Be master of the storm. Don't let it master you!"

But Cain, with his twisted perceptions and his contorted face, went right on. And he laid a trap. And he sprung it. And he did murder! He destroyed his brother! And Cain, who had been in touch with God, and who had God's promise that no one was free to destroy him—went away—from the presence—of the Lord.

Do you know that storm? Have you been in that storm?

Oh, yes, you have. We all have. We have known the wind of disappointment to come up. And waves of jealousy threaten to swamp us.

We have been warned. But instead of taking hold of ourselves and rebuking the corroding resentment, we have imagined to settle things our own way. And that way leads to the destruction of our brother! Then we, who have been in touch with God, have, like Cain, gone away—from the presence—of the Lord.

III. The Storm of Self-reliance that turns in to Wickedness.

There is a list of the descendents of Cain. And there is a list of the descendents of Seth. The two lists begin with different attitudes. When Cain was born, Eve said, "I—have gotten a man!" When Seth was born, Eve said, "God—has appointed for me a child."

The list of the descendents of Cain is a list of remarkable, competent, innovative people: the first builder of a city, the father of those who have cattle, the father of those who play the lyre and pipe, the forger of all instruments of bronze and iron. The list ends of Lamech's self-reliant boast: "I have *slain* a man—for wounding me. I have *killed* a young man—for striking me. I am *avenged*—seventy-seven-fold!"

The list of the descendents of Seth is a list of people about whom only two descriptions were given. They began to call upon the name of the Lord. They walked with God.

In the Storm of Doubt that led to Disobedience, Adam and Eve went the wrong way. In the Storm of Disappointment that became Jealousy, Cain went the wrong way. But in the Storm of Self-reliance—*some* went the wrong way, but some—called upon the Lord. They walked with God.

Do you know that storm of Self-reliance? Have you been in that storm of competence and innovation that leads to doing without God?

Oh yes, you know that storm. You and I are repeatedly feeling the winds of that storm arise. We, who have nothing but what the Lord has given us, we take delight in what *we* can accomplish— and we are all too eager to take credit for it. But *some*times—we go the way of Seth, and we call upon the name of the Lord—and we give thanks to God, and we walk with God.

You know, it was that same storm of Self-reliance that grew to such intensity of pervasive wickedness that God sent the Flood to clear the earth and start afresh—with one of the descendents of Seth—Noah, who believed God, and built the ark, and praised the name of the Lord.

IV. The Storm of Pride in Power that Defies all Others.

This is a storm that comes upon us in some of our finest moments—moments of vision and forward-looking planning. It came upon the people who built the tower called Babel. Great skill they had. Marvelous technology. And organization to take on the biggest project yet!

But the motive that they had, and the goal that they set—went far beyond that shining tower! "Let us make a name for ourselves." And they consolidated their power to defy all others—maybe even God.

They were so self-assured they didn't even know they were *in* a storm—until God's judgment came upon them. Then they were confused and scattered: their communication disrupted, their organization dismantled, their unity dispersed.

Do you know this storm? Have you been fooled into thinking you were so in control of everything that you didn't even notice your pride reaching to consolidate more and more power to defy all others—maybe even God?

Oh yes, you and I know the rise of pride—the confident assumption that we can get it all together—and make a name for ourselves! And we have sometimes seen the elegant plans we laid —come to nothing—all broken up: the power we gathered—dispersed, the pride we built so high—left unfinished—a ruin, an eyesore, a reproach.

Dear friends, you and I know what it is like to be in a storm. Even when we are with Jesus, we can be in a storm.

But when we are with *Jesus*—we can have his authoritative voice to say "Peace. Be still." We can call upon his name. We can rebuke the storm. We do not have to be driven before its winds of doubt all the way to disobedience. We need not be overwhelmed by its waves of disappointment all the way to murder. We need not not be swamped by the weight of self-serving pride all the way to defiance of everyone—even God.

We can call upon the name of the Lord. We can trust in him. For though his justice expelled from the garden—his mercy promised a Savior. Though his justice haunted the guilty—his mercy gave time for repentance. Though his wrath made an end to the wicked —his mercy saved out a remnant. Though his justice scattered the defiant—his mercy gave a new time to trust him.

He who rules the storms—responds to you!

Call upon him—for he is near.

Trust him—for he cares. He cares—for you!

Amen.

C. RICHARD EVENSON
American Lutheran Church
Huron, South Dakota

I SAY TO YOU, ARISE

Sixth Sunday after Pentecost
Mark 5:21—24a and 35—43

Grief over the death of a loved one is always most difficult to bear. The death of a child brings a questioning sorrow. It is an experience which appears in our text.

Some years ago I was asked to be at a hospital in the early morning hours. I was to be with a boy and his mother. He was due for an appendectomy at 8 o'clock. Somehow I felt that the operation would go well. It did. He is now a robust young man enjoying the vigor of life.

A Mother Grieves

However, as I walked the hallway toward the door I heard a cry I will always remember. It was the anguished cry of a bereaved mother. "O God, bring my little girl back. Bring her back to me."

All the pain of her grief was in those words. Her daughter had just succumbed in death. With her were a doctor and a nurse, seeking to console her. In those moments the cause of death was not apparent. But anguish and heartache filled the room and bore into the hallway.

Going into Mark's Gospel, chapter five, we come upon a somewhat similar scene. The daughter of Jairus had just died.

Many were gathered outside, "weeping and wailing loudly." The daughter of Jairus must have been precious to more than her family. The mother is not in view. Likely she was inside beyond the reach of consolation.

Understanding Death

Someone has said when death comes close to us we understand it for the first time. In Christian faith we make further affirmations. When death comes close to us we recognize more clearly what a gift life is daily. We reflect on the resurrection theme of the Bible more deeply.

In the pursuits of life—growing up, earning a living, maintaining a home, raising a family—death may not come near us for years. The passing of acquaintances reminds us that death is around but at some distance from us personally.

Life is a gift all right but it tends to be taken for granted. Resurrection is God's known promise but it seems so far away.

Likely, that's the way it was for Jairus. Being a ruler of the

synagogue suggests both a position and responsibility. His life
was full. Running a synagogue in a country under the dominion
of Rome was not always easy. He was not isolated from the
funerals of his time. Yet death stood at a distance from him. His
family was young.

Things changed quickly for Jairus. How hard it was to pursue
his work when his daughter became ill. Concern changed into fear
for her life.

Then it happens. His daughter reaches a crisis. Little life is
left in her weak body. The color of death is on her face.

Jairus Gropes for Hope

"What can I do?" In the emotion of agony he can hear his heart
thumping within him. "What hope is there?"

"Jesus! Jesus from Nazareth of Galilee, maybe he's the answer.
I have heard how he taught at the synagogue. All who heard him
'were astonished at his teaching, for he taught them as one who
had authority, and not as the scribes.' "

"Jesus! Jesus from Nazareth of Galilee, maybe he will help
us."

Jairus had heard when "Simon's mother-in-law lay sick with a
fever . . . he came and took her by the hand and lifted her up, and
the fever left her."

"Jesus! Jesus from Nazareth of Galilee, maybe he will heal our
daughter. Why, he healed a paralytic!"

Jairus heard that friends of the paralytic lowered him on a
pallet through the roof of a tight-pressed, crowded house where
Jesus was teaching. Jesus said to the paralytic, "Rise, take up
your pallet and go home." And he did just that.

"Jesus! Jesus from Nazareth of Galilee, maybe he will hear
my plea." Word had come to Jairus that Jesus stilled the great
storm on the sea with his, "Peace! Be still!"

When Jairus heard that Jesus was coming he had to be there.
Jairus anxiously made his way through the great crowd. "So many
people. Where is he?"

"There he is. I must speak to him!"

Jairus Pleas for His Daughter

"Jairus . . . seeing him . . . fell at his feet and besought him
saying, 'my little daughter is at the point of death. Come and
lay your hands on her, so that she may be made well, and live."

"And he went with him."

Another circumstance of need interrupted their way to the

home of Jairus. Jairus must have wanted to pull him away by the arm. But Jesus healed a hemorrhaging woman and commended her for the sincerity of her faith.

In the meantime all life had left the daughter of Jairus. A sad courier faced Jairus. "Your daughter is dead. Why trouble the Teacher any further?"

He stood in shock, complete grief.

Jesus Responds

Then, somehow, he heard words, words more kind than ever he had known. "Do not fear, only believe."

They turned together and left—Jesus, Jairus, and three disciples. Soon they heard that loud grieving lament at the Jairus home.

Jesus asked, "Why do you make a tumult and weep? The child is not dead but sleeping"

How quickly human emotions can change. They now laughed at Jesus, laughed at him of whom they'd heard so much. But they knew. They knew the girl was gone.

Then Jesus ushered them all aside and those inside, out. Taking Jairus, the girl's mother, and the three disciples, he went into the child's still room. "Taking her by the hand he said to her . . . 'Little girl, I say to you, arise.' And immediately the girl got up and walked; for she was twelve years old. And immediately they were overcome with amazement. And he strictly charged them that no one should know this, and he told them to give her something to eat."

A New Dimension

The raising of Jairus' daughter offers much to us as we seek God's counsel and hope in life today. The miracle is one of many which Mark includes in his concern to tell us there is a new dimension, a new force at work in the world.

Two reactions indicate that our Lord's healing ministry revealed a new dimension. There was the astonishment of witnessing divine grace at work. His words in the synagogue yielded the grudging response, "A new teaching!"

Following the return of health to Simon's mother-in-law, "the whole city gathered" around him. When the paralytic got up, took his pallet, and carried it home "they were all amazed."

As the sea's angry waves settled into placid calm they asked, "Who then is this, that even wind and sea obey him?"

When the daughter of Jairus arose "immediately they were overcome with amazement."

So we see that indeed a new force had entered the arena of life. For those who welcomed what they had not earned, yet somehow yearned for, there was new life, joy, and peace. Mark is telling us that the promised new age has arrived. We live in that new age. We live on the brilliant side of history. The light of love that makes life whole has come into the world. Its rays shine into every facet of life.

We Are Near Jairus

Our lives are both different and similar to those people in Mark's Gospel. We live in a distinctly different culture. We would be lost in their environment, and they in ours. However, human love for family, for children, is with us now as then. We stand at varying stations in life and have responsibilities to meet. Life is full. It is not always easy. We are much like Jairus.

God's disclosure of a new force, a new dimension came upon Jairus. In this we stand very near to him.

Another way whereby we are like Jairus and the people of his time is in the hope of the life to come. It is disclosed, prefigured in Jesus raising the daughter of Jairus. The Bible says that God gives us life and, after a time, receives it back to himself again.

Live Life Now and in the Future

The raising of the daughter of Jairus demonstrates a power beyond that of man. It is a forerunner of Easter. However, it says something important about the present time.

Jesus from Nazareth of Galilee reveals the love that God has for people in the present. This life counts. He loved Jairus as a brother. He loved his family. He knew their questioning sorrow over the girl's death. We remember, too, how he had felt about the brother of Mary, who washed his feet and dried them with her hair, and her sister, Martha. He became caught up on their sorrow upon the death of Lazarus. "Jesus wept." Then Lazarus was raised after four days in his grave.

These raisings to life recounted in the New Testament do prefigure the first Easter and the Easter to come. But they do also affirm life in this world and God's love for people in their present existence.

To live life whole, which is an abiding concern in Mark's Gospel, suggests that we live our lives in this world responsibly—in thought, word, and deed—to God, to others, and to the world. But life here is not the whole story. Life will be lived in keeping with God's timetable as we keep in our minds and souls his unfathomable love and resurrection power for ourselves and our loved ones.

However you view the raising of the daughter of Jairus, there the account is in Mark's Gospel. Think of it as you will.

"Little girl, I say to you, arise."

GILES C. EKOLA
Calvary Lutheran Church
Alexandria, Minnesota

THE WOUNDED HEALER

Seventh Sunday after Pentecost
Mark 6:1-6

Rediscovery

As Christians we often question our own relevance and effectiveness. Several months ago when I was feeling sorry for myself because things weren't going as they should, a friend gave me a very captivating and helpful book. It was entitled *The Wounded Healer*. Henri Nouwen, psychologist-priest, describes the ministering Christian as a wounded healer who must look after his own wounds but at the same time be prepared to heal the wounds of others. In the image of Christian vocation as wounded healer I rediscovered myself and my ministry. And I said, "yes, that's me—a wounded healer." Something became very clear, "The minister is called to recognize the sufferings of his time in his own heart and make that recognition the starting point of his service. Whether he tries to enter into a dislocated world, relate to a convulsive generation, or speak to a dying man his service will not be perceived as authentic unless it comes from a heart wounded by the suffering about which he speaks" (Henri Nouwen, *The Wounded Healer*, Doubleday, 1972, p. xiv). Who am I? Wounded healer! Who are you? Wounded healer! Who is Christ? Wounded Healer!

Jesus the Healer

Today's Gospel pictures Jesus as the Wounded Healer. The Gospel, and the other lessons as well, present a realistic view of the church and her mission, implying that within her earthly fellowship there may still be those who are far away from genuine faith in Christ, implying that the outward witness of the gospel is no pushover. The surprising indictment of Jesus can be repeated in our time, even among us, "he marveled because of their unbelief."

Surprising Unbelief

The experience of Jesus with his own people was good training for his disciples. They were to learn that faith in Christ is not dependent upon any external relationship except an openness to his love. They were to discover that there is no point at which the unbeliever is forced, even by the evidence of healing miracles, to confess Jesus as Savior and Lord. They were to see that the presence of faith was always surprising, likewise the presence of unbelief. They had seen the faith of Jairus who asked Jesus to heal his daughter and the devotion of the woman with the flow of blood who wished just to touch his garment (Mark 5), and now they were witnesses to the surprising unbelief of those who knew Jesus best.

The Carpenter

Why didn't they believe? It seems that their unbelief had to do not with Jesus' deity but with his humanity. They recognized the overwhelming significance of what he said and did. "Where did this man get all this? What is the wisdom given to him? What mighty works are wrought by his hands?" But they could not understand how this astonishing wisdom and power could be invested in someone so human. "Is not this the carpenter, the son of Mary and brother of James and Joses and Judas and Simon, and are not his sisters here with us?" They took offense at him. They couldn't accept that all the hopes and dreams of God's promises would dwell in someone like themselves, an ordinary man, a carpenter from Nazareth, with brothers and sisters who were at times all too human. They couldn't cope with the mystery of the incarnation—God manifested in the flesh (1 Timothy 3:16). And as Jesus marveled at the faith of some (Matt. 15:28), so he marveled at the unbelief of others.

Unbelievable Incarnation

Although there are many reasons for unbelief, the way God is and chooses to make himself known is still the biggest stumbling block to faith today. Man would rather think of God as other worldly, glorious, spectacular. Then things would really get done! But instead he takes on our humanity. He comes as a little baby.

He grows up in a poor family. He makes friends with common people. He takes it patiently when he is ridiculed and hurt. He submits to death on a cross. He comes not like flashing lightning to strike us down, but like humble love to absorb the world's hurts and build us up.

It is hard to believe in a God like that because by nature we would rather be ruled by law than by love. But God is love! That's the way it is! It is unbelievable, humanly speaking, that the Creator on whose freedom and power we all depend, should allow himself to be bound in swaddling clothes, pushed around by people, nailed to a cross—all for us! But that's what happened when according to John's Gospel "the Word was made flesh and dwelt among us" (John 1:14). Helmut Thielicke puts it like this, "Christ is not a figure from the twilight world of magic" (*How to Believe Again*, Fortress, 1970, p. 58). His incarnation makes him real, approachable. To that Christ one must dare to come even at the risk of being disappointed!

The Church's Humanity

Like Christ, so the church! If the church is the body of Christ, then its human side will invoke disappointment, doubt, and rejection. Why is she so frail, so weak, so human? Her very nature becomes an offense to those within and without. Because they do not know that the church follows the likeness of Jesus, they lose heart, they lose face, they lose faith. How can the church be like that? How can I believe anymore if the church is that way? She is all too human! That's what happens when we forget the humanity of Christ. We also forget the humanity of the church. Through her humanity, often a stumbling block to faith, great things happen. But to have faith is to accept humanity and to see beyond it.

Not to Let God Be God

But why this unbelief? St. Paul tells it like it is, "The word of the cross is folly to those who are perishing, but to us who are being saved, it is the power of God. . . . For Jews demand signs and Greeks preach wisdom, but we preach Christ crucified, a stumbling block to Jews and folly to Gentiles" (1 Cor. 1:22-24). Beneath the inability and unwillingness to accept Christ, the incarnation and the cross, is man's sinful nature, his rebellion against God, his refusal to let God be God, his desire to mold God into his image—all leading to God's judgment (Old Testament Lesson). But who cares? How difficult then the task of the healer!

The Tragedy of Unbelief

Jesus marveled because of their unbelief. The tragedy of unbelief is that the healer can't heal, few mighty works are done. St. Mark says that Jesus "could do no mighty work there, except he laid his hands upon a few sick people and healed them." This means that people did not give Jesus the opportunity to help. They did not trust him. They passed him by. And because of that mighty works were left undone, especially the most mighty work of all, the bestowal of genuine faith. Faith is God's mightiest work. Without faith it is impossible to please God (Heb. 11:6).

Unbelief is bad enough because it shuts out the love of God, the benefit of Christ's atonement and the power of the Holy Spirit. It makes salvation impossible and leads to eternal death (Rom. 6:23). But what is more, it keeps Christ from doing his mighty works in the world. There is a profound relationship between unbelief and the ineffectiveness of the church. Why the lack of missionary zeal? Why the lack of concern for the poor and needy? Why the lack of spirituality? It is unbelief. We need more faith. The New Testament records that the paralyzed man was forgiven and healed because of the faith of those who brought him to Jesus (Luke 5:17-26). They trusted him. They depended on him. Faith opens the door to Christ so he can work in us and through us. Where there is faith mighty works will be done. This is the promise that God gives.

In His Steps

Like Jesus and his disciples we have a ministry in the church and in the world. The church is God's mission to the whole world. We affirm "that God has sent us. We are not asked to choose whether we will be sent. If we are in the Church, then we have been sent." (*Mission Affirmations,* LC-MS). Therefore let us move forward and not be discouraged. Jesus gave his disciples a very realistic view of their mission. He inspired them by continuing his ministry in spite of apparent defeat. Rejected by his own people, St. Mark reports that he still "went about among villages teaching." He went as the Wounded Healer. And then he sent out his disciples two by two to do the same. (6:7) They had learned from Jesus that their task would not be easy, but they had also seen that faith would spring up in surprising places.

Let's Be Positive

In a delightful and stimulating book *What's This I Hear About Our Church?* Charles Mueller reminds us to have a more positive view of things. While noting that a recent study showed that 40 percent of all Lutherans seem to misunderstand the gospel, he looks on the bright side, "Isn't it fantastic that 60 percent rejoice in the truth of what God has done for us in Christ Jesus and seem to know how to flesh out our conviction in their daily life?" (*What's This I Hear About Our Church?*, Augsburg 1974 p. 15.) He suggests we spend too much time with nagging negatives and not enough effort actively seeking the positive.

Miracle of Faith

As Christians we can have a positive spirit because we see the miracle of faith in ourselves and others. Every congregation of God's people gathered around Word and Sacrament in order to do God's mission is a miracle. Every member of the church is a miracle. Every spark of faith is a miracle. Luther explains it like this, "I believe that I cannot by my own understanding or effort believe in Jesus Christ my Lord or come to him. But the Holy Spirit has called me through the Gospel, enlightened me with his gifts, and sanctified and kept me in the true faith. In the same way he calls, gathers, enlightens and sanctifies the whole Christian Church on earth and keeps it united with Jesus Christ in the one true faith" (*Explanation to Third Article*). In the words of Martin Franzman, "Men do not hatch out faith by brooding hotly over the eggs of their experience. Faith is a divine work in us" *Follow Me*, Concordia, 1961 p. 138). There are miracles of faith all around us. So we can be positive in our understanding of the church and her mission because God is alive and doing great things.

Servant Not Above His Master

To be a genuine Christian and a faithful witness to the gospel in our day, however, is no easy thing. Neither should we expect it to be. There is need for us to renounce our success mentality and recognize that our Lord was despised and rejected by men and that the servant is not above his Master. We will have our share of defeat. Even in the church not everyone will be responsive to the call of the gospel. Some will say no. Others will say yes, and never do what they promised. Even people close to you will care little about the quality of their faith. They will postpone repentance and commitment to a more convenient season. The words of Jesus hit home, "A prophet is not without honor except in his own country." "A door opens to me. I go in and am faced with a hundred closed doors" (*The Wounded Healer*, p. xiii). And when this happens to you, you will tear your heart out and say "Why, why, why!"

They Say Thank You

A poem by a member of ours reflects the heart-rending experience of the church's role as wounded healer today.

> We offer new life
> And they say
> Thank you for calling
> But the boys and their father go flying and . . .
> Thank you for asking
> But we have a farm and . . .
> Thank you for the news
> But our boat must be sanded—or dry docked—
> or painted—or raced—or traded and . . .
> Thank you for reminding
> But you know our children are swimmers or
> In soccer, football, tumbling, tennis, ballet,
> judo, scouting and piano, baseball, volleyball,
> pottery and . . .
> *Will they ever see Lord?* That you are more than
> another idol for idle time—Will they ever put You
> first on their schedule?
> *Will you be waiting Lord?* When they can't fly and
> sail and ride and sleep and be busy, busy, busy
> When all they want is to live.

Wounds That Heal

We need to remember the worth of our healing ministry. We are giving something that the world cannot give. We give, as St. Paul says, "what no eye has seen, nor ear heard, nor the heart of man conceived, what God has prepared for those who love him" (1 Cor. 2:9). Again, "what we preach is not ourselves, but Jesus Christ as Word, with ourselves as your servants for Jesus' sake" (2 Cor. 4:5). And even if in our healing mission we are wounded, our witness not accepted and our love not rewarded, there is great blessing in that. The thorn in the flesh, the insults, the hardships, the persecutions experienced by St. Paul (Epistle lesson) were to keep him humble and to let Christ be Christ. It was God's way of preventing his ministry from being an ego trip but keeping it authentically Christian. When he was weakest, then Christ was strongest. That's what God promised when he said, "My grace is sufficient for you for my strength is made perfect in weakness" (2 Cor. 12:9).

God allows us to be wounded in our healing ministry, and in this way authenticates us as faithful witnesses, like the prophets, like Christ. "If they hear or refuse to hear, they will know there has been a prophet among them" (Old Testament Lesson). In the wounded spirit we find the opening to effective sharing of the faith. Listen to this, "No one can help anyone without becoming involved, without entering with his whole person into the painful situation, without taking the risk of becoming hurt, wounded or even destroyed. . . . Who can take away suffering without entering it?" (*The Wounded Healer*, p. 72).

Let Faith Be Renewed

Therefore let us faithfully continue in our ministry to one another and to the world. Let us do those things that strengthen faith in ourselves and in others. Let us share the Word of God and his caring love. And let this be the primary purpose of our lives. When faith is renewed, then God's power is unleashed. Mighty works are done!

Pushing in the Right Direction

There's a story about an old farmer who was seeking the most modern means—contour plowing, crop rotation, terracing of land, drainage of low spots, fertilization, to bring farmed land back into full productivity. One day his pastor asked him, "Alex, why are you doing all this. After all you're not a kid any more and you're not going to be around many more years, and you're certainly going to have to give up farming soon." The man replied, "Pastor, someday, I want my grandsons to know that even though I didn't finish the job, I was pushing in the right direction" (*Emphasis*, C.S.S., January 1975 p. 4). And that's the surprising power of the Spirit that drives us on in our mission as we wait for God's purpose to unfold.

Send Us

The Prayer for the Day puts it well: "Father of glory, Father of love, only from you can come peace. Fill our hearts with joy in your promises of salvation and send us as peacemakers and witnesses to your promises."

LESTER E. ZEITLER
Pilgrim Lutheran Church
Bethesda, Maryland

DISCIPLESHIP MEANS INVOLVEMENT

Eighth Sunday after Pentecost

Mark 6:7-13

"I just didn't want to get involved."

It was said by a man who stood by while a girl was brutally stabbed to death by some maniac. There were over thirty other people who witnessed the same ugly tragedy. They also did nothing. They didn't want to get involved.

What would we have done had we been there? Have we acted much differently in the wake of the horrendous tragedies that transpire in the world about us? How about our politically oppressed brothers and sisters in our own country, the starving masses of Africa and Asia, even the people battered by pressures and beset by problems in the house or apartment next to us? Have we demonstrated any genuine concern for anybody outside of our own family in the last forty-eight hours? during the last week?

Some of us have. Others of us copped out; we just didn't want to get involved. We cozy up to the kind of Christianity that is equated with plush pews and pious prayers—even if it involves an offering-plate and a weekly pledge. The kind that was manifested by Jesus Christ and later reflected in his disciples is something that we can hardly comprehend. We tend to ignore it or relegate it to another age and bypass it.

They Were Commanded to Go

Our Lord's first disciples, in our gospel lesson for today as well as in the months to follow, were in the process of learning that discipleship means involvement. "And he called to him the twelve, and began to send them out two by two. . . ." The same Jesus that gave the invitation to "come unto me and I will give you rest" would ultimately give the command to "go into all the world and preach the gospel." They were destined to discover what Christianity today needs to rediscover—that the come-unto-me-and-I-will-give-you-rest type of God-person relationship must resolve into a go-into-all-the-world-and-preach-the-gospel kind of Christianity. We are called to "come" unto Christ, to "rest" in his grace-giving love. The same Christ who called us to "come" commands us to "go." Both coming to him and going out for him are essential to the total Christian experience. Thus discipleship means involvement.

They Were Expected to Minister

Jesus sent his disciples out—thrusting them into the secular world—for the purpose of ministering to their brothers and sisters in the human family. They were to involve themselves in the lives and affairs of people about them. Their ultimate purpose was to promote the purposes of God's kingdom, to oppose the forces of evil and introduce the rebellious hearts of men and women to God and his claim upon their lives. They were not, as we are often tempted to do, to remain forever within the warm and comforting confines of Christian fellowship or to be perpetually enriched and exhilarated by the tangible presence of their Lord. There was a job to be done and their Master and Teacher was testing their mettle and their motivation in ejecting them, like lambs amongst wolves, into a hostile world to learn how to do it.

Jesus first primed his following few with some instructions. For *one* thing, they were instructed to travel light. "He charged them to take nothing for their journey except a staff." On this particular excursion they were to take off without money or extra clothes. Perhaps this was necessary to teach them that their dependence was not to be focused upon the trinkets of this world or the rewards of this life. They had received their Lord's injunction and authority—and this was sufficient. They had no axe to grind, no budget to raise, no allotment to fulfill. They were to go—and to minister to people with whom they came into contact.

Second, they were to concentrate upon relationships rather than statistics. "Where you enter a house, stay there until you leave the place." This would most certainly mean relating, conversing, sharing, enjoying, being concerned about and caring for the people they visited. In other words, they were not to peddle the gospel as a news-boy peddles newspapers, but to promote the gospel and the life it offers through their loving concern for these people and through the sharing of their lives with them.

Maybe our Lord was telling his disciples that they were not to judge their success by statistics nor ascertain their value as disciples and ministers by the positive responses to their efforts to serve others. Their task was to minister—not to manipulate, to love—not to frighten or coerce people to turn to God. There may be conversions as a result of their ministry—and this because they were endowed with the authority and power of God—but the failures would probably outnumber the successes. Conversions, and perhaps these disciples did not learn this until much later, are the responsibility of the Holy Spirit. Their responsibility was loving proclamation. If their ministry is, indeed, loving and the response to such is scorn or indifference, the fault is not theirs—nor the responsibility.

Third, according to their Lord's instructions, their ministry was to be a ministry to the whole person, not just to his or her soul. Their concern was to include the physical well-being of the people as well as their spiritual needs. They were expected to proclaim the Word of God—his love for these people and their need of his forgiving love—but they were also to demonstrate God's saving love by ministering to their tangible needs. "And they cast out many demons, and anointed with oil many that were sick and healed them." These disciples were subsequently to discover that their divinely impelled, self-sacrificing love to meet people at the point of their immediate and obvious needs often spoke more loudly and convincingly concerning God's love than anything they would say.

We Are All Ministers

Our gospel lesson may well be taken as a stern reminder that Christianity without discipleship is Christianity without Christ; that everyone of us who follows Jesus Christ is called to be a minister. We may not have the power to exorcise or heal as did these disciples, but we have the gifts we need to do the job we are called to do. The task we are called upon and sent into our world to carry out certainly includes proclamation. It would mean, as well, that we stand up with the oppressed against their oppressors—the exorcising of the "demons" of life and culture that rob people of their self-respect and dignity, their rights and opportunities—even the demons of pride and prejudice and ignorance and apathy within us that serve to inhibit the claim of minorities to the same rights and opportunities that we enjoy. The disciples of our gospel lesson were to preach repentance, but their ministry was not confined to preaching. Nor is ours. Most of the people that we are called to minister to have heard the message of God's judgment and love, law and grace. To them our divinely impelled, self-sacrificing love to meet these people at the point of their immediate and obvious needs may speak more loudly and convincingly concerning God's love than anything that we can say.

The Meaning of Ministry

Our Lord and Master is, in this very hour, commissioning and commanding us to *go* and to *minister.* This means to go in scorn of consequences, without gimmicks or ulterior motives, trusting the Holy Spirit to overcome our fears and absolve our frustrations, to go in obedience to Jesus Christ, to serve him in and through our sacrificial service to all people.

It means that we *relate*, to reach people where they are, to communicate with them in the language they understand. It means to become *involved* with their hopes and needs, their strains and stresses, their human and physical and material concerns. It means that we *listen* to their joys and their agonies. We may not condone or always identify, but we must listen. It means to *love*—even at the risk of getting our faces slapped or our knuckles rapped. If they cannot receive our love, we must find someone who will, but we must risk loving others. It means that we must *respond* to the immediate needs of people in our path even when we know that their greater need is something they may not comprehend or even anticipate. It means that we *share*—our lives and our possessions—even when there are no visible returns. It means that we must *proclaim* the power and presence of God through Christ.

This is the ultimate purpose of our day-by-day mission even though it may take a very long time before we can arrive at this point with many of the people with whom we deal. And for some of us with some of the people we relate to, we may have prepared the way for the preaching of others. We have often been told that, as Christians, our primary task is to lead men to Christ. We don't convert people; that must be done by the Spirit of God. It is our task to draw men and women to Christ, and this is generally done through the phases of going, relating, involvement, listening, loving, responding to human need, sharing ourselves, and eventually to proclaim the redeeming power of God. And this is as much the task of each one of us as it was of those disciples that Jesus thrust forth so long ago.

Discipleship means involvement. Our Lord set the pace, and he expects his disciples to keep it. He identified himself with the agonies of mankind. He became involved in their crying needs. He even went so far as to bear the consequences of their sins. To be a disciple of Jesus means that we who accept him as our Savior must also accept him as our Lord and Master. To follow him means that we continue in his course for our lives. We are expected not simply to criticize the distortions of humanity from the pews and pulpits of our sanctuaries, but to become involved in the blood and tears, the sorrows and sufferings of God's creatures in suburb and ghetto, town and country, wherever they may be found.

Because we are involved in the sickness of our world, we must, as disciples of Christ, become involved in its cure. It will not be convenient or comfortable. It might even be dangerous. We may have to risk our reputations, wealth, status in society, our very lives in this involvement. But discipleship means involvement. As our Lord suffered on our behalf, we are expected to suffer on behalf of others, to lose our lives in service to them only to truly find our lives anew in the incomparable joy of being priests and servants of the living and eternal God.

LESLIE F. BRANDT
Trinity Lutheran Church
Victorville, California

THE REACH OF GOD'S CONCERN

Ninth Sunday after Pentecost
Mark 6:30-44

However one interprets the feeding of the five thousand—a miracle story included in all the gospels—the heart of the story is this: God is concerned with individuals as whole persons in his world. Nothing in Jesus' teaching or in his life-style suggests that the *material* is evil and the *spiritual* good. There is no dualism in biblical Christianity.

One can almost hear people in that crowd in that lonely place asking themselves and each other, "Who is Jesus? Where does he come from? What is he trying to do?" He came from God, indeed, God was in him reaching out to restore humanity to wholeness. He was the culmination of all God's action in human history. God, having created the universe and having fashioned human beings in his own image, looked on his whole creation, declared it good and rejoiced in it. When his highest creation, human beings, went astray through willful misuse of their freedom, he did not wash his hands of them. Instead, he set out to persuade them to come home for his sake and for their own. Toward that end, he revealed his purpose and person in the elemental give and take of human experience. In the fullness of time, he came as a human person, born of human parents and subject to human disciplines, human authorities, and the dominion of the secular state. The incarnation makes clear God's continuing concern for the whole person. The Word became flesh—touched with all our infirmities.

Christianity, as William Temple was fond of saying, is far-and-away the most materialistic of all the world religions. It does not treat human beings as "souls with ears." It accepts them as embodied spirits. Jesus spoke five times more often about our attitudes toward earthly goods and personal possessions than about prayer. The cup of cold water in his name was, he said, an act of stewardship. The Good Samaritan was, he said, the only real steward on the Jericho road that day "a certain man" fell among thieves. Jesus was earthy, enjoying God's creation; he was not a monastic. Except for a year or so in public ministry, he worked at a trade to support himself and his mother; he was not a mendicant. His appreciation of good food and wine prompted his enemies to call him "a wine-bibber and a gluttonous man"; he was not an ascetic. Jesus urged his followers to seek *first* the kingdom of heaven; he did not call them to poverty or celibacy or fasting as ends in themselves. Some followers would be poor and others unmarried and some would fast as a matter of choice or circumstance, but Jesus set down none of these as universal requirements for discipleship. His concern for diseased and broken bodies, for tired and hungry bodies matched his concern for disturbed minds and wayward wills and shattered spirits. The Christian God ministers to the whole person. Essentially, that is the truth revealed in the story of the feeding of the five thousand.

From the beginning, this particular miracle story, like the parables, has been interpreted in various ways. It has meant different things to the church at different times. For Mark, it was one of Jesus' "mighty works." In the Middle Ages when food was scarce the story was interpreted allegorically. Albert Schweitzer viewed it as an "eschatological sacrament." Mark's interpretation is more straight-forward: the people were hungry and Jesus saw to it that they were fed. Some interpreters see Jesus directly multiplying the quantity of food. Others argue that he motivated people to share the food which they were keeping for themselves. Either way, one side of the miracle is that the Christian God cares for the whole person. The other side is that the disciples *obeyed* Jesus' directive, they did God's will.

A Necessary Rest

First, this account does show clearly God's concern for the whole person. When the disciples, proud of themselves, returned eagerly to tell Jesus what they had done in many places, Jesus brought them back to earth with a practical plea: "Come with me," he said, "to an uninhabited place where we can be quiet; you need a rest." So God reminds us of what we forget so easily: we are *embodied* spirits. We are not supermen. We are not angels. We are mortal, finite, self-willed. It is true, of course, that strong spirits, relying on God's grace, can function creatively in spite of faltering bodies. But the hard reality is that we *are* mortals; we are not "souls with ears." God knows that human beings need physical rest and renewal. When Elijah, convinced that God had forsaken him, panicked, God advised Elijah to get a hot meal, go to bed, and get a good night's sleep! When Jesus lived in a human body he needed physical rest. He wearied often. Forced to carry his cross, he stumbled under the weight of it. He thirsted there on Calvary, like any battle-field victim bleeding to death.

There is a steady call on us Christians to press toward the prize of the high calling of God in Christ Jesus. There are seasons when failure to strain every nerve is to fail God. But God's call is answered by creatures; mortals do the straining. And no mortal can "put on immortality" in this world.

No matter how contributory one's work is, there are seasons when physical rest is more necessary than prayer. Jesus' counsel is needed: "Come with me to a quiet place; rest your tired body, your over-taxed mind, your raw nerves." The God who cares for the whole person calls us to care properly for ourselves and for others in the same way. Nonetheless, there are seasons when one cannot get away from Christian ministry even to get needed rest. The crowds were waiting for Jesus and his men when they got to their intended place of rest. So Jesus, always the good shepherd, taught them. As the day wore on, the disciples expressed concern for the people's need for food and wanted to send them home.

Go and See!

Jesus said to his disciples: "How many loaves have you? Go and see." Here, too, Jesus' focus is on the mundane, not the eschatological. As in other seasons and in other places, the disciples had not only forgotten that God's resources were available; they had also forgotten to consider their own resources. So, quite at their wit's end, they snapped out at their best friend: "What do you want us to do; go out and spend two hundred denarii for bread? You know we don't have that kind of money. Send these people back to their homes for their own sakes as well as ours."

Most of us get peevish with God when life gets out of hand, when situations overwhelm us, when pressing tasks over-match our immediate resources. Our defenses go up; our self-pity surfaces; our excuses pour out. And we have it out with God, then and there on our terms—like children given to temper tantrums.

But the Christian God, while he never gives up on us, declines to coddle us. He loves us wherever we are and in whatever condition we are. He loves us in spite of ourselves; and he loves us as we are for what we can become in him. His love is neither deserved nor earned; it is given. But God's love does not splatter gelatinously into history lacking a skeletal structure. His love is structured by his righteousness, his holiness. He does not traffic in cheap grace; his promises are conditioned by his demands. Anyone can claim God's grace but *only* on God's recreative terms. Any prodigal can go home, but *only* on the Father's terms. Jesus put it succinctly: "If you love me, do my commandments."

"How much food is on hand? Go and see." Investigate! Don't theorize. Act! To the lepers Jesus said, "Go. . . ." and as they went they were healed. Declining to debate his teaching, Jesus urged persons to test it for themselves.

There is a clear directive here for us. Our complex society paralyzes itself by too much analysis and too little bold action. Causes are talked to death. Church people rarely try Christianity in their homes, let alone in the market-place. The Good Samaritan acted. The cup of cold water, given, is a deed. "Love is a verb." So is stewardship. Directly and indirectly, God's resources are more than adequate in any historical situation and for every human need. But each person in his freedom must claim those resources and administer them in the interests of persons-in-society. Jesus enjoins us to hunger after righteousness; he also teaches us to seek daily bread.

"What food is available? Go and see." Churlishly, I suspect, they went. And that is the other side of the miracle—they obeyed! It is always miraculous—out of the ordinary, against the human bent—when any person deliberately dethrones his ego, conquers his willfulness, and does what God asks, testing God's promises for himself. That was the miracle in Gethsemane: a human being wrestled against his own will and decided freely to do God's will. That miracle, accomplished in the human spirit, is the ground for more dramatic miracles: feeding the multitude, healing the blind, raising Lazarus from the dead, breaking the shackles of his own death.

Do What You Can

You know the rest of the story. There was more than enough food for the thousands of people, and what was left over filled twelve baskets.

Human resources—which come from God's creative hand—linked with his immediate, unexpected gifts always turn out to be more than enough for everyone. And the miracle is always two-fold: the individual is motivated to go beyond his expectations; God over-matches the deepest needs of the whole person.

One is tempted to speak expansively about the bounty of God's material and spiritual gifts. But this particular biblical passage

206

makes a concrete thrust: a multitude of people had physical needs, and God was interested, and God was able to meet those needs through the obedience of his disciples.

Presently, specialists tell us that 40 percent of the citizens in the United States are ill-fed, poorly housed, inadequately clothed. Specialists tell us that the United States, having 6 percent of the world's population, consumes 40 percent of the world's natural resources. The first statistic linked with the second suggests dramatically that the comfortable in our nation are getting more comfortable while the hard-pressed are becoming impoverished. Specialists tell us that ten thousand people die daily by starvation on this planet amply stocked by God's creative hand. Now, some scientists and politicians and business leaders are suggesting that these conditions cannot be altered, that the poor will be with us always, that there is an emerging Fourth World so poor and so over-populated that people in it must be left to die while the rest of the world—like survivors in an overcrowded lifeboat who have pushed several of their own into the sea—save themselves. "Triage," caring for some and deliberately letting others die, is creeping into the thinking of some people in North America and Europe. So the real miracle, if it comes, will not be the feeding of the hungry; it will be the radical change in life-style of the minority on two well-stocked continents which will make that feeding possible.

Jesus' word to his disciples is a clear word to you and me. Don't lose yourself in the complexity of hunger and over-population and competing sovereign states. Go and do what you can; what comes of it lies with God. One fire lights another. The double miracle occurs when human beings, disposed to look out for themselves, decide to do what God commands and thereby provide the channels for God's resources to be matched with human needs.

WALLACE E. FISHER
Trinity Lutheran Church
Lancaster, Pennsylvania

WORKING MIRACLES WITH FOOD
Tenth Sunday after Pentecost
John 6:1-15

There's a homely little homily in that old chestnut about the pastor who preached the same sermon for several Sundays. When asked why he did it, he told the man that when the people started to do what God was asking them to do in this sermon, he would begin on the next.

For the second Sunday in a row, you have heard the same gospel lesson, the feeding of the five thousand, a miracle by our Lord. Last Sunday, it was taken from the Gospel according to Mark, and this week from the Gospel according to John. It seems to be rather clear by this time that the church, which established this lectionary, had a need to concern itself with bread.

If that is not clear, then listen to the eighth chapter of Mark, where a parallel is drawn between a situation very similar to the one before us and a point we would like to make in conclusion. Mark says:

> Why are you talking about having no bread? Do you not yet understand? Have you no perception? Are your minds closed? Have you eyes that do not see, ears that do not hear? Or do you not remember when I broke the five loaves among the five thousand, how many baskets full of scraps did you collect?
> They answered, "Twelve."
> And when I broke the seven loaves for the four thousand, how many loaves of scraps did you collect?
> And they answered, "seven."
> Then he said to them, "are you still without perception?"

On the battle fronts of war, the wounded are divided into three groupings—

—those who will survive without medical help

—those who will survive with medical help

—those who will probably not survive even with medical attention.

Available medical supplies are then assigned accordingly. The sorting process that determines how resources are to be allocated is called *triage*.

The Process of Triage

It seems to me that the disciples in our text came pretty close to discovering this process when Jesus asked them, "Where can we buy some bread for these people to eat?" We are told that he asked the question to test them, since he knew exactly what he was going to do. Then Philip responded with the amount of money they had, to date, in the common treasury, "two hundred Denarii would only buy enough to give them a small piece each." If that were the only solution available for the problem of world hunger, not enough money but to buy every man, woman and child just a small piece of bread, what would you do? Would you agree to the process of *triage?*

There are some leaders of the world who honestly feel this to be the problem as well as the only solution. They argue that more damage has been created in our world by those nations who have tried to do something for hungry people, than if they had allowed those hungry people to starve in the first place. If they were not part of the problem today, there might just be enough food for all to eat. In fact, the masters of *triage* would lead us to believe that the world would be much better off if it would predetermine that a certain number of people should be put in the category "those who will probably not survive with help" and that they be allowed to die. It's kind of shocking, but it has a little bit more than just the sound of truth to it.

When you consider that most of the population growth comes from the underdeveloped nations of the world, you begin to consider this aspect of *triage* more seriously. When you note how deeply engrained in the thinking of people is the need to have children, and if you're poor, to have *more* children to support you, then you give a second thought. When you tie these facts together with the ways in which "enlightened" countries, as they move up the scale to better living, begin to better understand the need for zero population growth, then you almost become certain that you are on the right track. *But how can you justify letting people starve to death when you have more than you need?*

The Ethics of Triage

TIME magazine (November 11, 1974), concluding its special report on the world food crisis, explains its support of *triage:*

> In the West, there is increasing talk of triage. . . . If the U.S. decided that the grant would simply go down the drain as a mere palliative because the recipient country was doing little to improve its food distribution or start a population control program, no help would be sent. This may be a brutal policy, but it is perhaps the only kind that can have long range impact. A triage approach could also demand political concessions. . . . Washington may feel no obligation to help countries that consistently and strongly oppose it. As Earl Butz told TIME: Food is a weapon. It is now one of the principal tools in our negotiating kit.

Food, however, is not the weapon. The denial of food—famine —is the weapon. At the present time it becomes obvious that our

Christian concern is motivated by an ethics of affluence more than by our practice of sharing and self-denial. Only surplus food is available. Under the terms of Public Law 480, the Food for Peace Program, food is given away only after all our commercial commitments are met. And there are indications that even these paltry amounts do not find their way into the areas of most need. During the Viet Nam war, nearly half of our food aid went to South Viet Nam and Cambodia. And in the crisis that developed in Chile when Salvadore Allende was still the head of state, three days before the coup d'etat, the United States turned down a request to sell wheat to Chile for cash. Yet one month after the government changed hands, the U.S. granted the new regime eight times the total credit ever offered to Allende to purchase wheat.

Such facts and figures, however, are never very convincing. They only seem to establish the fact that a little knowledge about hunger problems brings forth words of sympathy, while more knowledge tends to be boring. It certainly does not motivate Christ's people to establish a higher priority for hunger problems on a value scale already filled with, maybe even cluttered with, far too many "top" priority items. The process of triage only enables us to get out from under a pressing need for more and more brothers and sisters who populate this globe with us. For if we discover that the known need of today does not motivate us to share what we have with them now, then to reduce the need by assigning certain groups of people to die because their prognosis is not good would only alleviate the pressure we might feel to share what we have and more equitably divide the grain and food resources that are available gifts of God to the world in which we live.

"Where can we buy some bread for these people to eat?" is a needed question we all must face. But to face it, we dare not remove names from the list of the needy rolls of this world. Maybe we need to expose our lives to hunger exercises that will enable us to grasp the problem more effectively. Maybe if we knew what it meant to be hungry, rather than how to dispose of hungry people, we would feel the compassion which our Lord taught us to feel. Then we would take what we have and try to multiply it till all were fed.

It is very rational to decide that there are limits to the possibilities of food production. It is not at all difficult to see the connection between food production and population development. And our experience teaches us more and more that to grow more food, we will not necessarily reduce hunger, we may instead produce more people. More food leads to more population, not to less average hunger. We also discover that our ethical decisions in these matters are not tied so much to Christian concern for others as they are to our technology and our economics. What then becomes evident is the tight interrelationship between technology, economics, and politics *and* our ethical, moral, and religious principles. To prevent starvation and death in parts of the world we have never seen, important ethical, moral, and religious decisions have to be made in the world we do know, and have seen because we live there.

An Exercise in Hunger

In our text, the good news comes in the discovery that one possibility, namely, the using of a common treasury, was not the only solution. Another was also available. "There is a lad here who has five barley loaves and two fish; but what are they among so many?" It makes you stop for just a second and pose the question of which is easier, to multiply money or food? Would the multiplied money have been harder to give away than the multiplied food? Maybe the real question is what prompted the small boy to share. When we could know that answer, we might be on our way to eradicating hunger.

To be able to translate facts and figures about hunger into feelings, opinions, attitudes, and motivational impulses that do something about hunger is the task for a culture and a church that knows somewhere in this world there is starvation, but looks around at stores full of food, and sits down to tables groaning with excess. Our problem is not that we are about to starve, but that we need to diet, to reduce our intake. To accomplish that task as well as to experience hunger as most persons in the Third World are forced to do is an exercise for those willing to commit themselves.

There are various plans that have been suggested by various authors. As we gather this month for our congregational meeting to make plans for the Fall, I shall propose one that has caught my imagination. It will be done, I hope, by a group of families during the month of November in preparation for Thanksgiving Day. All are welcome to participate, the more the better. Four points will be stressed for those who share

1. The living on a hunger budget for two weeks

2. Written notes about your feelings and experiences

3. Sharing in group discussion several times during the two week experience and at the end

4. After the experience, to plan to make a gift which we will agree upon before we start.

(CHRISTIAN CENTURY, January 22, 1975,
"An Exercise in Hunger")

These points will be made more specific to those who will commit themselves in the congregational meeting and the weeks that lie ahead. It is our hope that you will give this your serious consideration, and will be willing to work with us to improve the plan, so that it opens us up to the possibility of becoming sensitive to hunger needs and to the implementation of those needs in a program of action.

At the end of the miracle, our Lord had sensitized people to the possibility of having a resident miracle worker in their midst. They began to dream about what this could mean for them. It didn't take long before they came to the conclusion that such a person would be mighty helpful, and they could even conceive of his being their king.

Now do you remember the reference we made to Mark's Gospel near the beginning of the sermon? The disciples in that situation were again wrapped up in a concern about bread. So Jesus reminded them of this miracle before us as well as the feeding of another group of people. "Are you not without perception?" He asked them, "Do you not understand? Do you not remember?" For us, who live lives filled with good things, like bread and wine, there is much to remember, and there is understanding. Should not our concern be this morning for those who have little to remember and therefore do not understand?

ROBERT L. GRIESSE
Lutheran Church of the Newtons
Newton Centre, Massachusetts

SHARE THE BREAD OF LIFE

Eleventh Sunday after Pentecost
John 6:24-35

Bread. The necessity of life. The symbol of the essential. Several vignettes come to mind with the thought of bread: A child, with a mischievous grin, saying to his grandpa, "Man does not live by bread alone—he needs peanut butter, too." A family meal during which an impatient child says too loudly, "Pass the bread!"

Hungry people along the roads to Ethiopia pleading, "Bread, mister, please. Because of Jesus Christ!" A community of persons celebrating a beautiful experience of trust and support breaking and sharing bread together, remembering that Jesus promised to be present in and with the breaking of bread.

Another vignette: Berke's face beamed with pride as Tadessa took a big knife and began to cut the two-foot diameter Ethiopian bread. The huge, thick loaf had been specially prepared and baked over the outdoor fire. We had been invited to share the holiday with Berke and Tadessa in their humble mud and straw home. These friends who are so often receivers were now joyed to be able to share . . . to give. The loaf was cut and shared, big hunks passed around to our whole family. With the 10 or 12 children that gathered at the open door they also shared big hunks of the coarse, brown delicious bread. Each child, in traditional Ethiopian style, received the gift in both hands with a grateful bow of the head. It was a beautiful scene . . . of bread . . . of sharing and of persons together. Jesus' words re-echo from cathedral pulpit to simple home: I am the bread of life!

Everyone Wants a Free Biscuit

Just preceding the account in today's gospel text from John in which Jesus declares, "I am the bread of life," there had been the feeding of the 5000. What a picnic that had been! Thousands fed on the sunny hillside. It was a great event. The people wanted more. Who wouldn't? Everyone wants a free picnic . . . something for nothing.

Just like the people in Moses' time who were murmuring in the wilderness the people followed Jesus to see more signs, more wonders, more tricks. But Jesus wouldn't be a trick-doer. He wouldn't let them make him king. He wouldn't be followed because of a few extraordinary things he did. Rather he called attention to the essence of his life . . . to his being. He was the bringer of the "way." So strongly and so directly was his own life tuned in to the Father that he was able to say, "I *am* the bread . . . I *am* the light . . . I *am* the resurrection."

He was critical of those who came seeking him because of their narrow vision. He tried to challenge them to see more than just a free picnic . . . to see the miracles of sharing. But, now—just as then—many have ignored his invitation to "follow me" into the joys and sorrows of the world and are still back on the hillside waiting for another course! He didn't call—and doesn't call—people just to have good feelings about being on his "picnic" or playing in his "team" but he calls to discipleship in the world.

Feeding 5000 . . . and Just a Few

There were thousands fed on that hillside. Some even followed him to the other side of the lake. Jesus also met and talked with them . . . with the few. He answered their questions and challenged their narrow vision. The needs of thousands were met and also the needs of a few.

There are times when we're called to respond to the *thousands*. There is need for bread for the thousands of hungry in the world. We need Lutheran World Relief, "Bread for the World," "Food for Peace," and other programs to help us break bread with all our brothers and sisters. But there is also a screaming and crying need for changes of lifestyle among the world's satisfied . . . to waste less, to consume less, to use less, to desire less. If that could happen for the sake of the brothers and sisters of the world . . . that would surely be a miracle of 5000-feeding dimensions!

There are also times when we're called to respond to the *few*, to those close to our own lives. Bread, the symbol of what is necessary, is sought by the few, too. The caring, sharing relationship is one way of giving the true bread which does not perish.

How Can You Eat Spiritual Bread?

It's an easy temptation to spiritualize the life right out of this gospel text. We can stretch it so thin that its meaning evaporates. Does it mean that we should just sit back and enjoy our faith in the spiritual Jesus, the bread of life? Did Jesus mean we should not be concerned for the hungry when he said do not be concerned with "bread that perishes?" Can we rightly interpret his words "believe in me. . . . I am the true bread" as an invitation away from the needs of the brothers and sisters, away from involvement with the needs of the world? Of course not. To do so would be waiting for another free picnic.

The immediate situation which prompted Jesus' words was the narrow vision of the people. They were people who could only see their own desire for another free picnic. That kind of narrow self-centeredness is the "bread that perishes." Jesus wanted to open their lives to new visions, new hopes, new horizons. He wanted to disclose a kind of bread that does not perish . . . but which truly fills and satisfies the deep hungers of the human person.

He turned the focus on himself, but not for personal gain. He just turned down kingship back on the other side of the lake. No, he turned their thoughts beyond their destroying preoccupation with their own comforts.

That's where this gospel ought to speak pointedly to those of us of the so-called "soulless western world." Where do we find our soul again? Is it not by heeding Jesus' call to the *way*? Does not that *way* call us to our brothers and sisters? We find ourselves again by seeking the *true bread* . . . and by *being* the *true bread* for one another.

Who, Really, Is the Bread of Life?

Jesus said it. He said, *"I* am." I believe that if we could have continued the conversation he would have also given us the challenge, *"You* are the bread of life," just as he also said to his followers, *"You* are the light of the world."

In the community of persons we *are* the true bread for one another. We have power to provide what is necessary, what is essential for satisfying living. We give the love which builds persons and binds lives together. We share the joys of living. We give forgiveness when someone has wronged us. We provide encouragement for the discouraged. We pick up the fallen. We lighten the brooding sorrowing spirit. We *are* the *true bread* for one another! Our lives have been given the power of that aliveness. We can, by our Creator's gift, be a generating, power-giving source of life for the brother or sister. We can be for the other what is *essential*.

We are the body of Christ in this time and in this place. It is right to say in the family of man, we are the bread of life for one another! Our brother, Jesus, has showed us the way!

To one who feels no trust, your trust can be his bread. To one who feels no worth, the encouragement that lifts and builds can be his bread. To one who feels downtrodden, an act of caring can be his bread. To one who sorrows, a genuine suffering-with can be his bread. To one who has a vision, a goal, an ideal, to have someone to share it with can be his bread. To one who feels deep guilt, forgiveness can be his bread.

Jesus lived that kind of life for others! He said, "I am the bread," and also, "When I was hungry you gave me to eat."

To one who is physically hungry, bread given in a way that does not demean, is true bread. To those in need of food, bread may be seed, or technical skill, or knowledge. *True bread* comes in many forms and shapes and sounds and textures. To those hungry for affection, you may be their bread of life!

What a privilege to be able to say . . . and to experience . . . "I am the bread of life for you . . . you are the bread of life for me." Jesus leads us into that community, that fellowship of persons, in which all are our brothers and sisters. What a joy to share that reality . . . that discovery . . . with Jesus our brother.

Yes, I remember that simple Ethiopian home. I remember the bread received by grubby little hands. I remember the thankful expressions on the little faces. And I remember the caring look of love on the faces of the givers.

I know a little better what Jesus meant when he said, "I am the bread of life!"

DANIEL W. OLSON
Mekane Yesus Church
Addis Ababa, Ethiopia

DECISION'S GREAT DIVIDE

Twelfth Sunday after Pentecost
John 6:41-51

Ultimately, it is either belief or unbelief. Finally, the option is commitment or rejection concerning the eternal matters of the soul. These alternatives toward the kingdom of God are precise. They are not matters of indifference or unconcern. The question that rings through the ages for humankind is: who shall have dominion over a person's eternal destiny? To what master or to what cause shall there be commitment? This is the inescapable either-or before each of us.

Running through the high country of western North America is a unique geographical phenomenon. It is one of the earth's great watersheds, the Continental Divide. In northwestern New Mexico it runs like a curving spine through the plateaus with the scrub junipers on its back. In the Rocky Mountains it might fashion the course of the highest crest of a mountain range. If a large drop of rain should fall precisely on a sharp rock at the apex of the Continental Divide, that drop would be cut in two. Half of it would roll down the eastern slopes into the Arkansas River and ultimately to the Gulf of Mexico. The other half would flow down the western slopes of the Rockies, down the long Colorado to the Gulf of California, eventually to unite with the waters of the Pacific. That majestic ridge in the Rockies divides the waters of a continent.

The sixth chapter of John is a mighty watershed. The Gospel suddenly takes on a new course. Our Lord begins to pin down the decision and the division that faced the people in his day. This chapter changes the course of attitudes. The crowds at Capernaum had to make a choice of ultimate allegiance, a choice that none of us can ever escape either, even today.

The Setting of the Drama

Because the sixth chapter of John is the Gospel's turning point, the text John 6:41-51 cannot be considered apart from its context; else, it is a gem lost from its unique setting. This chapter begins with the feeding of the five thousand. Our Lord fed the hungry because he had compassion on them. Compassion was inherent in our Lord's shepherding mission upon earth; neither dare this virtue be absent from the heart of today's Christian. As the fact of world hunger at home and abroad sharply thrusts itself into our consciousness, compassion must address itself to the grave and immediate needs. There is no time to offer complaint about causes of hunger or to rationalize about over-population or to deplore the lack of family planning or to blame irresponsibility and indolence. Hunger is there; it reaches out its bony fingers toward us. Hope, pleading pitiably from sunken eyes, is an imploring gaze we can't forget.

Our Lord even had concern for economy and ecology at the feeding of the five thousand. He directed his disciples to gather up the broken fragments after the meal. Twelve baskets full were gathered. Then Jesus began to notice an uneasy stirring in the throng. He surmised their intent at once. They would soon come to him in large numbers to make him king "by force." It was not the Lord's plan at all to be made a king, least of all by force. Nor was he interested in being the kind of king they had in mind.

Accordingly, he directed the disciples to go to the boats immediately and to ship out across Lake Galilee. Our Lord himself slipped away and departed into a mountain alone. It had been his custom often to go into a mountain or into the wilderness to escape the press of crowds in order that he might meditate, think, pray, and rest.

In the morning members of the previous night's crowd had crossed the sea also, or had gone around it, to face Jesus again. They were ready again to make him king. They could not understand in their wildest imagination why a man would not desire to be king. Wouldn't a person's soul soar to the stars to consider the prospect of being declared king? Wouldn't he receive adulation like that of a conquering Caesar returning home with slaves and spoils, and the acclaim of multitudes? Jesus had conquered the devil in the great temptation concerning rulership and allegiance and kingdoms. Now it seemed the evil one wasn't through with him yet. Here, now, a crowd was assembling to crown him king at once, but a king of this world, a bread king, a king of games and military conquests.

A New Bread

Now, then, the text speaks. Jesus speaks to crowds concerning a totally different kind of bread. Here is the apex of the Great Divide. The text is the key to the chapter's turning point. Instead of providing breakfast for the crowd, as he had provided supper the night before, he now says, "I am the bread of life," and further, "I am the bread which came down from heaven."

The multitude is puzzled. It cannot understand what he is trying to say. How could such words satisfy morning hunger? Isn't the greatest need that a person should have daily bread? Then, why such talk as "For this is the will of my Father that everyone who sees the Son and believes in him shall have eternal life"? But the vast majority yearn for baker's bread and material possessions. Our Lord's emphasis on the bread of life does not ignore the fourth petition of the Lord's Prayer. But there are also six other petitions. Intrigued by the material things the average crowd, even today, desires to hear proclaimed a demagoguery equivalent to three cars in every garage, a boat, a trailer, plenty of gas for all engines, and a steak on every griddle!

It was the time of the Passover. Pilgrims were even crowding Galilee. Most likely some of the leaders of the synagogues had asked for expert help from Jerusalem to deal with this pesky prophet who was planning to visit Galilee. At least, the Jerusalem wise men should be able to debate with this upstart, thought the local religionists. And sure enough, "the Jews," a term describing the church officials and scholars of that day, "murmured." They complained, they griped, because Jesus said something about coming down from heaven and something about his "Father" having sent him! But they knew this Jesus, they declared. They even knew his folks. This was none other than Jesus the son of Joseph the carpenter. What in the world was he trying to tell them with his strange figures of speech?

Suddenly, now, they were confronted with a total redirection of their thinking. Again, our Lord speaks of a greater need than earthly bread. He says this remarkable thing: "Truly, truly I say to you, he who believes has eternal life. I am the bread of life." This seemed like utter nonsense to many who listened.

There was a feeling abroad at that time that the Exodus miracle of manna from heaven would occur all over again; a new miracle was now due. So our Lord mentions that the fathers in the desert who ate manna from heaven died. But, if his hearers would believe in him, Jesus Christ, there would be the glory of an eternity. Is it any wonder, then, that some of the group turned away in disgust? The crowd at Capernaum could not fully understand what Christ meant. Some were confused. Others were offended. Those who remained with him continued in faith until dimness and confusion gradually faded.

After this, too, occurred one of the saddest occasions in our Lord's ministry for, "After this many of his disciples drew back and no longer went about with him." Thereupon Jesus turned to his immediate disciples and said, "Will you also go away?"

The turnabout had now been made. The program of the new kingdom had now been launched. A new life and destiny lay ahead. Who could follow now?

The Decision to Yield

What a difference it makes in our lives when we have made the great choice. Shall we choose the idols of the market place or will the Lord God finally choose us, after we have adopted a willingness to be chosen? Incidentally, let's keep quite clear how this process of total allegiance toward our Lord Christ develops. In our text Jesus said: "No one can come to me unless the Father who sent me draws him." The so-called decision, then, to "accept" Christ is rather a ceasing to resist the call of the Holy Spirit. This allows the path to be clear for the Holy Spirit to lead us to our Lord. Of course, often we hesitate to ascribe full validity of this process to any one other than ourselves, including God. Our ego wants to say *we* decide; we are the true decision-makers for our salvation; we provide our justification! True, we have the power to reject, and the power to cease resisting, so that the Father in heaven may "draw" us to himself.

Briefly, there are still those who would declare that this text establishes the first foundation for the sacrament of the Holy Supper. This is declared because our Lord said, "If anyone eats of this bread, he will live forever; and the bread which I shall give for the life of the world is my flesh." But Christ was not yet ready to introduce the sacrament. This was not the time nor the occasion for it. He here referred to his death upon the cross, his coming sacrifice. The institution of the Holy Supper was to come later in the presence of his disciples only. Many ancient fathers and the reformers concurred that this passage has no reference to the Holy Communion.

Helmut Thielicke writes that change from determination by the flesh to determination by the spirit is, in fact, a most radical change in lordship. Paul, writing in Galatians, says "Walk by the spirit and the desires of the spirit are against the flesh." The true spirit reveals and destroys the identity with the past. Men experiencing a new birth discover that a change of dominion takes place. Faust, meeting Mephistopheles, exclaims:

Faust: Who are you, then?

Mephisto: Part of that power which would the evil ever do, and ever does to the good.

Faust: A riddle! Say what it implies!

Mephisto: I am the spirit that denies.

So we are back again to developing our priorities, either deepening the priority away from our Lord or adopting a new lordship, a new discipleship with our Lord.

The Finality of Vital Decisions

Great decisions in life are precise and final. When the air raid sirens of a city sounded in World War II, the citizens pondered their possible fate as they entered the shelters. In a short while they may no longer be alive. Their places of business would either be standing or destroyed. Their homes and their families would still be intact or gone. Life was reduced to sharply defined eithers. So also in the highly important areas of our lives the watershed choices are simple but final. For example, one is either a citizen of this land or he is not. A person is either married or he is single. Before the bar of justice he is either guilty or innocent. He is either a child of God or he is not. Our Lord said, "He who does not gather with me scatters." "He who is not with me is against me." "He that loves son or daughter more than me, father or mother more than me is not worthy of me." It's just that simple in matters that matter ultimately. It's either God or idolatry.

There is finally belief or unbelief, allegiance or rebellion. Having changed our loyalties the mighty walk in faith begins. A new road looms; a new destiny beckons. It is the faith of absolute involvement with the way of Christ, the way of absolute commitment, of total allegiance, of complete discipleship. The sixth chapter of John is the outline of the turning point. And ever and always that haunting question burns into our souls, "Will you, too, go away?"

WALTER M. WICK, President
Indiana-Kentucky Synod
Lutheran Church in America

JESUS IS OUR BREAD

Thirteenth Sunday after Pentecost
John 6:51-58

Jesus Is Our Bread—Delicious!

It was quite interesting to watch a young girl select a treat from a variety of good things offered to her. There were cookies of various sizes and shapes, there were candies, and even a dish of chocolate chip ice cream. Each one irresistible, right?

Wrong.

She passed them all by with hardly any trouble.

Can you guess what she chose?

It was a piece of buttered bread. Can you imagine?

Actually her choice wasn't as strange as it might seem, because that bread was so fresh that it still was warm, soft, and fragrant.

Hmm, delicious; truly delicious.

This event brings to mind a quotation of Luther. He once said that God is an oven of love. That's quite a comparison, isn't it? It would be useful and encouraging if we could recall it the next time we're in a kitchen waiting to see and to bite into a slice of freshly baked bread, or cake. It would also be helpful if we could recall this comparison the next time we're down, depressed, or even angry over our thoughts about God and the role he seems to be playing in our world and in our lives. It might help us to rise above the moment and to return to a better frame of mind so that we're able again to love him, desire him, and worship him as we ought.

Our text suggests a slight addition to Luther's statement; it's just a few words; and I'm confident that he would welcome them. God is an oven of love, and Jesus is the bread he offers.

Jesus Is Our Bread—Strength for Our Wilderness

God has offered good bread to his people before.

We can't help but recall the manna which God sent from heaven onto his covenant people as they journeyed through the wilderness of Sinai. To recall what that manna did for them and meant for them is to have a description of what Jesus offers us today.

Jesus, however, is better nourishment and strength than that manna because the strength in him is more enduring than that found in the manna. The ancient manna maintained its strength for one day, or for two at the most, then it failed, it spoiled.

The strengthening power of our Lord Jesus has unlimited staying power. His ability to nourish us remains fresh forever. Even though the benefits which Jesus offer us are exposed to spoiling forces similar to those forces of the wilderness; for instance, the force of our fiery passion, the force of our parched spirits, the force of our rough pride, the force of our endless range of ignorance, he remains fresh, unspoiled, and strong.

Jesus Is Our Bread—Divine Purity for Us

The Old Testament people were quite familiar with another bread and it too offers a helpful insight into Jesus and his benefits. This bread was the bread used in the Feast of the Unleavened Bread. Once each year, at the time of the barley harvest, seven days were set apart for a time during which all the yeast-filled baked goods must be removed from everyone's home. It was a time for using only unleavened bread.

All this might seem meaningless to us, but it had great meaning for those people. They had been taught to see in yeast an example of their sin, and the sin of the world. The obvious power of the yeast mysteriously at work in the dough was an illustration of the way Satan and all his forces are able to work in us and in our world, invisibly but with awesome results.

I recall hearing a group of ladies talk about the experience of making bread from its basic ingredients. There was an elderly lady in the group and someone asked her if she used to work with yeast and dough. "Only once!" was her quick reply. "It was such a mess I never tried it again," she added. Everyone laughed. But, everyone understood her experience. The leaven at work does indeed symbolize the inner, invisible force of our sin. So it was a great relief to have it removed completely from the home—at least for seven days.

But those seven days were not breadless days. They were not days of fasting and abstaining. Rather they were days of feasting and sharing the good taste of that crispy unleavened bread! This yeastless bread was also powerfully symbolic. It represented the absence of sin and Satan and the perfect presence of God and all of his virtue. It was as though they were eating pure bread, bread from heaven, instead of the ordinary sin-filled bread of every day. This unleavened bread was itself pure, and it seemed to have in it a mysterious power that was able to purify everyone who would eat of it.

All of this worked together beautifully to make the week of the unleavened bread a gloriously rewarding week for all those who took part in it with awareness and with faith.

When we are offered Jesus as we hear the good news of his life, death, and resurrection, which he accomplished for our benefit, in

222

our place, to remove from us the power of our sin and the sin of the world, we are being offered the unleavened bread of God's grace and truth.

When we receive the good message of Jesus' grace and love with faith and trust we receive the pure and purifying presence of God in our lives. Thus sin and Satan are expelled and we are made holy and right with God and with one another.

All this goodness—this unleavened life—is not given to us for a limited time, but is given to us without any limits whatsoever.

Jesus Is Our Bread—It's Dangerous to Pass Him By

God's message for us today is not only the good news of the gracious nourishment which our Lord Jesus provides for us, but it is also a bold and blunt warning to us not to miss out or to misuse these benefits. No one could read the three lessons for today without feeling as though he had heard stern words of warning. So, in keeping with these lessons, let us draw to its close this sermon by speaking as clearly as possible to one another those same words of warning.

As in the Old Testament lesson's spirit, let us plead for *wise* use of the good food which God has prepared for us and offers to us. The only wise thing for us to do is to take that food into our lives and consume it totally.

The Epistle pleads also for *wise* use of God's spiritual food.

In the Gospel also, the last words which we hear from our Lord Jesus are words of warning about the danger resulting from foolish use of God's food. He calls to mind the tragic end for all those ancient people of the wilderness who, even though they received heavenly manna, nevertheless died along the way. They wasted the bread of God that could have sustained them all the way into the Promised Land. Tragically, foolishly, they died in the desert.

So let us all hear and heed these words of warning. Let us resolve to be as wise and discriminating as the young girl I described for you at the beginning of this sermon, the one who preferred freshly baked bread over all of those confections. Let us wisely select Jesus rather than spiritual candy and ice cream and cookies that are filled with power to weaken and even power to kill us. Let us derive our spiritual nourishment from Jesus, the living bread. "He who eats this bread will live for ever."

DANIEL W. FUELLING
The Lutheran Church of the Resurrection
St. Paul, Minnesota

TO WHOM SHALL WE GO?

Fourteenth Sunday after Pentecost
John 6:60-69

One of the phrases born in the private chambers of the Nixon Administration was—"Will it sell in Peoria?" This question was asked repeatedly on various occasions by the coterie of presidential advisors. When new and innovative policies were being examined, when action was planned that would affect the nation at large, when decisions were made or votes were to be taken— then the question was put—"Will it sell in Peoria?"

Even a casual examination of that query makes the reason clear. The geographical location of Peoria nudges up against the center of these United States. Also—the nature of the populace of that Illinois city probably represents a cross section of the attitudes and opinions of Americans at large. Thus if it sold in Peoria there was a pretty good chance that it would also sell in Los Angeles, Topeka, Hanover and Columbus. Peoria served as a symbolic gauge to measure the political winds and take the temperature of the national waters.

This political method is neither new nor sinister. Compromise is the name of the game. But when and where to compromise lest the political winds become a tornado—the national waters a boiling cauldron—that is the fine line for the discerning politician. "Will it sell in Peoria?"

Proclamation

Our Lord seemed oblivious to these kinds of mechanizations. He had just unleashed a bolt of jagged lightning upon his hearers. "Truly, truly, I say to you, unless you eat the flesh of the Son of man and drink his blood, you have no life in you; he who eats my flesh and drinks my blood has eternal life, and I will raise him up at the last day. For my flesh is food indeed, and my blood is drink indeed. He who eats my flesh and drinks my blood abides in me, and I in him." No matter how you read those words—no matter what kind of interpretation you draw from them—no matter how much symbolism you believe they are freighted with—those words are impossible. They stick in your craw. If our Lord had calculated a way of losing friends and antagonizing people he found it.

Response

He could have chosen better words. He could have fashioned an easier saying. He could have used more acceptable prose. But—he didn't. He well knew what effect these words would have on his audience. There were few things more abhorrent to a Jew than to eat the blood of an animal. Blood was life—life given by God. Yet here Jesus speaks of eating the flesh and drinking the blood of a man—created in the image of God. It was enough to make the belly of any son or daughter of Abraham churn and wretch. The effect those words produced seemed calculated, if not a foregone conclusion. "Many of his disciples, when they heard it, said, 'This is a hard saying; who can listen to it?' . . . After this many of his disciples drew back and no longer went about with him." Drew back indeed! The writer John seems a master of understatement. It wouldn't have sold in Bethlehem, Jericho or Jerusalem.

And Jesus' response?—a simple question addressed to the twelve disciples—"Will you also go away?" No apologies, no easy explanations, no convoluted interpretations common to religious discourse. He permits the words to stand even though they repel —even though they actively drive people from him. The mystery deepens.

If you would go about today telling people to eat the flesh and drink the blood of the Son of man—I dare say you would raise nary a hackle. You could not even stir a good discussion. The best you could hope for would be to be consigned to the fringes of the religiously queer—a fanatic if not a lunatic. It's not really one of the big issues confronting our world in this hour. It doesn't even grate on our sensitivities. The words were spoken on another day —in a distant era—to a different situation. But do we escape the offense of the gospel simply by relegating these words and others like them to antiquity? Has not the church in this day been intimidated by the charges hurled at her by the world and in defense succumbed to the—"Will it sell in Peoria?" syndrome.

Our Efforts

Let me illustrate. In recent times the church has been the target of a host of "slings and arrows" hurled at her by people both within and outside her ranks. Sentiments such as the following have been echoed. The church is more concerned about Bible verses than daily headlines. The church worries more about eternity than it does about time. The church has a lot to say about heaven and hell but is too often silent concerning the living accommodations of this earth. The church worries more about saving immaculate souls than about redeeming broken bodies. Her creeds are ancient—her music and hymns suffer from age—her organization is creaky and ineffectual. In short the church is irrelevant to today's world.

Whether or not the charges are true seems to make little or no difference. Many people believe it is so and dismiss the church out of hand as a relic from the past that is tolerated but no longer taken seriously. Then there follows the nervous response of churchmen who are stung by the charges. They scurry about in an effort to—"make it sell in Peoria." Get the preacher out of his chancel dancing costume and robe him in psychedelic. Turn off the organ and plug in the guitars and amplifiers. Throw out the liturgy—that impossible remnant from the past—and let each person do his own thing. Shut the preacher's garrulous mouth and cease his endless pulpit droning. Let's have dialog and discussion. Stop this morbid confession stuff and bring in the hilarity of celebration. All this and more in the fevered expectation that now—"it will sell in Peoria." Now we will turn people on lest they turn us off.

The Offense

These are only peripheral issues. But do they not betray our uneasiness with what really lies at the heart of the matter: this Jesus, this barn-born babe, this crucified failure, this resurrected Lord? Ultimately we are confronted by something—someone— that is offensive to us, that is absurd, that defies our every logic and invites only the children and the childlike. No matter how you cut it, the gospel always offends, always. We are ill at ease with its contradictions and mystery and strive to reduce the faith to simple and often maudlin categories. As if the whole gamut of biblical witness readily lends itself to an advertising slogan.

Let's face it! The gospel always confronts us with mystery, with miracle, with the majesty of God. We cannot lay hold of it with our intellects, our emotions, our much striving. God comes to us when he will, where we are, in ways that he chooses. As our Lord said to his disciples—"This is why I told you that no one can come to me unless it is granted him by the Father." To make it sell in Peoria"—to make the faith palatable is an exercise in futility.

Hang In There

Our Lord concluded with a single question directed to his disciples—"Will you also go away?" Peter replied with another question and his confession—"Lord, to whom shall we go? You have the words of eternal life; and we have believed and come to know that you are the Holy One of God." That is a response not exactly brimming with certainty and conviction. It seems to be more an admission that there are no other options to exercise at the moment. Until something better comes along they are going to hang in there as best they can and see what happens. And is that not also our proper stance? To hang in there with this Jesus —with whatever trust we can muster?

Our myriad questions still unanswered. Our many doubts still unresolved. The gospel still an offense to this world. We can never penetrate the majesty of God. We are at all times condemned to brief glimmers and flashes—experiencing but not explaining— glimpsing but not perceiving. Then to the drudgery and joy—the monotony and mystery of it all. Somehow trying to make do with this Jew from Nazareth—"his flesh and his blood"—a handful of parables and a pocketful of miracles. To realize that at all times before God and his Christ we can worship—stand in awe—bow in reverence—obey and trust. Never can we explain.

We had best never rest easy with our labels and categories— our pigeon-holes and casual explanations. We must always know ourselves as worshipers before the living God. The one who worships is the one who waits. He waits upon God and his Christ that he might be open to his gracious visitation. For—"to whom shall we go?"

KEITH KREBS
Emmanuel Lutheran Church
Walla Walla, Washington

TRADITIONS IN CONFLICT

Fifteenth Sunday after Pentecost
Mark 7:1-8, 14-15, 21-23

Amidst the social and political turmoil of our world, I wonder whether you have noticed how much of it is related to religious traditions in conflict? Do you remember the struggle between the Buddhists and Roman Catholics in Vietnam? Then, too, as our American involvement in the Vietnam conflict escalated, there were some people in this country who regarded it as a "holy" war to curtail the spread of communism and other people refused to participate in it at all on moral and religious grounds. The wounds caused by these traditions in conflict still are not healed. Turn to the Middle East and again you will find religious traditions in conflict, fanning the flames of hostile discontent. Add to the list Northern Ireland. One Irish man expressed his exasperation, "Would to God that we were all atheists so that we might live together as Christians."

But come closer to home, to our own community and our own congregation. Some people think that their neighbors who belong to that other denomination are much too lax morally. And then there are some in our own congregation who don't read the Bible literally and who don't seem really to have the Spirit. You know who I mean?

Religious traditions in conflict, a sign of our times, even though we are living supposedly in a secular, non-religious era! It might be helpful for us, therefore, to reckon with the conflict Jesus had with a religious tradition of his day. Oh, the issue at stake sounds so remote and primitive. And it is. But, then, the story of this century, *our* century, is not all that enlightened, is it?

The Tradition of Mr. Clean

The scribes and Pharisees ask Jesus bluntly, "Why do your disciples not live according to the tradition of the elders, but eat with hands defiled?" So, what's the issue? That's simple enough— "How to be Mr. Clean?" And the prescription? You're right, the tradition of the elders.

But we're making light of a tradition that had a considerable amount of religious earnestness in it—maybe too much earnestness, but that's no novelty for us either. The distinctions between clean and unclean were sharply drawn. There were, for example, unclean people: a woman after childbirth, a leper, an outsider—(a hippie maybe)—or an unchurched person. Moreover, you became unclean if you had any contact with these people, which was difficult to avoid in the market place—just as it would be difficult to avoid in the loop of Chicago. So, practically everybody was contaminated indirectly through contact with unclean people.

To compensate for this unfortunate state of affairs, the tradition of the elders prescribed ways for unclean people to become Mr. Clean or Mrs. Clean or Ms. Clean so that they could approach almighty God properly. The tradition contained rules and regulations for washing one's hands, e.g. dipping one's fingers into water and then pointing them upwards, followed by rinsing from the wrists as the fingers were pointed downwards. And all of this, not in the interest of hygenic purity, but in the interest of ceremonial cleanness, i.e., in the interest of approaching God purely and honestly, not as a dirty bum but as a clean person.

And the Conflict

Jesus found himself in conflict with this venerable tradition for two reasons. One had to do with his refusal to divide God's good world into clean and unclean, sacred and profane. This very division lies behind the ancient practice of ceremonial cleansing and Jesus calls that tradition into question in a radical way. He contends that it leads to hypocrisy, enabling people to honor God with their lips but not with their hearts.

The reason for this duplicity is quite simple: the tradition provides a structure of division and alienation among people. It offers criteria for separating the good guys from the bad guys, the clean people from the unclean people, the okay people from the not okay people. You see, it's part of that devilish game of separating, evaluating, and condemning people.

And the dynamic which makes it all work is our deep-seated desire to justify ourselves, to prove by means of our traditions that while others are not okay, we are fundamentally okay, while others are in error, we have the truth, while others need to change their habits and ideas, we are okay just as we are.

Jesus calls this attitude hypocrisy. It involves the effort to honor God with our lips and have him confirm our values, prejudices, ideas and business but not allow him to alter and change our hearts so that we might become his people in the world. We want God to say Amen to us, not us say Amen to him. That is hypocrisy.

We need, therefore, to examine carefully our own cherished traditions. In what sense are they a structure of alienation, causing us to separate ourselves from others as well as judging and condemning other people? How are we using our traditions to make us special in comparison with others? Make no mistake about it: religious traditions that separate and alienate people are not the work of God in our midst. They are the work of the devil. The final demonstration of the fact that Jesus abolished the difference between the sacred area and the profane area, the good guys and the bad guys is his freedom to keep company with sinners. Yes, company with sinners, outcasts, despised and rejected people who were living outside the scope of a religious tradition.

Related to Jesus' concern to abolish the difference between the sacred and the profane was his radical understanding of the nature of defilement. He put it succinctly, "There is nothing outside a man which by going into him can defile him; but the things which come out of a man are what defile him." In other words, Jesus seems to be saying, that *things* cannot be either clean or unclean in any significant way. Only *persons* can be defiled depending on what comes out of their heart, their very being. This was his radical new doctrine. With one simple pronouncement Jesus declared that uncleanness has nothing to do with what a person takes into his or her body (despite what the W.C.T.U.

claims) and everything to do with what comes out of his or her heart.

And the list he gives of what comes out of a heart is enough to make one shudder with horror. Listen to it again, "evil thought, fornication, theft, murder, adultery, coveting, wickedness, deceit, licentiousness, envy, slander, pride, foolishness. All these evil things come from within, and they defile a person." Evil is not out there in some thing or some group of people. It is in us. And until one locates evil properly and honestly, there isn't much chance of doing battle against it. We begin to do battle against it only as we acknowledge and confess the venom we have in ourselves, the destructive impulses and instincts which twist and pervert relationships and life. Only as we face our own heart of darkness will we have the honesty and humility to be open and accepting of others.

But this is not quite the end of the matter. For God knows not only the worst about us but also the best. Think of those flickering impulses of love and understanding and compassion which you and I have had toward other people even though we didn't express them very well. Think of the decent motives, the high motives we have had to serve other people in our community, motives that probably became twisted in the process. Think of that inner core of sensitivity and courage and hope which we sometimes keep hidden from others. You see, there is, in each of us, the makings of a better person than you and I have ever known.

And only that tradition which releases the makings of a better person is valid and true. For the sake of that tradition Jesus contended with other traditions which twisted and crushed human potentials. That is why in the company of Jesus, men and women have found coming to birth in them something stronger and kinder and gladder than they could ever have known without knowing him. That's the final test of a godly tradition.

MORRIS J. NIEDENTHAL
Lutheran School of Theology
Chicago, Illinois

THE SIGN LANGUAGE OF GOD

Sixteenth Sunday after Pentecost
Mark 7:31-37

It is easy to miss the "secondary characters" in the gospel because we watch Jesus so much. Not that we should overlook Jesus by any means, but the fact is we can see what he is doing with new eyes when we watch him through the persons of those with whom he is interacting. Our text today is a case in point.

Seeing Jesus Through the Eyes of the Deaf Man

Put yourself into this man's shoes. We know very little of him, but we could conjecture that he is a Gentile since he lives in the region of the "Ten Towns," an area inhabited chiefly by Romans and Greeks. If he is a Gentile, the very term "Messiah" would likely not have meant much to him even if he could have heard what was happening. Since he had an "impediment of speech" we might further conjecture that he could hear at one time since hearing is quite important to learning to speak whether with or without an impediment. With a little guesswork, then, we can flesh out a little information about the man.

But imagine his situation in the moment we find him in the text. You will know how isolated from society a deaf person is if you have ever known such a person. He can see what is happening, but he does not know how to react since he cannot interpret what he sees without the faculty of hearing.

So he is pushed and pulled by a crowd of people rushing to see Jesus whom they have heard is passing through the area. But the deaf man doesn't know what all the pushing and pulling means, and since he possibly doesn't know who Jesus is because of a Gentile background he must have been thoroughly bewildered. His gutteral attempts at asking what was happening would likely have been overlooked in the rush. Caught up in a crushing crowd dragging him to see Jesus as they hoped to see a miracle, he was a pawn in their hands and he must have been frightened out of his wits. His uncertainty must have struck Jesus almost immediately. Fear and consternation deep in his heart must have surfaced in signs that drew Jesus' compassion forth at once.

So Jesus immediately tries to restore some semblance of calm in his heart. Jesus takes him away from the crowd that was pushing and pulling at him. He draws him gently to the side and restrains the crowd. He speaks as best he can to the man with a form of sign language. Putting his fingers into the man's ears, he indicates an awareness of the man's problems. Spitting with his own mouth and then touching the tongue of the man indicates further recognition that the problem is also tied to his speech. One can almost sense the man settling down and starting to nod his head. His eyes light up with an awareness that somebody knows how deeply this trouble afflicts him, how totally it cuts him off from the society of men.

Then a look to the heavens tells him that only God can help him in such sore troubles as he carries. A deep sigh indicates a concerned prayer to the Father who alone could help.

Then . . . a sudden word broke the silence of his ears: "Ephphatha!" "Be opened!" For the first time in years (perhaps ever!) sound broke into his being. The man must have almost leapt out of his skin. Now the miracle is multiplied, for without hearing language had become almost foreign to him. Even if he could write he didn't know the sounds, but we are told that he immediately spoke clearly as a coordinate to the hearing clearly! Can you imagine how the man felt?

A whole new world opened to him! He was returned to human society. His isolation was broken with this gift. It was new life!

What did the man perceive in Jesus? Whether he knew him by prior reputation or not, he must surely now have seen a man who brought the earliest dawning of the kingdom of God into his life. We sense this idea astir throughout the crowd as they say, "All that he does, he does well. He even makes the deaf hear and the dumb speak!" Whether they wittingly or unwittingly said it in this way, they were speaking words filled with Old Testament imagery. We hear it in today's Old Testament reading where the coming of the kingdom is announced as the time when blind men's eyes shall be opened and the ears of the deaf will be unstopped. They saw in Jesus the coming of the king . . . and if the king is at hand, can the kingdom be far behind?

Seeing the Deaf Man Through the Eyes of Jesus

Let us backtrack a bit to see the love and compassion of Jesus as he takes this bewildered, frightened man and prepares him for the coming of the kingdom. Separating him from the crowd was an act of compassion itself, for Jesus saw how he was pressed and afraid. Jesus' deep respect for the man's situation was accompanied by a care and compassion for his needs. But the first need was to relieve the immediate problem of his fears generated by a crowd he did not understand.

Once settled, the man could read Jesus' sign language through which Jesus shows the direction of this miracle . . . and all of his miracles, for that matter. Jesus wants above all to show *himself* to the man through what he does for the man.

What, then, is the miracle pointing to? Power is, of course, inherent in a miracle (it hardly being possible to perform a miracle without power). But power is really a side issue in Jesus' miracles. Behind and underneath the miracles of Jesus was the sign language of God—the pointing beyond this present world to that kingdom that is breaking in upon the world through the coming of Jesus. That is why Jesus refused on occasion to do miracles for a person wanting only a freak show. The miracle was to speak of God's grace and mercy. The present situation of the world is broken, unlike that for which God's creative hand made it to be. What is presently should not be . . . and to show what ought to be . . . and will be . . . and *can* be for anybody who follows the king, the miracle becomes a signpost for the glories of the kingdom. That is why the scriptures can speak of creation as "standing on tiptoe" to use Phillips' paraphrase in translating Romans 8:19. It is waiting for the coming of the full glory breaking in on creation already now. It is as though we were stretching to see over a wall presently separating us from a glory whose light streams over to our side. We yearn to see the source of that glory and strain our eyes. The miracle is the sign language of Jesus to signal the coming of the kingdom!

So Jesus takes the time to gently explain as much as possible what he is about through such sign language as his hands and mouth and body could bring to bear on the man. Then . . . the man is released from his slavery to deafness and all that has stood behind this fallen situation signaled by the deafness!

God's Sign Language to Us

Is this much different from the situation we all find ourselves in? Do you not feel the pressures and uncertainties and fears of life? It is almost frightening to realize that none of us is more than a breath away from death; few of us are more than a paycheck away from poverty; an accident at the next street corner can spell disaster in any number of ways. A host of events and possibilities and fears bring us before God in much the same way this poor unfortunate man was pushed and pulled before Jesus.

Nor is it enough to say that we need fear none of these because God is on our side. Such an escape clause is far too glib a response even if God is not opposing us! For when a man is confronted with the living God himself the first response is hardly comfort, but fear and awe. Isaiah felt unstrung when he envisioned himself in the throne room of God. "Woe is me, for I am undone" is his response. Until God put the pieces back together (as we hear so beautifully in our Old Testament Lesson for today) the prophet remained unglued. We dare not take God for granted under any circumstances.

For what hold do we have on him that he *ought* to keep our

lives whole and together (or mend them when in disrepair)? The man of faith knows above all that God is not required to do anything that he has done for us. Therefore we receive all things as a gift . . . the very breath that keeps us alive, the word of forgiveness . . . *all things!*

To assume the contrary, namely, that God "owes" us anything we have from our life to our forgiveness and hope is to place ourselves in a totally alien position over against the Christian faith. Lest we thus take God for granted, we need constantly to realize, therefore, that the God who deals with *us* is the God whose Son deals here with this frightened and uncertain deaf man. As with him, so he deals with us in respect and with concern, but he does it in the light of our complete helplessness so evident to him who loves us with such a great love! This man laid no claims on Jesus, and in that moment Jesus felt the greatest responsibility for him. We come in like manner.

And we are received by God as Jesus receives this man. The one who hates sin becomes the chief sinner for us; the judge becomes the judged in our behalf because he knows our helplessness and takes up the responsibility of our life for us as a loving Father for a child. He speaks the word to our heart, "Ephphatha," "Be opened," and our ear and life is filled with forgiveness and new hope. A whole new life is set loose for us and in us when we hear the word of the king!

All this is communicated to us in the feeble forms of sign language, to be sure. Our poor human words, the things that make up the biblical literature and message, are not enough to show us the full glory of the coming kingdom. It is God's touch that causes those words to come alive and draws us to them. Words are pitiful little windows through which to see what is yet to come. So Jesus draws pictures for us . . . parables and miracles . . . to show us what the words promise to us. "The kingdom of God is like. . . ." How many parables begin like this! They are pictures to help us stand on tiptoe and preview the glory that is coming.

A deaf man is made to hear while his impediment of speech is removed. Sign language of a most vivid form previews the coming glory yet to be revealed in its fulness! Water is poured as a sign and symbol through which God opens the doors of the kingdom for us with power! Bread and wine become the visual images through which the body and blood, once shed for us, are offered anew as a preliminary taste of the great wedding feast where we shall all sit at meat, basking in the splendor of the glory of the Lord. The kingdom is at hand! It must be spoken of, proclaimed, signed, made visible in any way possible as an invitation to participate in the greater fulfillment yet to come!

Our Sign Language to Others

The invitation goes out to everyone! And we are the "sent ones" to proclaim the coming of the kingdom! How shall we do it when even Jesus seemed to "get through" to so few? Are not our means of communication far more puny than the mighty miracles of Jesus?

Yet . . . is not our life itself a miracle, a sign of what is yet to come? Our words tell something of the miracle, but words can only tell so much. Is not our very life itself a part of the network of communication God is spreading across the face of the earth? That we should live by grace . . . that we should show love . . . that we should come with the word "be opened" to lives closed in by sin and loneliness . . . this is the miracle of renewal that is for our world "the sign language of God."

HUBERT BECK
University Lutheran Chapel
Texas A & M University
College Station, Texas

ON THE SIDE OF GOD

Seventeenth Sunday after Pentecost
Mark 8:27-35

Am I on the side of God, or of men? I wonder about that at times. You see, I like a little bit of *both* sides. Both God *and* mammon look good to me—I like the ways of God, and I like some of the ways of men.

Am I a disciple, Lord? Am I on the side of God? And can I be sure? Is God the central certainty of my soul?

Perhaps you wonder also. You believe in God. You confess that Jesus is indeed the Christ, the Son of God. The seeds of God's grace were sown in you at your baptism. You *want* to be a disciple, a follower of Christ. You pray; and you pray, "Thy kingdom come, thy will be done." You want God on *your* side. You want him to influence all that you are—your thoughts and your words and your deeds.

But somehow it all gets muddled up. You are plagued with doubts. The apparent silence of God in the face of your prayers makes you wonder if he really cares about the little things in your life. Trying to live out each day in the harsh realities of this world—this community—you wonder if God has washed his hands of the whole mess and has withdrawn to the friendly courts of heaven to play cards with the angels and archangels.

And the ways of men, the devices and desires of our own hearts, seem very attractive. *And they are!* The scientist, the medical doctor, the psychiatrist have all contributed greatly to the relief of human suffering. Farmers, production men, and transportation experts have filled so many of our needs. And I'm all for that. The ways of men are dynamic, interesting, and when directed to good causes, very satisfying.

But enthralled by the ways of men and enrolled on the side of men, I am easily led to believe that in this space age, God is really quite irrelevant. In a sophisticated, technical world, God seems so naive and impotent. And I can easily wonder if I want to be a disciple at all. To be a disciple is a costly thing, *and I know that.* To enroll on God's side means a cross, a cross of suffering love, and that seems an awesome thing to bear. To enroll on God's side means I must lose my life for *his sake and the gospel's,* and that is an embracing commitment. Are there not more glorious ways to invest your life? The secular life produces its heroes. Where are the Christian heroes?

Whose side are *you* on? Today, at this moment? Are you on the side of God or of men?

Before we rush to answer that question, we ought to consider our response quite carefully in the light and in the fire of today's gospel passage. What does it mean to be on the side of God?

It's a Personal Enlistment

You don't enroll by proxy—it's a very personal thing.

The preliminaries were over. Jesus knew who he was; now he had to know if anyone else knew. The reconnaissance phase was ending; the main battle was drawing near. So at Caesaera Philippi he asked his disciples quite bluntly, "But who do *you* say that I am?" It wasn't enough what other men said. Jesus wanted to know if anyone had been captured by the godliness that was in him.

Peter had seen it. "You are the Christ," he said. He did not understand all that that confession meant, but at that moment, he saw clearly that *all* of the Old Testament promises of God were somehow fulfilled in this Messiah who questioned him. In a strange way he knew that God himself stood before him. *In the flesh, full of grace and truth.*

And that's precisely where your enlistment on God's side begins. No one can enlist for you. It's not like the American Civil War days, when a man could get another to serve for him (for a price). Your enrollment on God's side begins as Christ presses home to you that question, "Who do you say that I am?" As you are gripped by the certainty that Jesus Christ is the reality of God among men, as you see in him the searching, seeking grace of God, then you see also that enrollment on God's side is open to everyone—*even you.* That endless cross is your personal forgiveness before God, and through the Christ who died there, you know that God will have you, that God wants you very much to be on his side.

Yes, it's a personal matter. Your husband, your wife, your mother, your father cannot come to this realization for you. "Who do you say I am?" will always be the very personal and individual invitation from God the Son to those who would enroll on the side of God.

It Means You Trust Him

Your enlistment on God's side calls for a measure of trust that passes all understanding. Peter had trouble at this point, and so do we.

You see, there's more to it than just the confession, "You are the Christ," or "Jesus is Lord." That's only the beginning. One swallow does not make a summer; one solo flight does not make an airline captain.

Faith in God, faith in Jesus Christ, is a trust *above all else.* Peter wanted to do things *his* way. He sought to stand between Jesus and the cross, and the Lord blistered him. In effect he said, "I do the will of the Father. I trust him, and no one—neither you, my beloved Peter, nor Satan—will alter my trust in him. So get behind me, you are not on the side of God, but of men." Peter learned a hard lesson that day.

The total loyalty of the soul to God—that's what enrollment on God's side means. It means that you trust the Christ of the cross as your full forgiveness before God. You trust Jesus Christ, you trust his authority (his lordship), and you trust him *most* when you seem to be so much in command of your own personal situation.

It's not an easy thing to do, but the central fiber of your faith in God rides in your trust of him. It's not easy, and it may take time. It took Peter a long time. But it comes through trusting him over and over again. As you trust God, he weaves a compelling bond between you and him that puts certainty and confidence in your heart. The more you trust, the surer you become. It snowballs that way, until your trust in God outruns your ability to comprehend it.

And when this happens, you know that you are enrolled on the side of God.

You Lose Your Life in Him

On the side of God you lose your life for *his* sake and the gospel's. Enrolled on the side of God, you invest your energy in the *concerns of God*.

And that puts you squarely *at* the side of men! At Bethlehem, Christ was enrolled in the human census, and to this day he works the tasks of the Father in the broad human enterprise.

Discipleship is not some mystic leap into the lap of God. Enlistment on the side of God is no warrant to turn your back to the deep and the hurting needs of other people. "I belong to God" does not mean that I do not belong to my neighbor.

All of us—here in this church today and throughout this community—are so very much alike. Our need for God, for certainty, for purpose, for love, for peace, for understanding, for acceptance, for forgiveness, for hope, for *grace*—these needs weave through all of us. And the dwelling place of God is among us in order that he can reach and fill these great needs that we have.

And the call to "follow me" puts you squarely in this arena of human need. It's costly. It takes time and energy. It requires love, forgiveness and much grace. But that's the nature of the cross that Christ invites you to take up. Your cross, you see, is much related to his. He bore a cross of forgiveness, love, and grace. He died there that God could come to us, and we to him. That's the gospel! That's *good news*, and he invites us to invest our lives in this same good news, that God may come to others, and they to him. As we come to the side of God through our rendezvous with God the Son, he points us to our neighbor. That's where he leads us.

Where Do You Stand?

Now we can return to the question, "Whose side are *you* on? Today, at this moment? Where do you stand?"

Clearly the answer lies between you and God. But that you may be counted on God's side *at all* is the good news for today. As the Holy Spirit sounds that eternal question, "Who do you say that Christ is?" we are at the same time invited to enroll on God's side. As Jesus Christ captures our trust, we yield to him. He knows what he's doing. And as we embark on the grand venture of faith that involves us with the human family, we know we are investing in the concerns of God.

You believe in Jesus Christ, you trust him, you follow him into the human cauldron. When these three come together for you, *you are there*. All of a sudden you are gripped by the certainty that you are on the side of God.

And that's exactly where God wants you! Amen.

JOHN W. COFFEY JR.
Hope Lutheran Church
Walker, Minnesota

TRUE GREATNESS

Eighteenth Sunday after Pentecost
Mark 9:30-37

He Talks About the Cross

He knew what was in store for him. The one for whom the world had waited, waited now for what he knew the world would do to him. He talked about it. They heard him; but they were not listening.

"The Son of man will be delivered into the hands of men and they will kill him, and when he is killed, after three days, he will rise." Jesus could not have said it more clearly. The deliverer was soon to be delivered. The disciples did not understand. They never got beyond the stabbing focus of the word *kill*. There was no arresting assurance they could claim in the promise that, "after three days he will rise."

St. Mark says, "They did not understand the saying." Although not understanding fully, they understood too much. "They were afraid to ask him." Putting off going to a physician because we know too much and are afraid to learn more is an experience many of us have had. Like hearing about the announced lay-off of workers at the mill, none hurried to the bulletin board to find out if his name was on the list. And some of us have known the terrible length of the hospital corridor leading to the swinging doors of the intensive care unit. We wanted to know the answer to the question, "How is she this morning?" But we were almost afraid to ask. We can get hold of the disciples' feelings.

It wasn't he about whom they were really concerned. It wasn't his mission about which they were anxious. They did not listen because they suspected that perhaps some of the accumulating death would spill over and reach out to engulf them.

They had been identified with him in life. Would they be marked like him for death? Had they promised too much in their confirmation? Had they been too quick to enthuse about the joy of following him? Could he really be the Son of God? What happened to the idea of his being the kingly Messiah on whom they had pegged their hopes for the restoration of Israel? Was their hope of sitting at his right hand in the coming kingdom to be hammered to death on a cross?

They were afraid to ask the specific questions. The answers might get them in too deep. Like the disciples, many today find the cross as the law of life unthinkable. Nothing in the world in which we live seems to support the idea of the triumph of defeat. The meek shall inherit the earth? Really?

Sam Levinson's Papa seemed to say it all when he put his hand on his son's shoulder and said, "Remember, my son, if you ever need a helping hand, you'll find it at the end of your arm." It is in clenching the fist that the dynamic tension which develops muscle is created. It is in stoking the furnace which manufactures the steel which makes the guns that makes a nation strong. It is the annihilation of the competition that gets a company into the top ten profit makers in the nation.

Even in the church, the list of the outstanding congregations is made up of those whose measurement is based on the criteria of "how many?" and "how much?" When pastors talk to one another about their "good members" we all know what they mean. The pillars of the church are those who support it best. "The new members I take in never replace the losses that move out," writes a pastor in his parochial report. It was written to account for the fact that while there was an inflation of growth figures, there was at the same time a loss in income. The high cost of serving people was outrunning the income! What a pity that building was deteriorating because it was being used by so many non-paying persons! And our blessed Lord keeps talking about a cross.

They Talked About Greatness

The best way to stop listening is to start talking. It's the intermission that brings some people to the concert. The disciples started their own conversation when the orchestrated theme of his sacrifice proved too disturbing to them.

To overcome their anxiety, their ability to fear that had been welded to their ability to imagine, they attempted to fortify their spirits with talk about their own net worth. Recapitulating for one another the assets each of them possessed, they argued about who was the greatest among them.

When persons sense that they have misseed the mark, the easiest way to restore respectability is to compare themselves with other persons. The Pharisee in the temple could find cheap absolution in comparing himself to the publican. Each of us can easily find someone with whom to compare ourselves and in the process make ourselves look good. "It may be true of me that I have loved things and used people rather than loving people and using things, but look at *him*. He's got twice as much as I have. Everybody he ever met was used to help him acquire what he's got. By comparison, I look pretty good."

The disciples' uncomfortableness in making a wide conversational detour around the subject of the cross was exposed by Jesus' question, "What were you discussing?" None was willing to share with him the subject of their conversation. They were intuitively ashamed. Their discussion had wandered into a very distant place from the area he had suggested. He had hoped that they would reflect upon his death and resurrection. They were conversing about greatness without reference to the cross. They could not know on their side of calvary what we know about it from our side in time, but they had been with him long enough to know that the life Jesus came to bring was to be found in losing life on lesser terms. If they were to follow him, they were to deny the self in order to liberate it.

The understanding of this denial has been distorted for many of us. To deny the self is not to hate one's self. Jesus became a man not to deny our humanness but to reveal it. There is an ancient legend which tells of the day when the gods felt themselves in the presence of a real threat to their positions. There were persons, they were aware, who fashioned themselves to have the potential for divinity. So a convention was arranged (at the heavenly Hilton?) and all the gods were invited. The agenda was focused on one question, "Where shall we hide the spark of divinity where mortals can never find it?" There were all kinds of answers, but none satisfied the convention. At the bottom of the sea? Hardly, for it would only be a matter of time before humans reached the ocean depth. In the far residence of the galaxies beyond the highest reach? Would the spark be safe there? Not really, these mortals who had learned to outswim the fish, and soon would learn to outrun the gazelle, would one day outfly the eagle. The meeting was about to adjourn in frustration (as so many conventions do!) when one of the more timid delegates suggested that he thought he might have the answer. "Let us hide the spark of divinity where mortals will never think to look. Let us hide it in the human heart." The vote on the recommendation was unanimous.

Jesus came to reveal the spark of divinity; not to hide it. In him was revealed God's possibility for persons. No one could think of herself or himself in the same way now that he had come. A liturgy composed for use in a congregation of black persons has the congregation antiphonally responding to a series of depressing facts which reveal "man's inhumanity to man" with the repeated chant, "I am *somebody*." We have a lot to learn from our black sisters and brothers. There is glory and promise in what it means to be a human being in the world today. For too long we have demeaned it. "Mere humanity," "only human" we are prone to declare in reference to that which Christ assumed in the incarnation. God knew that we could only love that which we could get our arms around; so he became a babe and was wrapped in swaddling cloths. Then people could say, "This is Emmanuel. This is God with us." As Bishop Sheen had said, "What happened was not so much the conversion of the godhead into flesh, as the taking of manhood into God." I am somebody!

The Cross Defines Greatness

Jesus meets people where they are. Not in unevaluative acceptance, but he receives them in his name. In his reception, he frees persons through the liberating power which releases, in their full humanity, the newly directed capacities.

The disciples were discussing greatness. He did not condemn them. There was a greatness he expected in them and had previously told them of it. There on the mountain he had included in their ordination sermon the injunction "Unless your righteousness exceeds that of the scribes and Pharisees, you will never enter into the kingdom of heaven." The impulse to be first has accounted for all manner of calamity when being first is prostituted to the enthroning of a person at the expense of other people. There is a firstness, however, that lets a person's God-given ambition become not the master of life but a servant of it. Jesus seems to be saying, "All ambition is God given, and is intended to be harnessed to service." Let it motivate our commitment to high spiritual enterprise.

In a kingdom where the last shall be first, our estimates of worth are in need of constant revision. We are not, however, without examples to enlighten our understanding. There are all about us, in spite of the media's inability to spot them, those persons whose greatness is measured not by what they can claim as possessions but by what possesses them. Like the apostle Paul who never evaluated his life by that which he laid hold of, but by that which laid hold of him, there are those who find their renewal not in saving their strength but in giving their lives away.

"I wouldn't do what you're doing for a million dollars," said a member of an inspection team to a missionary nurse whose potential for helping was seriously hampered by the meager equipment in the hospital which opened its doors to thousands in need. Without a moments hesitation, she replied "Neither would I." The significance of her life and that which supplied her joy was in being enlightened by the cross as to the meaning of greatness.

A friend of mine owned a nursery for the growing of roses that bordered the nursery owned by a family who had immigrated from Japan. When that day that shall "live in infamy" occurred and Pearl Harbor was struck and the destructive seeds of hatred were sown throughout America, my friend's competitor and his family were soon taken off to a concentration camp. Instead of rejoicing in the demise of the competition, arrangements were immediately made to take over and operate the business for the absentee owner. The roses grew to maturity and were marketed. Books were kept and profits deposited. Love bloomed and life opened up for the neighbor who was called a fool. And he was. He was a "fool for Christ's sake."

When the war was over and the imprisoned family returned, they expected to find the shambles which neglect had promoted. Instead they found a thriving business maintained and a neighbor who had almost killed himself guaranteeing the future of his friend. When I pass that nursery now and see through the windows of those greenhouses the crossed beams that mark the rows of plantings, I think of the way the cross was preached in that place.

"Whoever receives one such . . . in my name receives me." True greatness, indeed.

A. HOWARD WEEG
Assistant to the President
Pacific Southwest Synod—LCA
Los Altos, California

THE PAIN THAT WORKS PEACE
Nineteenth Sunday after Pentecost
Mark 9:38-50

Nobody likes pain. We avoid it whenever possible. We take aspirin at the first sign of a headache. But there is much necessary pain, pain that is not to be avoided. The cross Jesus suffered for us was that kind of pain. The peace we know in his name would not have been possible without it. And so we must take him seriously when he invites us today not to run away from the pain that makes for peace. Notice his two illustrations.

Salted with Fire

In other texts Jesus speaks of salt as a seasoning. Here his point is that salt is medicinal. When you "rub salt into a wound" it burns "like hell" we sometimes say. That's right. There is a sting to it, which makes the wound hurt worse than ever. Therefore we avoid the salt. We prefer to keep our sore than to use salt for its healing. Jesus says there will be no such escape in the end. "Every one will be salted with fire," he promises. If you avoid the pain now, it will only catch you later.

With this medicinal imagery of salt goes that of the "worm." "Worm" is a way of describing infectious and deadly diseases. King Herod was stricken with worms, says Acts 12:23 in describing his death. The infection shows in sores on the body. They are abhorrent, fearful. The medication for such sores is salt. That is why Jesus says "Salt is good." However much it hurts, it is good. By the salt "the worm dies," and the body is healed. Although the salt burns like fire, the burning is not forever. The fire is "quenched." The contrast is hell, for in hell "their worm does *not* die and the fire is *not* quenched," as Jesus observes in reminiscence of Isaiah 66:24. You have the wound for ever. You suffer the burning and the abhorrence of it for ever.

Therefore Jesus pleads, "Have salt in yourselves." Suffer the pain in yourself for the healing of your own wounds. Don't try to escape it by rubbing the salt into the wounds of other people, by accusing them and exposing their wrongnesses. If you take the salt for your own wounds, you will discover a great wonder. Not only will you yourself be healed, but your whole society too! You will then "be at peace with one another!"

Amputation

The other illustration of pain in our text is amputation. The members of the body which Jesus suggests might need amputation are the very ones accident insurance policies today cover with full indemnity—a hand, a foot, an eye. We don't want to be without these. But Jesus suggests that amputation may be called for, that it can be a good thing, just as salt is good. Once in a while we know it. If a doctor can save your life only by amputating a foot or leg, you suffer it. Therefore Jesus says, "If your hand causes you to sin," that is, if it becomes a stumbling block for you to keep you from entering the kingdom of God, then "cut it off." For "it is better for you to enter into life maimed," or with one hand, or with one eye, than to be "thrown into hell."

But What Does All This Mean?

The illustrations are physical and have to do with bodily life and healing. What Jesus is really getting at, however, is the power of sin and death that works in all of us, even when we are physically healthy.

For example, you naturally desire *glory*. You love to feel good about yourself, and to have people admire and applaud you. King Herod was like that in the little story of his death at the end of Acts 12. He made a speech, and everybody applauded. "The voice of a god, and not of man!" they shouted. And Herod believed it! He thought he was really great! That's when the Lord smote him with worms, and he died. But it is so very human. Jesus' disciples were like that. They wanted the glory of high places in his kingdom.

We are like that too. We want to be king of the hill. We fight jealously to keep any advantages we have. But God says, Give it up! This love of glory is like a deadly wound. Put the salt on it, and burn it out now, so that you don't find your glory turned to shame and suffer the burning for ever! Amputate it now, so that it doesn't carry your whole self into hell and death for ever! Because you have one glory only, that is the glory of being named children of God, baptized into the name of Christ, bought by his blood, sharing his life and eternal glory. Any glory you get for yourself is a cancer, a deadly wound, not only for yourself but for your whole society. Why do people fight one another? Is it not because each seeks his own glory at the expense of the other? Let the salt of God's truth burn out the glory in which you boast! Then you will be healed, and then you will also have peace with people around you.

Or again, you naturally want to be *right*. You think you are wise and know the answers. Other people who disagree with you are the fools, they are wrong. Therefore you can readily accuse them. The way you think, the way you were brought up, that is the measure by which you measure the whole world. The hardest thing for you is to discover and admit you are wrong. But now Jesus pleads that this kind of rightness is deadly! It poisons you. It shuts out the word of God and the truth about yourself. It creates war and bitterness between you and other people. Cut it off, amputate it. Even if it's your right eye, pluck it out. Because you have only one rightness, that is the forgiveness of your sins in the love of God, through the redemption that is yours in Christ Jesus. Be the child of God with him and in him, wear the family robe of his rightness. Then you are alive, and well, and at peace with God and the people around you. But if you cling to your own sense of rightness, it will kill you not only now, but for ever!

Try one more. Your *desire,* your *ambition*—these too are a great sore, a corrupt member, needing God's salt or his amputation. You see what you want in life and set out to get it. You harness God to your ambitions, as the disciples tried to harness Jesus to theirs. You don't really want God's kingdom and life, you only want God to help you achieve your goals! If he doesn't come through, then you have no use for him. What good is religion, you say, I can do it myself! But it is deadly. If you cannot give up your ambitions and private desires for the sake of the will of God for you, how can you love his life and kingdom? You will not treasure his promises and inheritance. You will rather set your heart and life on the things you see and boast of and desire. To satisfy the lusts of your flesh and the pride of life, that will be your constant endeavor! Will you not listen to Jesus? Amputate that desire! Rub the salt of God's truth into that wound, before it utterly destroys you and leaves you in the eternal fire!

The Wholesome Outcome

Let the salt do its work! Suffer the amputation! That's what "repentance" and turning to God is really about! It changes you, makes you into a different kind of person. But it's great, when the Spirit begins to get that kind of thing done in us. No matter how much it hurts for the moment, its effect is beautiful and wholesome. Jesus points to the newness of it when he says, "Have salt in yourselves, and be at peace with one another!" The text itself signals how different things will be then. For example:

The Man Casting Out Demons

The disciple John is proud of himself. He reports seeing a man who was casting out demons in Jesus' name. "We forbade him," says John. And why? Because "he was not following with us." The disciples around Jesus are becoming a closed group, a clique. Already they think of themselves as an institution with a fixed and registered membership. The preaching of the Word of God must be administered by the institution. This man has not asked for institutional certification. Therefore he cannot be allowed to preach, until he has been brought into the system. What he says does not matter. He may indeed be preaching "in Jesus' name," and casting out demons in his name. But if anybody can start preaching that way, we will have anarchy! Therefore he must be properly certified, commissioned, ordained first.

Strange! That's exactly the argument the scribes and priests used against John the Baptist and Jesus, and later against the early church. Who authorized you to preach? Show us your divine credentials if you have any, because you obviously have no credentials from us. But if you don't give us a sign from heaven, then either submit to our system or else be silent! Thus what we call the "institutional church" uses the power of institutional pressures to silence the word of God! That is a sickness, a deadly sore. It calls for salt, for amputation, whenever it begins to occur among us.

Notice Jesus' reply. "Do not forbid him!" Jesus is not worried about creating an organization, but only about getting the word out! Woe to the church when its organization gets in the way of the message! "No one who does a mighty work in my name will be able soon after to speak evil of me." Therefore this strange preacher who casts out demons in Jesus' name is hardly an enemy! Surely he will not be among those who soon will cry, "Crucify him, crucify him!" "For he who is not against us is *for us*," Jesus adds. But if he is for us, then we had better not be against him!

Do you see what is happening? There is a wound of institutional glory in the disciples, and Jesus is applying the salt of God's truth to heal it. Let the salt burn! If some of the salt rubs into our own wounds, let it burn us too! For the salt is good! It is not meant to burn for ever!

A Cup of Water

To give a disciple a cup of water to drink is hardly a great work of love and sacrifice. Jesus' disciples apparently even found cause to criticize it, the way we tend to criticize the minimal participation of some members far out on the fringes of congregational life. Think perhaps, of persecution times, when people had reason to be fearful of the authorities and could not openly confess or support the name of Christ. A secretive cup of water to a courageous disciple is all the confession such a person may be able to manage. We are tempted to view his action as a sign of weakness and equivocation, and to demand greater boldness. But Jesus is tender. The tiniest sign of life gives him joy. That man is already living by God's promised inheritance! His reward shall not be denied him! Let the disciples learn tenderness from Jesus, how to cherish the bruised reed rather than trample it, how to nourish the tiny spark on the lamp's wick and not smother it.

But do you see what this means for the disciples and for us? The salt has healed the wounds of self-glory, self-rightness, self-ambition, and institutional power. All these have been amputated. And life now means to love, to rejoice in the least of God's little ones, to become small and meek so that others may be built up, and to live by nothing other than the treasures of divine hope and promise.

Have Salt Within Yourselves

Let it happen to you, this hurt that works change and healing. Then you find yourself thinking and acting the way Jesus did, the way these disciples also learned to think and act through his Spirit.

Jesus was meek, small, the servant. He took the hurt into himself, even our judgment of fire and wrath. He did not want to be our accuser, not even when we were altogether wrong. He took the death for our sakes when we by our blindness were simply unable to repent or to ask for mercy and forgiveness. He took the salt in himself. By it he created *peace* between us and our God. By it he empowers us also to "be at peace with one another."

PAUL G. BRETSCHER
Immanuel Lutheran Church
Valparaiso, Indiana

COURTROOM OR COURTSHIP?

Twentieth Sunday after Pentecost
Mark 10:2-16

In a class session with a group of ninth graders, a pastor posed the question,

"Which two commandments out of the ten do you consider of least importance?"

Without hesitation, one of these young people responded,

> "Honor your father and your mother" and "You shall not commit adultery;" these two commandments are of least importance because no one keeps them anyway!

Posing the same question before a group of adults, after much deliberation it was finally concluded that the two commandments which warn against coveting would have to be set aside as of least importance. Then the adults were reminded that the New Testament tells us that covetousness is idolatry (Col. 3:5 and Eph. 5:5). If we eliminate the two commandments which are concerned about coveting, then we must also set aside the first commandment which warns us against idolatry. With this information before the group, one of the adults responded,

> It doesn't make much difference how we look at the Ten Commandments anyway. Jesus told us that the minute we break one of them, we have broken all of them.

In conversations with young people or with older people, when our concern centers in the commandments, it soon becomes apparent that the setting in which these sacred words are seen is that of a courtroom. In this courtroom, we stand beneath the awesome authority of a Supreme Judge who is seated in solitary splendor high above the heavens. In the courtroom, there is no jury made up of people like ourselves who may sympathize with our human frailty. God alone will judge our case. He has made it clear that when we break one of his commandments, we stand guilty of breaking all of them.

When this is the setting in which Christian people see the Ten Commandments, then, like the Pharisees in the Gospel text for today, we spend our time looking for loopholes in the Law. Some of these men came to Jesus one day with the question, "Is it lawful for a man to divorce his wife?"

Jesus responded, "What did Moses command you?"

They said, "Moses allowed a man to write a certificate of divorce, and to put her away."

Our Lord could easily have demolished their shallow, self-centered interpretation of what Moses commanded in the Book of Deuteronomy. Moses spoke out of love; these people saw his words as a loophole in the law. Moses wrote in behalf of mercy; the Pharisees manipulated his words to justify what they wanted to do without mercy.

Jesus could see it would not be enough to win a debate. More decisive action was required. The Pharisees of every age must be shown, once and for all, that there are no loopholes in God's law. He took them beyond the commandments and back to creation. When two people are united in marriage, they become one.

"What therefore God has joined together, let not man put asunder."

Even the disciples of Jesus were disturbed by these blunt words. All of us can understand their concern. Instinctively, we would like to find some loopholes through which we could crawl out of a difficult situation without feeling guilty about it. There is no way out. Jesus told his disciples,

> Whoever divorces his wife and marries another, commits adultery against her; and if she divorces her husband and marries another, she commits adultery.

In our Lord's day, adultery was punishable by death.

Listening to the Gospel for today, if you were asked to name two commandments out of the ten which are of most importance, which ones would you choose? Over the centuries, whenever the church has placed the commandments within the setting of a courtroom, then great importance has been given to these words, "You shall not commit adultery" and "You shall not steal."

People who broke these commandments were harshly condemned. Idolatry, profanity, failure to keep the Sabbath, dishonoring parents, lying or coveting were more easily excused. There have been times when the church has deliberately broken the commandment, "You shall not kill" to justify itself in the fight against heresy. It is also a sad part of our history to admit that when the charge was adultery, women have been more severely condemned than men.

Against this background, there are three things of great importance we need to keep clearly in our mind. The first is this: on that day in our Lord's ministry, the conversation with him revolved around marriage, divorce and adultery. This conversation could have applied to any of the commandments, and the conclusion would have been just the same! There are no loopholes in God's law.

"All have sinned and fall short of the glory of God" (Rom. 3:23). Whenever man tries to justify himself by the law, by the law he will be condemned.

The second item is this: whenever, like those Pharisees, we place the Ten Commandments within the setting of a courtroom, then we have set aside the Gospel. To live by the Gospel is to see the Ten Commandments, not in terms of a courtroom, but rather in terms of a courtship. These commandments become the guidelines within which this courtship between God and man can be carried out.

People in love do try to find loopholes in the commitments they make toward each other during courtship. Imagine two people whose wedding date had been determined saying to each other:

> Darling, once we are married we shall spend our lives together. Between now and our wedding day, I want to be free to give my devotion to someone else. I want your permission to say whatever I want about you. Only occasionally do I want to see you between now and then. If you or your parents try to stop me, that will be dangerous. Don't expect me to be faithful to you sexually until we are married. I want to be free to cheat and lie and covet whatever pleases me. Once we are married, then I will mind my manners.

Obviously, in the wake of such a conversation, the courtship would come to an abrupt end. No human being in his right mind would put up with that kind of arrangement.

I said there were three things which needed to be heard today. What needs to be said now is so incredible, you may feel crushed by it. The fact we must face is that God has been putting up with this kind of courtship over all of the centuries of human history! We have said to him:

> Lord, I want to be with you in heaven when Christ, the Bridegroom, takes the church, his bride, to be with him forever. But, for now, Lord, I hope you will understand if I have other gods, and profane your name, and forget your day, and dishonor my parents. I want to be loved even when I hurt other people physically, when I am sexually irresponsible, when I steal and lie and covet. Lord, I am like the apostle Paul. In my inmost self, I want to do that which is right, but day by day, I discover that what I do is what I hate.

Under these conditions, we would assume that the courtship would be over and God would simply forget about us. Yet, the courtship has continued across the centuries. Our Lord's love goes beyond our understanding. We violate every basic guideline for an honorable courtship. In response, he gave his Son to fulfil the law for us that we might be forgiven and reconciled to him once more. When Jesus had this conversation with the Pharisees, he was on his way to Jerusalem to suffer and die for us.

Walking with him on the way to that cross, we discover something of the depths of his love. When the Pharisees and the disciples talked to him about marriage and divorce and adultery, he did not become angry. It was nothing new for him to be confronted by people who were trying to find loopholes in the law.

But when the disciples tried to prevent some people from bringing their little children to him, then our Lord became indignant. He had to make it absolutely clear there are no loopholes in his love either! There is no one here, no matter how young or old you are, how rich or poor, how pious or profane, whether you are single, married, divorced, or widowed, even if you are living in open rebellion against God, you still are not living beyond the boundaries of his love. If you want to respond to his unfailing love, then stop trying to justify yourself in terms of the law. No person can do that. God offers his love to us as a gift of grace. To receive the gift of his love, we must become like children. We don't pretend to deserve so great a gift. We simply open our hearts and lives to receive it openly, freely, enthusiastically, with praise and thanksgiving.

To love him is to keep his commandments as faithfully as you can. When you fail, you confess your sins. He has already paid the price for your forgiveness. Then strive again, in response to his love, to find your freedom within the guidelines of his law. Christ summarized the commandments for us when he said,

> You shall love the Lord your God with all your heart, and with all your soul, and with all your mind. You shall love your neighbor as yourself (Matt. 22:37, 39).

The good news for today takes us out of a courtroom and into a courtship. We discover there are no loopholes in God's law. We also discover there are no loopholes in his love.

LOYAL E. GOLF
St. John's Lutheran Church
Northfield, Minn.

THE POVERTY OF WEALTH

Twenty-first Sunday after Pentecost
Mark 10:17-30

The Cutting Edge

If there is one hallmark of the contemporary body of Christ in our world today, it is radical discipleship that is a revolutionary commitment to the person of Jesus Christ. This is a unique sign of the frontier obedience of Christ's incarnate presence in our world today. At a moment in history when structured ecumenical form is corroded and jaded, a bright and glimmering evidence of hope is the emerging of the call for obedience to the lordship of

Jesus Christ that is beyond legalism and beyond institutional loyalty. It is a relationship in which witness and service are no longer in false polarization. Our text, in Mark 10:17-30, witnesses to this.

The Poverty of Wealth

Our textual encounter with Jesus Christ starts with a question and a counter-question. We note Jesus with the distinctive Markan emphasis of activity starting on his way, when a wealthy man in haste kneels at his feet, and with respect asks, "What must I do to receive eternal life?" Jesus counters with the question that is never answered because in its answer lies the revelation of who he is: "Why do you call me good?" Jesus is incarnate good.

Jesus then lists six moral prohibitions: murder, adultery, stealing, lying, cheating, and the positive demand to honor one's parents. The man's moral wealth became his spiritual poverty, for his answer, "Ever since I was young I have obeyed all these commandments," shows the inner bankruptcy of false self-acceptance. The outer had never become inner. Every person's problem of hatred, lust, covetousness, loss of integrity, taking advantage of other people, and respect that is taking a second look of reverence to one's elders—all these never "repentasized" him.

Wealth Meets Poverty

The man who had the most had the least; and the man who had the least—only the robe on his back—had the most. Jesus looked straight at him with love, and he fulfilled the demand of the relationship of love. He focused in on the man's greatest need. He told him, "You need only one thing." When Jesus Christ focuses in on the areas of our life that are so expansive that they have become a god or have become a cluster of gods, then he has fulfilled in our life, speaking the truth in love.

Jesus articulates the meaning of the radical discipleship so needed in an affluent community. Five verbs articulate this encounter. The first is the active verb "go." Rip yourself from the domination of the present god that holds you. Verb number two is "sell." The selling was not at the Palestine equivalent of the stock market. The selling was to take place in God's market place. The prophet in the Old Testament declares it this way: "Come, buy wine and milk without money and without price" (Isa. 55:1). Let there be a new Sovereign of all of your resources. The third verb of action is "Give." "Give the money to the poor and you will have riches in heaven." This is not merely symbolic, it is the fulfillment in the Christian's life of what is said of Jesus in 2 Corinthians 8:9—"For you know the grace of our Lord Jesus Christ; rich as he was, he made himself poor for your sake, in order to make you rich by means of his poverty." The "selling all" is my realistic commitment of all that I have and can be—to be poured out that other people might have the wealth of letting go and letting God. The fourth verb is "come." It is the opposite of the first verb "go." It is coming, stripped of all pretense of moral wealth, physical wealth and spiritual wealth. The fifth verb is the object of radical discipleship, "follow me." It is the fulfillment of Jesus' word, "No one is good except God alone." For Jesus is good and Jesus is God. Thus I follow him.

The Wealth of Poverty

Gazing profoundly at the back of the man he loved and who had turned down his invitation, Jesus words his grief, "How hard it will be for rich people to enter the kingdom of God." The disciples were shocked; and Jesus counters one of those sayings that is almost exegeted out of existence: "It is much harder for a rich man to enter the kingdom of God than for a camel to go through the eye of a needle." The disciples' shock turns into amazement, and they blurt out, "Who, then, can be saved?" And the good news of the Gospel is, "This is impossible for men, but not for God; everything is possible for God." Shock and amazement are regular companions on the road to self-discovery in Jesus Christ.

Peter Demurs

"Look, we have left everything and followed you." Then Jesus articulates the wealth of poverty. First he affirms Peter. He lovingly strokes even the feeblest commitment to radical discipleship that you and I are capable of with one word, "Yes." Jesus does that with people. He affirms them. He encourages them. He accepts them.

Then he states the truism, "Anyone who leaves relationships to people or places receives a hundredfold." For the moment I become a living part of the committed company of God's very own, I inherit as my own family the love and the resources of a community that is far above what I can ask or think. In fact, it is a serious conjecture as to whether a person knows what it is to be a Christian if he hasn't tasted of the fulness of the life of the family of God, and all of its love, acceptance and resources.

The other gift is the gift of persecution. This is not self-imposed evangelical masochism. It is not a paranoid looking for opposition and condemnation. It is, rather, facing the utter realism that I cannot live in a world in which evil is such a powerful force without paying the price of pain, of sensitivity, of suffering. It is said of Jesus in Hebrews 12: "Who for the joy that was set before him endured the cross." We have purpose in life in a day when the second cause of death for young men between 16 and 24 is suicide—this is wealth. If you please, the wealth of poverty.

Jesus concludes, "And in the age to come he will receive eternal life." All this and heaven too. What a gospel for the day in which we live. But it is not other worldly escapism. It is the very opposite. It is the eternal complement of a fulfilling relationship already begun here.

Lord Jesus Christ, give us the grace to be bankrupt, and in the cashing in of our false assets at your cross to discover new life in your kingdom with yourself as our Lord. Amen.

CARL J. JOHANSSON
Trinity Lutheran Church
of Minnehaha Falls
Minneapolis, Minnesota

SUMMONED TO SERVE

Twenty-second Sunday after Pentecost
Mark 10:35-45

It appears to be reckless and irresponsible for disciples to be demanding that Jesus give them what they ask. The pupil cannot tell the teacher, "Here is the assignment for you to do." The child cannot tell the parent, "In this way you are to be obedient." Such sounds insolent and audacious. "When you complete your suffering and enter your glory, grant us to be on your right hand and on your left hand." The request, if that mild word could be used, seems to ignore good etiquette. It disregards the anticipated suffering feelings of Jesus. "When you come in that glory-kingdom, after you have been beaten and killed, then give us the honor, not only to enjoy the fruit of your battle and victory, but to share in all the glory and honor. Let one of us be at your right hand and the other at your left hand." Can't you see these two exalted in their aggrandizement and enjoying being a celebrity. Human vanity knows no bounds.

Surprisingly, Jesus, in his response, diverts the direction from that of being exalted to that of being humbled and humiliated,

from being a lord to being a servant. The change is not to provide the disciples with another alternative, but it is really a
transposition. The first is placed last and the last first. This is
what you might term "normal" for the Christian faith and life,
in the light of all we heard before. Jesus has his own way of telling us to get our priorities in the proper order.

They Didn't Understand

Jesus tells them they do not understand what they are asking.

If this is a foolish request, what can we say? Are we to be
excused and say that we have never asked God for foolish things?
If this is a request of their own pride or haughtiness, what about
our oft-spoken requests which build up our ego. One thing about
these two is that they are not afraid to ask. There is no timidity
about their approaching Jesus. They may not be humble, but at
least they are bold. When our Lord summons us to pray or to ask
him he invites us to call upon him as loving children speak to their
loving father.

But they did not understand that for which they asked. Not
too long before this he had spoken also of his suffering before
death and resurrection. At that time Peter rebuked him and said
that should never happen to him. He understood what was going
to happen, but he did not like it. These two heard what would
happen and they found much pleasure in it because of the outcome. They understood what he said, but, as Jesus said, they did
not understand what they themselves were saying.

Had they asked for something wrong? If a son asks a father
for a fish, he would not give him a scorpion, but what if he asks
for a scorpion? Was this a deadly thing for which they asked?
If a child asks for bread is his request to be answered with a
stone? But what if he should have bread and ask for a stone?
Was this request of James and John the wrong thing for which
to ask? Do not men strive for honor? Is glory undesirable? To
play an athletic game means victory, to run a race is to achieve
success, to work for a mark in classes is to seek out an honor.
Are these to be classified as shameful? To be near the Lord, as
close to him as possible, is that all so wrong? Yet our Lord says
they do not understand that for which they are asking.

Victory Through Suffering

Listen again what he said to them before. Jesus would come
into glory by the road marked with a cross. Jesus would wear the
crown after he would go through the bloody battle in which he

would give his life. He would be glorified but he would be forsaken. He would be honored but he would be rejected first. The gold medal would be his only after he had defeated all his opponents and all of our opponents. Christ is the victor over sin, all sin, over death, all death, over darkness, all darkness, over the grave, all graves. Nothing, no one, can win again over him.

For anyone to share the honor and the glory which is his is certainly an unworthy honor and request. It is his and his alone. Only he came through the battle. And yet Jesus says you do not understand what you are asking—not for that reason—but because there is another question which needs to be met.

Share in the Suffering

Can the follower of Jesus, James or John, or any of us, drink the cup which he drank and be baptized with the baptism with which he was baptized?

All of us share in what he suffered in that we use the benefits of his suffering, we reap the harvest of the work he has done. But he is saying here that to share in the glory we are to share in the cup of sorrow and in the baptism he had.

Christ firmly says his followers will drink that cup and will be baptized with that baptism. The pupil is not above his teacher. If the teacher is mocked and ridiculed, so also the pupil. As he is the vine so we the branch will be as he. If we suffer with him we will be glorified with him. If we are to be glorified with him we suffer with him. Through tribulation we enter his kingdom. Someone said that tea was made for hot water and Christians are to suffer, here but not hereafter.

James and John wanted the position of honor and glory but that was not for Jesus to give. He had other positions to offer, that of being servants. They again must learn the priorities in the kingdom—the first are last and the last are first. He gives to whom he pleases. He is charitable and full of grace. He has a right to do what he chooses.

Perhaps that position is to be ours or theirs, who knows. But to whomsoever it is given it is by grace, as are all of God's gifts. I suppose our greatest joy is to trust and to learn to be content for contentment with godliness is great gain. And whatever the suffering that comes the Lord allows no more to come to us than we are able to bear. In all sufferings under his hand he chastens to make us more chaste and purges us to make us more pure.

Children are great imitators and learn to walk the way their parents walk. And when our Lord invites us to come, follow him. There are some things we cannot avoid or leap over. And every cup of sorrow he has not only tasted but drunk, every baptism of pain he has already endured. And as we go about confessing him, in speech or in life, the very reaction which he received and still receives is the reaction we too receive and obtain.

So positions of honor come later, right now it is suffering. When the other ten disciples heard the two, James and John, make this amazing request they were indignant. If they were indignant at the two for asking what they themselves wanted, we could understand that. We could also understand it if their request brought up the subject again about their suffering, for after all they would just as soon not talk about that too much. Who would want to bring that up? And our Lord is just as patient with the ten as he was with the two. For, after all, he wants us to be his followers. So he endeavors to mold us, reshape us, renew us, redeem us, restore us to be what he intends us to be.

Don't Lord It

And to be like him we must learn of all things not to be so lordly, lording it over people. It would be lordly to say to Peter, or James or John—"Shame on you for asking for rewards for following the Christ. Shame on you for asking for positions of honor." It would be lordly to cry shame for the Davids in our own day who commit adultery and murder and say that God will never forgive them and God will never accept them into his kingdom. It would be lordly for us to denounce Noah for his drunkenness and say he is outside the kingdom and can never return. It would be lordly to take a Peter who curses and denies Christ and refuse to offer him the hand of forgiveness and of love.

How easy it is—or is it really difficult—to say about some one who has done wrong as we believe it to be wrong, "I just cannot go to him and offer him the hand of love. I cannot go to him and speak to him of forgiveness and grace. I cannot forgive him for the hurts he has done." And it is very lordly if we condemn even such a person for appearing to us to be so lordly.

We Are to Serve

We are to serve—not to be top person, number one, but bottom person, whatever the number might be. To serve those whom we like and do not like, who have favored us and who have disappointed us, who have agreed with us and who have hurt us. If we see a child of God hesitate to be steadfast, vacillate in his conviction, waver in his purity, falter in his following the Lord —ours is to serve, to come to his aid and assistance.

Jesus came to serve all, the entire world, and even more to serve all, giving his all, keeping back nothing, not even himself, giving himself as a ransom, fully and completely for all.

For us to be with him, since we belong to him, we die to our self, we lose our self in service for others. The highest achievement of our life is to lose ourselves for him and others and in so doing we will find ourselves. If we avoid discomfort and annoyance, building our nests and making our money, believing we are safe, we lose even what we have gained.

Samuel heard God's voice at night calling him to service; Gideon protested he could not serve for he came from a poor family; Moses complained he was unequal to the task; Jeremiah said forthrightly he was but a child and unable to serve; Paul noted that he was the chief of sinners and God summoned him to serve. Our Lord summons us to serve. He, God's own suffering servant, is wounded for our transgressions, bruised for our iniquities, chastened for our sins—all this as our Old Testament lesson says—and he takes us mortals, vessels of clay, and cleanses us. He tells us that we will drink his cup, but we will also share in his glory. Humbly we follow, as we are summoned to serve him.

GEORGE W. BORNEMANN
Redeemer Lutheran Church
Elmhurst, Illinois

OUR VULNERABILITY AND THE KING OF TRUTH

Last Sunday after Pentecost—Christ the King
John 18:33-37

Human Vulnerability

All of us have been witnesses in recent times to some rather outstanding examples of human vulnerability. We have noted a number of shocking events: the bankruptcy of the Penn Central Railroad, an American economic giant; the collapse of the Franklin National Bank system; the deposing of the President of the United States of America; and the demise of a very powerful congressman from Arkansas. In this parish we have witnessed tragedy, through illness and death of the young as well as the old.

Human vulnerability: people great and small toppling from positions of trust and power. How do we respond? Some stand back, watching a person meet defeat or destruction, looking on with a kind of gleeful joy. Some recoil in horror that such tragedy could be. Neither of these reactions is proper nor helpful. As Christians we ought rather to look upon human vulnerability and accept it calmly and without cynicism. Human vulnerability is a given fact of life in our world. Further, we need to come to a calm realization of our *own* vulnerability and accept our human fallibility with wisdom and understanding.

We do have feet of clay. And unless we recognize and deal with that fact as a given reality, we are setting ourselves up personally for some kind of fall and disillusionment. Each of us has dramatic points of personal weakness, our own "Achilles' heel." Not only are we vulnerable physically and mentally, we are especially vulnerable morally and spiritually.

Christ the King

The story from the Gospel of John, where Jesus appears before Pilate in the praetorium, is an illustration of human vulnerability. Pilate is interrogating Jesus and asks, "Are you the King of the Jews?" Jesus answers with a question: "Do you say this of your own accord, or did others say it to you about me?" In disgust, Pilate says, "Who do you think I am? Your own people turned you over to me; what have you done?" And then Jesus begins to reveal his power: "My kingship is not of this world; if my kingship were of this world, my servants would fight, that I might not be handed over to the Jews; but my kingship is not of the world." Pilate pounces, "Ah! so you are a king?" Jesus answered him saying, "You say that I am a king. For this I was born, and for this I have come into the world, to bear witness to the truth. Every one who is of the truth hears my voice."

Who Is Vulnerable Now?

Think of that setting in terms of power and vulnerability. Jesus, the rabbi, is arrested, bound, charged with a crime, taken before the High Priest and then ushered before the Roman ruler, Pilate. By all accounts Jesus was in a terribly vulnerable and helpless position. We know that Pilate is about to condemn him to death and that crucifixion is impending. It appears that Pilate is in charge and that Jesus is the victim.

Then, as they begin to discuss power, Jesus acknowledges that he is, in fact, a king and that a kingdom and sovereign authority are his by right. But, he points out, the *source* of this authority is *not of this world.* "My kingship is not from the world." He is the king of *truth.*

The Source Is the Key

Suddenly the tables are turned! It is Jesus who is in charge and Pilate is being interrogated. The clue is the *source* of power. Jesus is not vulnerable—Pilate is. Pilate served as the Procurator of Judea at the pleasure of the Emperor of Rome. Presidents serve the United States at the pleasure of the electorate. History tells of rulers basing their power on force or intrigue. But, Jesus tells us, no matter what the base, *all* power is vulnerable at its source, except that power which finds its source in truth. Jesus' source of power is not from this world, his validation is from truth—God. His power and authority are not of human origin—they are from God.

In, Not of the World

This statement of Jesus has caused concern and disagreement: "My kingship is not of this world." Does it mean that God and Christ have no concern for the earth? Does it mean that to have faith in Jesus means to show no concern for this world, but rather to be concerned only with the world to come? No! Jesus does not say the world is not the sphere of his authority. He says that the source of his power comes from *beyond* this world. Therefore, the source of his power is beyond vulnerability. In light of that, the authority and power of Pilate are trumped. The whole power of Rome is perplexed. The earth is put into perspective . . . under God, the ruler of the universe.

Thus, Jesus needs no soldiers or armies to march on his behalf. He is simply not vulnerable, even though he is condemned and crucified . . . yet truth triumphs! Jesus is the king of truth. His sovereign and royal power is manifested not by force, but by his witness to the truth. His subjects are not those who fight on his behalf; his subjects are those who know the truth and obey the king. Jesus Christ is the incarnate Son of God, full of grace and truth. He manifests in himself the knowledge of God. Those who believe in Christ are born of God, therefore they are of the truth and they see Christ's glory.

The Source of Our Vulnerability Is the Lie

Jesus is of the truth, and is therefore not vulnerable. Why are we so vulnerable? Is it because our lives are based on that which is false and untrue? Jesus says, "I tell the truth, I bear witness to the truth." That does not mean that his words are simply in conformity with reality, but that his very words are the manifestation of God himself, that sovereign event that approaches us to expose the lie that is within us.

What is that lie? It is that we do not listen to God. We want to live independently of him and to slay Jesus, going our own way. You see, Jesus and his kingship, calls everyone to submit to God, and thus find life and truth. Pilate found himself under the scrutiny of truth and the claim of God.

When we are confronted by God we must submit, finding the truth and the life. Truth is the grace which frees us from our sin. Our sin is that we live under the lie that we control our lives, that we are invincible, that we are not vulnerable. To discover our vulnerability and to accept it is the first step to salvation and life, because we open ourselves to God's truth, forgiveness and grace. When we do not accept our vulnerability, we continue to live under the lie and the illusion that we are not vulnerable, which is death. When we accept our human fallibility we throw ourselves upon God's grace.

The Role of the King

Jesus is the king of truth and he is invincible. He comes, not as a political king or a royal pretender to the thrones of Pilate or the palaces of Herod, but rather, he comes to rule in the hearts of his people. He will influence our will, our desires, our mind, our imagination and our loyalty. Jesus doesn't want to be president or prime minister, nor does he want to take over the state legislature. He wants vulnerable humans to listen to his voice— the source of true power. He asks us to acknowledge that the highest government is of God and that we must be honest, straight and attentive to that final power.

The King Makes a Claim on All

Jesus told Pilate that the only power Pilate had over Jesus was the power given to him by God. Jesus' kingship makes that claim on us and on all who rule with authority in the world. That claim reaches well beyond any political power, beyond any political revolution, because that claim calls for a revolution in values, calling us to reassess that which is the very center of our lives. That claim calls us to acknowledge the very God-centeredness of the whole world.

Jesus has laid claim on Pilate, on every human authority and on each one of us. He is the true bread of heaven. He is the true vine. Jesus' flesh and blood are the *true* meat and drink, in opposition to that which is false, perishing and vulnerable. To encounter Jesus Christ is to confront God, and his divine judgment upon the falsehood of our lives—that which has made us so vulnerable. Jesus is the way, the truth and the life. Jesus illuminates that which is eternal. His grace exposes the falsehood under which we live. When we open ourselves to his truth, we acknowledge that he can rule as the king of truth in our lives.

Christus Rex

The classic picture of Jesus the King, of Christus Rex, in Scripture, in sculpture, in painting, is that of a strong Christ, crowned, holding the whole world in the palm of his hand. How can we come away from that picture with the notion that Jesus was not concerned with the world and its problems? How have we, in our practice of the Christian faith, perverted the *message* into a practice of simply "saving souls" or dealing only with "spiritual matters?" How can we have diminished the gospel into an oral activity of essentially preaching?

Gnosticism is an ancient—and modern—heresy which limits our faith to a god who is interested only in the spirit, but who is not of this world. It limits "god" to the soul, and has no concern for the body. But true faith in God does not allow us to compartmentalize faith from life or faith from the earthly matters of daily living. True faith proclaims that "Christ is the King" . . . over *all* of life. He is the King of kings . . . Lord of lords . . . President of presidents . . . Governor of governors . . . Ruler of rulers. His sovereign reign is over all matters.

Lord of All Creation

God simply will not be confined to a corner of our lives or of the world. He is integral to all of life and he calls upon us, his people, the church, to also be involved, to be a part of all of creation: in government, in family, in personal relationships, in employment, in the economy, in taxes, in energy, in hunger, in freedom, in justice, and inflation. God has called us to be good stewards of his world, on his behalf. We are his managers. To be obedient servants of the king of truth is to be responsible managers of the world. As Carl Braaten writes: "The message of the Christian faith is concerned not merely with the private things of the soul; it embraces the public realities of life in the world." (*Eschatology and Ethics,* Augsburg, 1974, pp. 19-20.) Christ is king of the whole creation. *Christus Rex.*

Are Christians Exempt from Vulnerability?

We must learn to live with and accept our human vulnerability. In the process, we learn that to accept our limitations is to become free in God's grace and truth, receiving his forgiveness and salvation. Does faith in God make us less vulnerable? Probably not. What is the difference then?

The difference is the message which calls us to be the church, to be a part of those who acknowledge their/our vulnerability before God and one another. Together we seek God's forgiveness and his help. We find our hope, our rest and our salvation in our God-given faith in Jesus Christ. Our confidence is no longer in our personal invulnerability, but rather in God's eternal power, in his authority as the *King of Truth.*

WARREN A. SORTEBERG
Our Saviour's Lutheran Church
Minneapolis, Minnesota

THE GIFT OF GRATITUDE

A Day of Thanksgiving
Luke 17:11-19

The phrase, "Just be thankful," is heard many times. We say it to point out that things could have been much worse than they really are. But it should also be a very positive statement. One of our basic needs is to be thankful—to be able to express gratitude. The lack of that gift causes a great deal of trouble, because your life should be an expression of appreciation. Inability or unwillingness to share feelings of thankfulness causes all kinds of difficulties. Whatever amounts of turkey and stuffing you consume this Thanksgiving cannot cure the problem of ingratitude—or gratitude unexpressed. We are like a child being told, "Say 'Thank you' to the man." There isn't genuineness in such thanks.

Hiding the Gift

In the church I am often disappointed by the lack of gratitude on the part of youth. They so easily forget what parents and others have shared. They attend Sunday school, youth activities, basketball games, church camping, and then just drop out, without ever really feeling that they should be thankful for every opportunity given. Such tender wisdom wears thin as they say, "I believe in God, but not the church or organized religion." Such a voice expresses no thanksgiving for the church that baptized and taught them all about God. Young couples seek the counseling of pastors, the beauty of a chancel wedding, the prayers of a congregation. They in turn often forget to even remember the church with a gift, while spending hundreds of dollars on an unnecessarily large reception and an exorbitant number of pictures. Many of us with added years and experience still do much complaining about the prodigals who are not as faithful as we. We lack hearts of thankfulness to God, and we are thereby poorer. We are just selfish prodigals still at home with the "haves"—unable to love the "have nots"—especially if their faith is not as great as ours.

"Now abide faith, hope, love—these three," but gratitude scarcely abides at all, and never for very long. Dr. George Buttrick points out that the nine lepers in the story of our text, Luke, Chapter 17, suffered the disease of ingratitude. He says that their ingratitude was a worse leprosy than the physical disease which they carried outwardly. The leprosy of their bodies gave them a common misery which even a Samaritan could share with them, so their prejudices were forgotten in the sharing of pain and disfigurement. But just one leper, the Samaritan, who could praise and thank God, was really made whole and complete. Would you guess that a tithe of real and genuinely thankful people are listed in good standing in your congregation? The gift of gratitude helped the leper to remember, and the seed had been planted long before the miracle of healing. Grateful spirits need to be cultivated and helped to produce joyous appreciation.

Gratitude for the Most Obvious

In the 9th chapter of 2 Corinthians, Paul reminds the Christians that they were rich enough to be generous. Very probably he did not mean earthly possessions, because they had little. But they were rich in God's love and blessings. Is not this the goal that we should be seeking? Before all else there is completeness through gratitude. For instance, have you really thought very much recently about good health? Time and time again, I have fretted and strained and been concerned, only to suddenly realize how unimportant everything else was as compared to genuine good health. So your home, your "one" talent, your job—you can continue the list—how much you have when you really open your mind and life to the reality of how much is yours, and what joy it brings. Just be thankful! In everything give thanks to God with the constancy and contentment that St. Paul urged upon the Philippians, and which he exhorted Timothy to express.

At this season we are reminded of the trials and difficulties of the first settlers in Massachusetts—beautiful but cold in November. But still the first Pilgrims really had much to be joyous about on their first Thanksgiving. To be sure there was much trouble before them, difficulties would still be with them; but one year after anchoring in the frigid waters of Provincetown Harbor, one year after the first meeting with the Indians, one year after their first testing of the bitter cold of the wilderness, they could look ahead. From then on it would not be a question of bare survival. They could be thankful for the obvious and the daily goodness of God. Come, now, and remember all that you have day after day— and no leprosy.

Gratitude for Forgiveness

When Paul wrote to the Romans about the things he did and knew he shouldn't, and the things he left undone that should have been accomplished, he wondered aloud who would get him out of that mess. Then he shouted, exultantly, "Thanks be to God through our Lord Jesus Christ!" All of his shortcomings, failures and sins were not to be held against him. He would never be the most able apostle or the perfect preacher, but he could be thankful in God's loving forgiveness. This could also include thankfulness for the great victory over death which he writes about so beautifully in the 15th chapter of First Corinthians. "Thanks be to God who gives the victory." Do you really think about that as an active reality? Be thankful for the gift of gratitude that remembers forgiveness. In fact—be happy for the common sense which helps you to be honest about sin and failure—and then leaves it with God.

Gratitude for the Lives of Others

When Senator Harold E. Hughes left the U.S. Senate at the end of 1974, he sent a letter to his Iowa constituents with a heading, "Thanks and God bless you." His transfer from the political realm to full-time religious work was marked by the expression of a fortunate individual, one who was thankful for others. He appreciated their trust and their warm personal kindness. The dedicated Senator—with much thankfulness for forgiveness himself—felt inadequate to express it fully—but within was the gift of gratitude.

Even though we are not always kind to one another, we can be thankful for the quality of human love. Again it was to the Corinthians—to the church that St. Paul could say, "I always give thanks for you" (1 Cor. 1:4). He reminded the Colossians in a brief and specific phrase, "Be thankful" (Col. 3:15). There is a healthy gratitude for your family, for the Christian congregation, for the United States. This is not a matter of worship or claimed faultlessness. It is just being thankful for the variety and excellence of people. It is people that Christ has shown to be the church, people with their faults. So it is people that make a nation great—not the power to bomb Hanoi or to spy on radicals. Be thankful for that! Express gratitude for people.

Gratitude in All Circumstances

I return to our opening reminder of the sickness of ingratitude. Sometimes it is almost like a fever. It disappears when we feel good and our hearts are full. The Thessalonians were reminded that thankfulness is to be expressed in all circumstances. You really are aware of the blessed gift of gratitude when you can be thankful when all is *not* going well—when the reasons are not obvious, when God's forgiveness seems distant, and when you are separated from others.

Pray and Work

The November 1958 issue of the CHRISTIAN CENTURY told about the churches of Hungary which had planned a Sunday of thanksgiving for the few days of freedom that they had had. Then came the Russian tanks and the smashing of their brief freedom. Oppression and terror came back again. There could be no celebration of gratitude for freedom now shattered and lost. Stark reality challenged the worship of words—a nation was captive. How could anyone sing joyous thanks? The 1958 article challenged Americans who might be tempted to sing because we had been spared. It spelled out for us that Christian thanksgiving must be that of straight-seeing, sober joy that is not vulnerable to circumstance, not just due recognition of abundant blessing. There is much about the activities of man in history that disturbs us. We give thanks not only *because* of what we have, but just as much *in spite* of what has happened. *Thanksgiving is not simply an obvious response to obvious goodness.* Gratitude is a gift for this season, of response to God, and through days which leave us wondering. Thanks are not just party manners. They are a token of faith, a pledge of allegiance, a declaration of dependence, a vote of confidence, an expression of hope. I wish that kind of gift for you and me.

I'll be thankful if our talking together has revealed the infection of ingratitude to each of us and has helped open our lives to the gift only God can give—healing. Each of us can be healed. Saying "Thank you" will make us complete persons—whole.

On the first Thanksgiving of our nation, the Pilgrims read

from Psalm 24: "The earth is the Lord's and the fullness thereof." We live in a day in which the fullness of God's earth seems unequally distributed. The gift of gratitude should help each of us to have a burning desire to share with others. The good gifts which God has provided, including the obvious and the unrecognized, are truly his gifts. The world is God's, and we are stewards.

Blessings come to us in order that we might thankfully share them. Let us keep the emphasis upon the giver of the gifts rather than the gifts themselves. Gratitude to God will help make possible the full, rich use of his gifts. Happy Thanksgiving!

Almighty God, our Heavenly Father, we do give you thanks for all the very special gifts and bounties which we can plainly see, and which are obvious to everyone. We thank you also for the gracious gift of life and forgiveness. Thanks be to you for all people who enrich our personal experiences. Grant us gratitude to truly appreciate the gift of faith through which we are able to accept lovingkindness and guidance, even when we do not see how it works together for good. Thank you, God, for your presence in our lives. Amen.

CHARLES V. BERGSTROM
Trinity Lutheran Church
Worcester, Massachusetts

WORSHIP AND PARISH RESOURCES FROM AUGSBURG

AUGSBURG SERMONS/Gospels, Series A

Sermons based on Matthew. 280 pages. Cloth. $7.95

AUGSBURG SERMONS/Gospels, Series C

Sermons based on Luke. 288 pages. Cloth. $7.95

SMILE! JESUS IS LORD

50 Messages for Children to See and Hear

by Lavern Franzen

These 50 messages use a child's terms and images to bring Jesus' messages to small children in church. Each talk is about five minutes long and can be given by any worship leader—pastor or teacher. Simple props such as cardboard, flashlights, bricks, and paper dolls may be used. Also popular with senior members in the congregation!
112 pages. Paper. $2.95

SMILE! GOD LOVES YOU

59 Gospel Talks for Children to See and Hear

by Lavern Franzen

More than just object lessons, these messages use young images to communicate the Bible's stories of Jesus' love for his people.
128 pages. Paper. $2.95

IDEAS FOR BETTER CHURCH MEETINGS

by Jerold Apps

Direct, practical suggestions to pastors, committee leaders and members on improving meetings. Step-by-step directions for planning the meeting, organizing the agenda, and stimulating discussion to obtain efficient productive meetings.
128 pages. Paper. $2.95

HOW TO IMPROVE ADULT EDUCATION IN
YOUR CHURCH by Jerold Apps

This book provides tangible guidelines for understanding the adult personality and learning process, implementing the education program, defining a suitable approach, and selecting exciting and rewarding subjects. Includes case studies of successful programs and suggestions for further reading.

110 pages. Paper. $2.95

BAPTISM: A Pastoral Perspective
by Eugene L. Brand

The biblical, historical, liturgical, and pastoral aspects of baptism are discussed in this book. A fresh approach.

128 pages. Paper. $3.50

FAITH FOR TODAY
A Brief Outline of Christian Thought
by William D. Streng

A concise, basic introduction to the Christian faith for the interested inquirer. Addresses questions of modern readers and relates these questions to Luther's Small Catechism.

64 pages. Paper. $1.25

LET THE PEOPLE KNOW
A Media Handbook for Churches
by Charles W. Austin

Will help pastors and congregation leaders to recognize news, prepare news releases, publish parish newspaper, and use the resources of radio and television. Plus ideas and helps for many more church communications projects.

95 pages. Paper. $2.95

AUDIOVISUAL IDEA BOOK FOR CHURCHES

by Mary and Andrew Jensen

A practical and concise book containing hundreds of
ideas on how to use audiovisuals more effectively in
the congregation.
160 pages. Paper. $3.95

GROUP COUNSELING IN THE CHURCH

A Practical Guide for Lay Counselors

by John B. Oman

A how-to book on setting up group counseling programs in the church. Discusses the need for such
programs, how to start, enlisting and training lay
counselors, insights into the human character and its
problems, and the special role of the church in such a
project.
128 pages. Paper. $2.95

YOU CAN HELP MAKE IT HAPPEN

by Wilfred Bockelman

A stimulating book that speaks directly to the layman
—the officer and committee member especially—and
challenges him to find new excitement and fulfillment
in church work.
96 pages. Paper. $1.75; $19.25 doz.

EFFECTIVE COMMITTEES AND GROUPS IN THE CHURCH

by Ernest G. Bormann and Nancy C. Bormann

This book demonstrates how practical use of communications theory can help church groups and com-
mittees become more effective. Analyzes elements of
cohesiveness, group norms, objectives, leadership, and
feedback patterns.
112 pages. Paper. $2.95

WHAT'S THIS I HEAR ABOUT OUR CHURCH?

An Action Guide for Congregation Leaders

by Charles S. Mueller

A down-to-earth guide providing new insights into decisions you must make about your church. Maps, graphs, and charts aid in determining the real needs of your congregation and community.

104 pages. Paper. $2.50